¡VIA!

¡VIVA LA RAZA!

Readings on Mexican Americans

Julian Nava

California State University, Northridge

D. VAN NOSTRAND COMPANY
New York Cincinnati Toronto London Melbourne

Cover design by
RICHARD VINCENT NUNZIATO

D. VAN NOSTRAND COMPANY REGIONAL OFFICES:
New York   Cincinnati   Milbrae   Dallas

D. VAN NOSTRAND COMPANY INTERNATIONAL OFFICES:
London   Toronto   Melbourne

COPYRIGHT © 1973 BY LITTON EDUCATIONAL PUBLISHING, INC.

Library of Congress Catalog Card Number: 73–1234

ISBN: 0–442–25918–2

Published by D. Van Nostrand Company
450 West 33rd Street, New York, N.Y. 10001

Published simultaneously in Canada by
Van Nostrand Reinhold Ltd.

10 9 8 7 6 5 4 3 2 1

ACKNOWLEDGMENTS

(In the order which documents appear)

Part 1: "The Birth of Cueróhperi" reprinted from TARASCAN MYTHS AND LEGENDS by Maurice Boyd with permission of the publisher, Texas Christian University Press. Copyright © 1969 by the publisher. "Maya Numerical Notation" reprinted from THE ANCIENT MAYA, Third Edition, by Sylvanus Griswold Morley (revised by George W. Brainerd) with permission of the publisher, Stanford University Press. Copyright © 1946, 1947, and 1956 by the Board of Trustees of the Leland Stanford Junior University. "The Spanish People" reprinted from THE SOUL OF SPAIN by Havelock Ellis with permission of the Society of Authors of Great Britain as literary representative of the Estate of Havelock Ellis. "The Social, Political, and Economic Situation in the Fifteenth Century" reprinted from A HISTORY OF THE JEWS IN CHRISTIAN SPAIN by Yitzhak Baer with permission of the Jewish Publication Society of America. "Generalizations on Spanish Culture and Literature" reprinted from A NEW HISTORY OF SPANISH LITERATURE by Richard E. Chandler and Kessel Schwartz with permission of the publisher, Louisiana State University Press. "A Selection from The Cid" reprinted from THE POEM OF THE CID by Lesley Byrd Simpson with permission of the publisher, University of California Press. Copyright © 1957 by the publisher. "The Second Dispatch from Cortez" reprinted from CONQUEST: DISPATCHES OF CORTEZ FROM THE NEW WORLD by Irwin R. Blacker and Harry M. Rosen with permission of the publisher, Grosset & Dunlap, Inc., Copyright © 1962 by Irwin R. Blacker and Harry M. Rosen. "The Messenger's Journey" reprinted from THE BROKEN SPEARS by Miguel Leon-Portilla with permission of Beacon Press, copyright owners in the United States. Copyright © 1962 in the United States by Beacon Press; originally published in Spanish under the title VISION DE LOS VENCIDOS and copyrighted © 1959 by Universidad Nacional de Autonoma. "A New People in Mexico" reprinted from THE RISE OF THE SPANISH EMPIRE by Salvador de Madariaga with permission of the publisher, the Macmillan Company. Copyright © 1947 by Salvador de Madariaga. "Contract of Don Juan de Oñate for Discovery and Conquest of New Mexico" reprinted from Part I of ONATE: COLONIZER OF NEW MEXICO, 1595–1628, by George P. Hammond and Agapito Rey with permission of the publisher, University of New Mexico Press. Copyright © 1953 by the publisher. "A Letter from Junípero Serra" reprinted from WRITINGS OF JUNIPERO SERRA, edited by Antoine Tibesar, O.F.M., with permission of the Academy of American Franciscan History. "A Report from Francisco Garcés" reprinted from ON THE TRAIL OF A SPANISH PIONEER: THE DIARY OF FRANCISCO GARCES through the courtesy of Harper & Row, Publishers, Inc. Copyright © 1900 by the publisher. "Province of Texas" reprinted from DOCUMENTS OF TEXAS HISTORY by Ernest Wallace and David M. Vigness with permission of the publisher, Steck-Vaughn Company. Copyright © 1960, 1963 by the publisher.

PREFACE

The Mexican American is a true blend of the Old and New Worlds, and he shares with Mexicans and other Spanish Americans a rich and socially-important cultural background that is his essential heritage from Europeans and native American Indians who developed highly-advanced civilizations hundreds of years before the first voyage of Columbus. Unfortunately, much of the Mexican American's cultural past has been ignored or neglected by many historians, and so, too, has his history in the United States.

Although the Mexican American has been part of American life for a century and a quarter, the history of his struggles, his achievements, and his contributions to the unique American culture are largely untold. The Mexican American's cultural heritage and his past in the United States are stories that are long overdue. And it is to that task that this work, although necessarily limited in scope, is dedicated.

Obviously, such a short volume as this cannot be all-inclusive, and it is not intended as a comprehensive study of the Mexican American. Rather, it is a highly-selective collection of documents that will introduce readers to some nearly-forgotten chapters in the rich and diverse history of the Mexican American and his forebears, and, hopefully, will stimulate these readers to further investigation.

This collection of readings will enrich studies in government, sociology, and literature, as well as history. By such readings, the student may overcome some artificial barriers to general understanding which have been raised and perpetuated by our traditional curriculum.

The selections, which are taken from such varied sources as original documents, secondary scholarly works, literature, and the press, reflect the author's perspective which stems from his background and activity in the Mexican-American struggle for justice since 1948, a struggle that later became known as *El Movimiento* (The Movement). It is a perspective that is broad and not commonly found in other works of this nature to date.

This anthology cannot correct all distortions and omissions about Mexican Americans. It does, however, offer a rich collection of primary and secondary source material that can enrich the reader's knowledge and set many records straight. And it offers the objective reader a chance to determine for himself the near-sighted and chauvinistic nature of much of United States history.

The book uses terms relevant to time and place. Thus, the term *Mexican American* is commonly used because it is sociologically useful and accurate. However, it also uses the term *Chicano*—a term which more and more Mexican Americans seem to prefer. The author proudly proclaims himself a Chicano and urges others to adopt the term.

CONTENTS

¡VIVA LA RAZA!

1

OLD AND NEW WORLDS MEET

Mexican Americans truly have a fascinating and unique heritage. In ancient Mexico Indian tribes built a rich civilization. During the years of exploration, many Europeans came to Mexico; however, it was chiefly the Spanish who settled there and brought their culture to it. The readings in this chapter focus on the Indian and Spanish heritage—the meeting of the two worlds. Mexican Americans are truly a fusion of the Old and New Worlds.

The civilization which the Indians built in ancient Mexico was magnificent; some early Spanish explorers believed they had stumbled on the Garden of Eden or some marvelous corner of God's creation. Gradually, as our incomplete knowledge of the past expands, the splendor of Indian civilizations emerges as unique in world history. Indian history is now accepted apart from European history and is viewed as a highly important and vital aspect of Mexican history.

The Maya and Aztecs dominate what we know about Indians in Mexico before the discovery. But they are only the tip of the iceberg, beneath which other tribes like the Zapotecs, Olmecs, and Chichimecs laid a rich foundation which others later adapted (somewhat like the Roman relationship to the Etruscans or Greeks). More knowledge of Indian history from its beginnings will lead to a greater understanding of what happened when Europeans came into contact with Mexican Indians.

Although it is fashionable among Mexican peoples to reject and ridicule Spain, the fact remains that all Mexican peoples owe much to Spanish civilization. The Spanish origins reveal the Roman, Visigothic (Germanic), Islamic, and Jewish elements present on the Spanish scene by the sixteenth century. After over 700 years of struggle to free Spain from the Islamic peoples and the Jews, Spaniards achieved success in their Reconquest (la Reconquista); however, Mexico never escaped the beneficial effects of intermarriage and cultural enrichment. A proud, confident, and religiously zealous monarchy worked closely with the Catholic Church in Spain to implant its civilization in American lands.

This opening section briefly outlines the conquest of Mexico and the formation of a new society in America. Spaniards and their offspring from Indian women undertook to explore, conquer, and civilize the vast regions to the northwest (our Southwest). While New Spain developed a colonial Mexican society with features as diverse as African slavery, new cities, scientists, playwrights, and universities, viceroys abandoned the attempt to settle the northwest due to distance and Indian resistance. Not until Russian and English footholds threatened the lands did Spain order their settlement in earnest. The last wave of pioneers including Indians, Spaniards, Negroes, and their complicated mixtures trekked across endless deserts to found missions, pueblos, and presidios to hold the frontier. About this time, the United States came into being, and soon its people streamed over into the Ohio and Mississippi River valleys where Spanish outposts like St. Louis hung on in the face of Indian resistance.

The selections in this unit offer a brief picture of the Indian and Spanish cultures as they developed prior to the fifteenth century and explain how they combined to form a new people after 1492.

The Mexican American has a distinct and unusual history—he is the product of two worlds. Mexican Americans embody not only the physical but cultural heritage of many civilizations and races. They are not all alike, and in most cases they are mestizos. This reality raises problems in the eyes of some. In the eyes of others, it is an asset.

INDIAN CULTURE

Most Mexican Americans embody an Indian past more complex than we imagine. Each Indian tribe had a culture of its own, and Spaniards who came to Mexico settled in many different regions. Thus the mixture of Spanish and Indian blood varied greatly as Spaniards mixed with different Indians over three centuries. As more pre-Conquest Indian history becomes evident much of the past takes on a new light.

Many Indian groups have survived in Mexico, and to some extent much of the Indian culture lives on. Mexican Americans of first or second generations display Indian life, manners, and physical features. Unfortunately, for the most part Indian history has been cast into the background, distorted, or looked upon as merely romantic and curious rather than real and relevant. Recently, however, the importance of Indian history to both Mexicans and Americans has come to be recognized. New knowledge about the ancient Indian civilizations of Mexico will shed light on the Mexican American.

Preconquest Tarascan Myths

The Indian past of Mexico is only partly known because Spaniards destroyed many buildings and objects in their effort to replace Indian religion with their own. Indian population dropped drastically after the Conquest and thus Indian culture declined. Fortunately, however, Spanish clergymen and some scholars preserved Indian writings and ideas. As archeology reveals more about the Indian past we find that successive waves of Indian conquests in Mexico destroyed much before Cortés arrived. There is much more to Mexican Indian history than the Mayas and Aztecs, who are fairly late arrivals on the scene. Thus nowhere is it more true that history is tentative knowledge about the past than with the Indian past of Mexico.

The Tarascan peoples of Michoacán, like many other distinct Indian groups, preserved their culture. Their ideas included concepts of how the universe was formed and how man was created. The poetry and drama of Mexico's Indian civilizations, rather than being entirely replaced by Spanish culture were enriched by it and thus Mexico's unique culture must be seen as a blending of the best of both the New World and the Old World. The following selection from *Tarascan Myths and Legends* by Maurice Boyd offers a brief view of the rich Indian civilization that existed long before the arrival of Europeans.

Tarascan Myths and Legends

THE BIRTH OF CUEROHPERI
(The Tarascan Myth of Creation)

The Tarascans, like other cultured peoples of Mexico and Central America, had knowledge of the calendar. Counting from one full moon to another, the native calendar contained eighteen months of twenty days each ($18 \times 20 = 360$) plus five intercalary days presumably inserted at a time appropriate for several days of fiesta. Fortunately the ancient Tarascans left us with the names of fourteen of their months, and they identified four of the months with the corresponding dates of the Christian calendar.

In the days before the Conquest, at the annual Tarascan fiesta of *Uazcata conscuaro* (June 27), the chief priest donned his ceremonial regalia to

3

recite the history of the Tarascan people for all the assembled natives. Standing atop a great pyramid near the present village of San Gerónimo, the priest or Petámuti told his people about the marvels of creation performed by their god, Cueróhperi. In the Relación de Michoacán, a work written probably in 1540–41 by a Franciscan monk in Tzintzuntzan, the annual recitation was recorded for posterity. The Relación tells of the miracle of creation, today known throughout the countryside as the tale of the birth of their great goddess Cueróhperi, who represents the creative principle and earthly fertility.

THE LEGEND

In the beginning of time there was no light. The silent dwelling place of Curicáueri, the only god at that time, was full of minute (*atómica*) particles which slowly moved around without any order of harmony. Curicáueri realized that his enormous circular eyes could not penetrate the darkness nor contemplate infinity; therefore he created four concentric orbs of light, each burning in one of the cardinal points of the universe, and light existed.

Great shapeless masses from the depths now were reflected in the eyes of the powerful god. From some of the mass Curicáueri created Huriata, the sun god, naming him father and overseer of the universe. Then Father Huriata formed the heavenly bodies, ordering that they light the heavens in their own manner.

Day and night thus came into the world.

Through his golden mask Curicáueri smiled upon seeing the light of the four orbs, and, viewing the orderliness which Huriata had given to the four orbs, and viewing the orderliness which Huriata had given to the universe, he desired to reward Huriata. He created the moon goddess, Cutzi, and presented her to Huriata as his wife.

The contract of the two—Father Sun and the Mother Moon—brought darkness to the cosmos. From the two joined bodies, three rays of light broke forth upon the firmament to form three concentric circles around the dusky body of Cutzi.

From the three circles was born Cueróhperi, the creative principle or Mother Nature, the daughter whom Father Sun endowed with beauty, and wisdom.

The three rays of light were extended through space, and they caused colors to be reflected from the heavenly bodies and the organized atoms.

Curicáueri had created light; Cutzi and Huriata created harmony.

Curicáueri heard the hymn which the heavenly bodies intoned in their movement through the sky. In addition, the slow, rhythmic beam of the atoms added to his conviction that his work was perfect. Retiring to his dwelling place amidst the four orbs, he sat upon his crossed legs and assumed a contemplative attitude. From this vantage point he beheld Cueróhperi, and, upon seeing how beautiful she was, he launched from his eye four beams of light which shielded her from the sight of the world. One beam rested upon Cueróhperi's forehead, another upon her heart, another upon her hands, and the last upon her womb.

The daughter of Huriata felt herself pregnant. Below on earth, amidst the crashing of a furious tempest, she gave birth to the mountains, the seas, the lakes, the trees, and the flowers. Father Huriata and Mother Cutzi carefully attended Cueróhperi throughout her ordeal and afterwards maintained the closest vigilance over her, he by day and she by night. The gift of fertility which Curicáueri had given Cueróhperi encumbered her always with the responsibility of deliverance.

Next she gave birth to the animals of the earth. Then came mankind, to whom she gave wisdom and the name of Purépecha.

The wisdom of the Purépecha was so great that they immediately began to govern the land with a knowing hand, cultivating and populating it in every direction. They created art and brought forth musical tones on magnificent instruments, such as the sweet-sounding *ocarina* and the sonorous *quiringua*. They painted with the colored plumes of birds, and they worked with stones to construct their dwelling place.

Very soon these men learned of their origin and displayed their gratitude to the gods by making sumptuous altars where they could worship the images of their gods. Curicáueri was represented as seated, with eyes and ears of the finest polished gold. They wished to denote that, in addition to being invisible, he had large eyes and ears in order to see and hear the sufferings of mankind. Besides this deity, the only things capable of seeing human beings were the four orbs residing in the heavens.

THE DANCE OF THE *Viejitos*

Related to the above legend is the still famous Dance of the *Viejitos* (little old men). Its origins lay in the ancient past, but how old it is no one knows. Such a dance existed before the days of the Conquest, and the influence of the legend of creation is discernible in it.

Each of the Tarascan dancers carries a heavy staff with an animal's head carved on the handle. They wear white cotton trousers, tunics with red sashes tied at the side, wide-brimmed hats with low crowns, and painted wooden masks depicting old faces.

The musician directs the dancing Viejitos, usually disguised youths, who dance collectively and individually, each trying to outdo the other in steps and clowning. In one of their serious figures, called "the cross of the four stars," the dancers form four files, each pointing in one of the cardinal directions. The four stars presumably represent the four orbs within which rests the abode of Curicáueri.

Today in the little village of Peramba, sometimes as many as 40 viejitos take part. One dancer wears the mask of a pretty white face symbolic of Cutzi, the moon goddess. The dancers form two files and each one dances individually with the woman wearing the white mask; then they form a great circle around her; in pairs, they pay reverential respect to her and perform a special dance. The circle, the reverential respect, and the dance are repeated until the participants grow weary.

The Dance of the Viejitos is performed chiefly during the religious fiestas of December, especially in the town of Pátzcuaro, a short distance from the old imperial village of Tzintzuntzan.

Maya Arithmetic

Like the Tarascans and other Indian peoples of Mexico, the Maya had developed a highly-advanced culture long before Spanish explorers arrived in the New World. The Maya mathematical system was no less advanced than that used in Europe, and, in some ways, it was better than the European method. It enabled the Maya to build great cities of beautiful buildings, to understand the movement of planets, and to fashion a calendar more accurate than the one we use today.

The following selection from *The Ancient Maya* by Sylvanus G. Morley briefly describes Maya arithmetic. While it may seem strange to us, we must remember that the Arabic system we use is comparatively recent and that peoples in other parts of the world today use other ways to count and measure.

Maya Numerical Notations

The ancient Maya used two types of notation in writing their numbers: (1) bar-and-dot numerals, and (2) head-variant numerals. In the first notation, the dot o has a numerical value of 1 and the bar _____ a numerical value of 5, and by varying combinations of these two symbols, the numbers from 1 to 19 were written. (See the chart below.) The numbers above 19 were indicated by their positions and will be described later.

5

Maya bar-and-dot notation was simpler than Roman notation and superior in two respects. To write the numbers from 1 to 19 in Roman notation, it is necessary to employ the symbols I, V, and X, and the process of addition and subtraction: VI is V plus I, but IV is V minus I. In order to write the same numbers in Maya bar-and-dot, it is necessary to employ only the dot and the bar, and one arithmetical process, that of addition.

The second notation employed in writing Maya numbers used different types of human heads to represent the numbers from 1 to 13, and zero. The Maya head notation is comparable to our Arabic notation, where ten symbols represent zero and the nine digits. These Maya head-variant numerals are heads of the patron deities of the first fourteen numbers. The head variant for 10 is the death's head, and in forming the head variants for the numbers from 14 to 19, the fleshless lower jaw is used to represent the value of 10. For example, if the jaw is applied to the lower part of the head for 6, which is characterized by a pair of crossed sticks in the large eye socket, the resulting head will be that for 16. It is probable that the heads representing numbers 1 to 13 are those of the Oxlahuntiku or Thirteen Gods of the Upper World.

MATHEMATICAL SYSTEM

In order to escape rapidly mounting calendric chaos, the Maya priests devised a simple numerical system which even today stands as one of the brilliant achievements of the human mind.

Some time during the fourth or third centuries before Christ, the priests devised a system of nu-meration by position, involving the conception and use of the mathematical quantity of zero, a notable intellectual accomplishment.

The unit of the Maya calendar was the day or *kin.* The second order of units, consisting of 20 kins, was called the *uinal.* In a perfect vigesimal system of numeration, the third term should be 400 (20 x 20 x 1) but at this point the Maya introduced a variation for calendric reckoning. The third order of the Maya system, the *tun,* was composed of 18 (instead of 20) *uinals,* or 360 (instead of 400) *kins.* This was a closer approximation to the length of the solar calendar.

Above the third order the unit of progression is uniformly 20, as will be seen from the numerical values of the nine known orders of time periods:

20 *kins*	= 1 *uinal* or 20 days
18 *uinals*	= 1 *tun* or 360 days
20 *tuns*	= 1 *katun* or 7,200 days
20 *katuns*	= 1 *baktun* * or 144,000 days
20 *baktuns*	= 1 *pictun* or 2,880,000 days
20 *pictuns*	= 1 *calabtun* or 57,600,000 days
20 *calabtuns*	= 1 *kinchiltun* or 1,152,000,000 days
20 *kinchiltuns*	= 1 *alautun* or 23,040,000,000 days

MAYA GLYPH FORMS

Every Maya hieroglyph occurs in two forms in the inscriptions: (1) the normal form and (2) a head variant, this being the head of a deity, man, animal, bird, serpent, or some mythological creature. Very rarely there is a third form where the glyph is a full figure.

SPANISH ORIGINS

Most Mexican Americans are mestizos, part Spanish and part Indian to varying degrees. As with the Indians of Mexico, Spaniards varied greatly at the time of the conquest. Spain was becoming a political unit under the dual monarchy of King Ferdinand and Queen Isabella, but all their subjects were not yet one people. There were many different groups and cultures throughout Spain: the Andaluz, the Gallegos, the Basques, and the Catalonians—to name a few. Thus, the complex and varied backgrounds of the Spanish brought many different influences to the New World.

Many other groups came to colonial New Spain (Mexico) and contributed to Mexican blood—Asians, Africans, and various other European groups—although Spaniards were the major colonizers. In studying Mexican history an understanding of Spanish background is most important, but it must also be realized that many races and peoples came to Mexico and mingled with the Indians. As a result, Mexicans became a varied and complex group of people.

An Insight Into the Character of the Spanish People

What makes a people great is a subject of constant discussion. Many today ask why America has such great influence in the world. Spain and its people left their mark on world events, but in time that once-powerful nation became a small power of modest importance. Many Spanish writers, philosophers, artists, and musicians continue to make great contributions to a universal culture, but, as a nation, Spain is no longer the great world power that it once was.

In the following essay from *The Soul of Spain* by Havelock Ellis, Salvador de Madariaga, a Spanish historian, looks to the history of his people and points to the complex origins of Spanish blood. He believes Spain is a bridge between Africa and Europe. He also feels that Spain has been a victim of its power and success. As those of Spanish background seek to understand themselves, the ideas contained in the following essay are of considerable interest and relevance.

The Spanish People

It has been said that a Spaniard resembles the child of a European father by an Abyssinian mother. Whether or not the statement is literally true, the simile may be accepted as a convenient symbol of the most fundamental fact about Spain and her people. Just as Russia and her people are the connecting link between Europe and Asia, so Spain is the connecting link between Europe and the African continent it was once attached to and still so nearly adjoins. . . .

THE WOMEN OF SPAIN

There are some countries, one is inclined to assert, peculiarly apt to produce fine men, others peculiarly apt to produce fine women. That this is so on the physical side all who are familiar with several countries have had occasion to observe. It is so also on the mental side. I have elsewhere pointed out, when investigating the genius of Great Britain, that while the men of Scotland have contributed more than their share to the sum of British intellectual achievement, and the men of Ireland less, as regards women the case is reversed, and the women of Ireland have contributed more than the women of Scotland.

The Spaniards, if we take their history as a whole, have been a peculiarly virile people, yet at the present day one is tempted to think that the women of Spain are on the average superior to the men. In the past, the men of Spain have been distinguished by the most brilliant personal qualities. In the Spanish men of today, however, it is sometimes difficult to recognize the splendid and restless activities of their forefathers. There is often a certain air of lassitude about them which is reflected in the comparative absence of brilliant adventurers or highly endowed personalities among the men of modern Spain when compared with the men of the great ages. It cannot be said that this must be set down to "degeneration," for then it would affect the feminine half of the race; but the women are full of energy and vigor even to advanced age; the Spaniards also are certainly a healthy people, and centenarians are by no means rare.

While the problem is somewhat complicated, we may perhaps appeal to selection for its explanation. Everything has happened that could happen to kill out the virile, militant, independent elements of Spanish manhood. War alone, if sufficiently prolonged and severe, suffices to deplete a people of its most vigorous stocks. "The warlike nation of today," says President Jordan, "is the decadent nation of tomorrow." The martial ardour and success of the Spaniards lasted for more than a thousand years; it was only at very great cost that the Romans subdued the Iberians, and down to the sixteenth century the Spaniards were great soldiers; but the struggle in the Netherlands against the Dutch finally wasted their energies, and when at Rocroy, in the middle of the seventeenth century, the Spanish infantry that had been counted the finest in Europe went down before the French, the military splendour of Spain finally vanished.

It is not war alone, however, that has tended to crush Spain's manhood: the Inquisition, an institution apparently alien to the spirit of the race and only established—by Spaniards indeed—with great difficulty, killed, banished, and drove out all the varied, vigorous and independent stocks on the intellectual side, just as war had on the militant side. And a third great cause of the depletion of manhood was the vast colonial empire "on which the sun never set." All the ardent adventurers, in search of gold or fame or eager to convert the heathen, rushed to the new world and made the old world poorer. When Ferdinand and Isabella conquered Granada almost at the same moment that they succeeded in firmly establishing the Inquisition and that Columbus returned from his great expedition, Spain seemed about to reach the summit of her worldly glory, but at the same time she was preparing to plunge into an abyss.

Jews in Spain

Jews became a basic part of Spanish life as Roman power declined after 500 A.D. However, many Jews preserved their language and religion. Many Spaniards did not accept Jews fully, and discriminated against them for several centuries. In spite of discriminations, however, Jews became Spaniards and loyally served their kings and cities. They were valuable subjects who enriched Spanish life.

The old resentment against all foreigners or non-Catholics grew in time. Finally, the Catholic Kings, as Ferdinand and Isabella were called, ordered their complete Christianization or expulsion in 1492. Soon after Jews were ordered to leave Spain or to become Christians, the Moors suffered the same fate.

This selection from *A History of the Jews in Christian Spain* by Yitzhak Baer explains how a decision was made to expel them.

The Social, Political, and Economic Situation in the 15th Century

Sudden changes in the Catholic Church and the royal courts of Spain saved the Jews at a moment

8

when they were on the verge of destruction and made it possible for them to build up their life anew. In Castile, John II (1406–1454) took over the reins of government and considered renewing the war against the Moslems. In Aragon, Alfonso V (1416–1458) ascended the throne. He also inherited the crown of Sicily and devoted his best energies to that country. Both kings were more interested in secular culture than in religious fanaticism, and showed willingness to restore the Jewish communities to their former status for the benefit of their own countries. Pope Martin V, a mild-natured man, was ready—and all the readier for his opposition to the schismatic, Pedro de Luna—to revoke the latter's edicts. Delegates from the Jewish communities of all the European countries appeared at the papal court in Rome, and emissaries from Spanish Jewry negotiated at the royal courts of Spain with favorable results. As early as 1419–1422, the Spanish kings and the pope abolished the whole series of anti-Jewish edicts that had been promulgated during the previous generation. The Jews' copies of the Talmud and their synagogues were returned to them. Some of the economic and social restrictions were abolished by law, while others fell into desuetude. Nevertheless, things were no longer as they had been before 1391. A glance at the map of the Jewish communities in fifteenth-century Spain confirms this statement.

In the Kingdom of Aragon, only the communities of the province of Aragon escaped disaster. The continuous conversions notwithstanding, the Saragossa community still numbered about two hundred families. In all the other provinces of Aragon, however, only tiny groups remained, refugees from the sword and apostasy. In Catalonia—particularly in Gerona and Cervera—there were some small communities, and in the province of Valencia only tiny communities, like that in Murviedro. As already mentioned, all attempts to reestablish Jewish communities in the great seaports of Barcelona and Valencia resulted in utter failure. And the Jewish community that went back to the capital of Majorca and reestablished itself there was presently dispersed in disgrace and apostasy as a consequence of the blood-libel trial of 1432. At the time of the Expulsion, the Jewish population of the Kingdom of Aragon was estimated at about six thousand families —not a large number in proportion to the total population.

The Jews paid taxes to the royal treasury, but exerted no influence on the political life of the country. There were no Jews except *conversos* in the service of the State. Only a few of the many Jewish physicians achieved recognition—by serving the Gentile authorities—as did Cresques, the physician and astrologer of John II of Aragon, or R. Abraham Shalom, author of *Neve Shalom,* whom the Christians of Cervera chose as their municipal physicians. . . .

The great majority of Spanish Jews lived in Castile. As a result of natural growth and the opportunities for diffusion in the villages and small towns, the Jewish population of Castile again began to rise in the fifteenth century. According to the most modest estimates, there were living in Castile at the time of the Expulsion 30,000 Jewish families, i.e., about one or one-and-a-half percent of the total population. This figure is considerably higher than the estimate of Jewish population in Castile in the thirteenth century. To it should be added the conversos, whose number ran into tens of thousands, and most of whom were Jews in fact. The political prestige of the Jews had sunk considerably, but they still enjoyed a certain economic and social standing. Central communities, like those which had been renowned before 1391 for their wealth and spiritual stature, no longer existed. Seville, Toledo, Burgos —the glory had departed from them all. The center of gravity in Jewish cultural life had shifted from the large cities to the small towns. Only in a few communities were there more than fifty or a hundred families, but in the small towns these formed from one-third to one-half of the total population.

As before 1391, the Jews in such localities were merchants, shopkeepers and, in the main, artisans. The economic and social character of most of the communities was heterogeneous, as in former times.

Every community had a few physicians, tax collectors, and other men of education and wealth who had financial connections with the government, or with the nobles and the bishops. There were many Jewish physicians who served the municipalities under contract at fixed salaries. The other Jews supported themselves by selling goods in their shops and, mostly by handicrafts. In towns like Hita and Buitrago, a number of Jews owned vineyards, fields and pasture lands, and the wealthier among the landowners held a substantial number of vineyards in their possession. At the time of the Expulsion, there were fifty or sixty Jewish house and landowners in these two towns. The economic development of each community took a different form, depending upon local conditions; for most of them no data are available. In Toledo, at the time of the Expulsion, the Jews owned forty houses. They were still living in their handsome old quarter, but were evidently unable to occupy its whole area; some Christians also lived in their midst. On the other hand, the community of Talavera de la Reina, formerly attached to Toledo, definitely flourished. Royal tax officials continued to record in their registers communities whose populations had dwindled and sunk into poverty, and which were therefore unable to pay the taxes levied upon them according to the official assessment.

In course of time the Castilian communities revived their autonomous institutions, which had been models of their kind in their day; but they certainly did not regain all those rights of jurisdiction which had set them apart from the other Jewish communities. In most of the Castilian cities there were some Jews who were conspicuous for their wealth and close connections with the court, and whose wisdom and culture enhanced the prestige of their communities and also of their cities; but now such intellectuals were to be found among the Christians as well. Owing to the conversionist trend, the old communal aristocracy had decreased in numbers, and only after some time did other wealthy and cultured men step forward to take its place. . . .

In some of the towns Jewish physicians treated their Christian neighbors either on behalf of the municipality, or unofficially. In most of the cities a few Jews farmed the royal or municipal taxes. At the courts of the nobles, Jews could be found serving as physicians, stewards . . .

The historian Alfonso de Palencia, who, as a good Christian, despised the Jews, but yet had such interesting things to tell about the life of the conversos, tried in vain to blot out the religious background of the conflicts of his age. During these conflicts—in the year 1473—the Inquisition again tried conversos in its courts at Cordova and Ciudad Real, and information concerning those trials has been preserved in the records of Torquemada's Inquisition. A direct line extends from the savage methods of the civil war to the method finally adopted by the Catholic Monarchs.

In 1474, when Henry IV passed away, Isabella and Ferdinand began to reign as equal partners in Castile. In 1479, Ferdinand inherited the crown of Aragon from his father and the two countries were united for a time under a personal alliance with co-ordinated policies. These Catholic monarchs rank with the foremost statesmen of the Late Middle Ages and the Renaissance. Once their regime had been firmly established and they had overcome opposition at home and abroad, they proceeded to stamp out the widespread anarchy in Castile, to repress the mutinous nobles and to maintain law and order. The entire reorganization of the state was carried out under the peremptory and explicit instructions of the indefatigable royal pair. They were assisted by highly educated men—jurists and bureaucrats—who had helped them to the throne and continued to merit their confidence. The king and queen strove to establish the State on foundations of law and justice, and with this in mind had a definite codification made of all the laws of Castile. This was their reason for interfering in the internal conduct of the municipalities and depriving them of their last vestiges of freedom. Moreover, they considered it their sacred duty to improve the status of the Spanish Church in the spirit of Catholic tradition and to stiffen the slackened discipline in the monasteries. In planning their religious policy, the Jewish question loomed up before them as a highly important problem which demanded an immediate solution. The sovereigns were profoundly moved by the conviction that, just as they were in duty bound to obliterate every trace of Moslem rule from the soil of Spain, so it was also incumbent upon them to restore the old unity of religion within their borders.

In the beginning, a distinction was drawn between conversos and Jews. In itself, the Jewish question was the simpler of the two. The Christian reforms were not, in fact, intended to undermine the ancient rights of the Jewish community, though these rights might have been subject to restrictions or change. As we have already mentioned, Ferdinand and Isabella were helped to the throne not only by conversos, who were regarded as devout Christians, but also by professing Jews. It was to their own advantage to rely upon such men, as most of the Castilian rulers had done before them, in the future as in the past. It was quite feasible to continue the traditional policy of relative toleration where the Jews were concerned. Indeed, at first the administrative policy of the State and its supporters in regard to the Jews was no different than it had always been. In general, the authorities protected the Jews against the outbreak of mounting anti-semitism and intervened in their favor when unlawful attempts were made to prevent their settling in certain localities or to restrict their trading rights. The authorities kept a watchful eye on the Jewish *aljamas,* supervising their elections, the apportionment of their taxes, and their administration of law and justice. At certain intervals the government convened assemblies of representatives from all the Jewish communities of Castile. The agenda of these conferences included not only taxes, in which the government had an interest, but all internal administrative affairs. The affairs of the Jewish community and Jewish lawsuits were still conducted in accord with talmudic law, which was officially recognized by the State.

Now and again the Catholic monarchs, like their predecessors, would appoint their Jewish favorites to important communal posts. . . .

BEGINNINGS OF THE INQUISITION IN SEVILLE AND ANDALUSIA

The king and queen visited the city of Seville in 1477. The time and place were considered opportune for opening the eyes of the rulers to the destructive effects of Jewish heresy: the clergy had tried in vain to persuade the conversos to repent. Alonso de Hojeda, head of the Dominican monastery of S. Pablo in Seville, "Fray Vicente the Second," and others persuaded Ferdinand and Isabella that only the Inquisition could remedy the situation, since leading personalities had been infected with the plague of heresy, a plague that had spread to the local populace. The rulers concurred in this view and sent a report to Pope Sixtus IV on the spread of heresy and its consequent incessant civil war. On November 1, 1478, the pope issued a bull investing Ferdinand and Isabella with extraordinary powers to appoint inquisitors in all parts of Castile. No details are available concerning the course of the negotiations, which were doubtless continued for two years thereafter.

At a session of the Cortes held in Toledo in May, 1480, the sovereigns included, among their various reforms, the reenactment of the law of 1412, which provided for segregating Jews and Moslems from Christians, and for the Jews' removal from all localities to separate quarters within two years. By means of this legislation the Christian extremists achieved an objective they had long cherished. On this occasion, moreover, they achieved it in its entirety, and in an orderly and legal manner at that. The intent of the law was to make it impossible for the Jews to exert any influence upon the conversos. . . .

EXPULSION OF THE JEWS FROM ANDALUSIA

The year 1483 marked a new phase in the liquidation of Spanish Jewry. On January 1 of that year the Inquisition issued an edict for the expulsion of all Jews from the archbishopric of Seville and the bishopric of Cordova, in other words, from the entire province of Andalusia. The original text of this edict is not exact; but the edict of 1492 for the expulsion of the Jews from the whole of Spain refers to the edict for partial expulsion promulgated nine years previously, and mentions the fact that it was issued by the government because there was only one way of ridding the country of Jewish influence: by expulsion. True, the expulsion of the Jews from Andalusia alone had been deemed sufficient at the time because their influence was strongest in that area. There are other indications that a kind of segregated Jewish enclave in the northern part of the country was then under consideration. The idea of total expulsion was thus rooted as early as 1483, but was not seriously entertained for the time being either for humanitarian reasons or owing to the war with Granada. Though the edict of 1492 attributes the order for the expulsion from Andalusia to the government, it is obvious that it was promulgated on behalf of the Inquisition. . . .

THE APPOINTMENT OF TORQUEMADA AS GRAND INQUISITOR

In the autumn of 1483, Thomas de Torquemada, prior of the Dominican monastery of Santa Cruz in Segovia and confessor to the queen, was appointed by the Catholic Monarchs and the pope, inquisitor general for all territories under the rule of Ferdinand and Isabella. Torquemada had been an inquisitor since the previous year, and it is probable that he may have been among the proponents of the idea of expelling the Jews from Andalusia. As inquisitor general, he presided over the *Consejo de la Suprema y General Inquisicion* ("Supreme Council of the Inquisition") which, like all other central administrative bodies in Castile, had been founded by the Catholic monarchs.

In the years that followed, Torquemada issued to the examining judges instructions based on the principles of the old papal Inquisition. . . .

Spanish Literature as a Foundation for Mexican Culture

Literature expresses the feelings and experiences of a people. Just as English literature has served as the foundation for most literature in the United States, so, too, has Spanish literature molded much of that in Mexico. The cultural tradition of Mexican Americans contains much that comes from the feelings of the Spanish people. We read in their literature many things about earlier Spanish cultures that have survived the centuries and made the journey to the New World where they have become part of the Mexican tradition.

This survey from *A New History of Spanish Literature* by Richard E. Chandler and Kessel Schwartz gives us a general view of major ideas and styles in Spanish literature over the centuries.

Generalizations on Spanish Culture and Literature

Many attempts have been made to define the nature of Spanish literature, some of which contradict one another. Any listing of the so-called essential characteristics of such a vast and complex field of human endeavor as the literature of Spain, which covers a period of ten centuries and includes thousands of writers and every type of writing known to the world, will necessarily remain incomplete and imperfect. Nevertheless, we shall attempt to point out those characteristics which seem to be typical of the literature of the nation as a whole, although it must be said that exceptions to generalizations of this nature are easy to find. . . .

POPULAR SPIRIT

The popular spirit underlying Spanish literature through the years has been a source of refreshment and inspiration for her poets. *Popularismo* is easily recognizable in the repeated use of traditional folk themes in all ages and in the Spaniard's preference for the simple, least artificial verse forms. The truly national creations—the epic, the ballads, the popular lyric, and the theater—use simple assonance, frequently with the easy-to-manage eight-syllable line, imparting thereby a folk flavor to their style. The popular spirit is also evident in the anonymity of many works; the epics, the ballads, and the cronicas; the *Celestina*, which was published anonymously; *Lazarillo de Tormes*, still of unknown authorship; and many plays of the Siglo de Oro, such as *La estrella de Sevilla*, ascribed to Lope de Vega, and *El condenado por desconfiado*, whose authorship has only recently been established. This popular note, which is a unifying thread running through the literature gives it a special flavor quite unlike that of any other literature and contributes in part to the markedly national character of Spanish letters and culture in general.

INDIVIDUALITY

Spanish literature, in addition to being national in spirit, has also been traditionally free and self-forming. The literary masterpieces of the land have been the products of an unrestrained spirit, free of rules, unfettered by dogmas, and scornful of imitation of foreigners. Examples of this are the picaresque novel, a purely Spanish development; the *comedia nueva* of Lope de Vega and his followers; romanticism, which lived a long life in Spain before it was discovered by other European nations; and the Generation of 1898. The paradoxical nature of Spanish culture resists all new importations and yet often tries them out before other countries. One might point, among such paradoxes, to the Copernican theory, Greek culture, education for women, romanticism, and others fused temporarily onto the medieval framework, only to be rejected and reaffirmed after a long sojourn elsewhere. The Spaniard has turned to foreign sources only in moments of literary sterility when national resources have dried up and are momentarily unproductive; but the imported elements are frequently not entirely assimilated and are disgorged, when possible, as repugnant and incompatible with national spirit and taste. . . .

IMPROVISATION

The Spanish genius is for the most part undisciplined, impetuous, uncalculating, given to quick improvising and verbosity. Rather than concentrating on a single work it prefers to scatter its energies over a number of minor pieces. One sometimes hears the complaint that Spanish literature is hard to know because of its extent. It would take almost a lifetime, for example, to study in detail the works of a single author such as Lope de Vega, who wrote an incredible amount, or of Pérez Galdós, whose novels frequently run to several volumes. This inclination to improvise rather than refine and polish has perhaps reduced the number of universal masterpieces which Spain has produced, but at the same time it has freed the Spanish genius to astonishing flights and great outbursts of passion and exuberance. And one must not believe that because of improvisation all Spanish literature is careless and slipshod, for the foreigner who can read the language is amazed that so much that is so good could come from the pen of a single author. . . .

OTHER CHARACTERISTICS

1. Democracy is reputed to be more characteristic of Spanish literature than of any other. Certainly it is true that the outstanding types of writing and those which exhibit the genuine national spirit of Spain are closely related to the folk of the nation and are, consequently, democratic in nature. The epic, the ballad, and the drama were created for the people and, with the exception of the drama which began as an aristocratic entertainment, were directed to the commoners. Even the drama was soon taken over by *pueblo*, and dramatists of the Golden Age catered to its tastes. Patronage in Spain was never so widespread as elsewhere, and literature there has been an avocation rather than a fulltime endeavor. Until very recently few writers have devoted themselves exclusively to letters. The continuing influence of the simpler forms of art associated with the people, such as the epic, the proverbs, the folk

legends, and the ballads, is further evidence of the true democratic spirit which prevails in the literature. Yet through contradiction, which is a major facet of Spanish letters, later writers have exhibited certain antidemocratic feelings.

2. Stoicism has been a mark of the Spanish character since the days of Seneca. The Spaniard is able to maintain a stoic attitude when confronted with the joys of life or with its adversities, and in the end he is able to face death serenely. Menéndez Pidal lists as one of the primordial characteristics of the literature of his nation a certain moral austerity which may be descended in part from his countrymen's renunciation of vanities. The Spaniard's grave, serious, dry, sometimes harsh, bitter, and sententious manner only serves to accentuate this facet of his personality. Perhaps no better example of this type of Spaniard could be found than Francisco de Quevedo, the great critic, satirist, and wit of the seventeenth century.

3. Humor is injected into almost all Spanish writing, for the Spaniard is not all seriousness, stoicism, and discontent, and his nature is not forbidding. Even in the most adverse circumstances, the Spaniard has his joke. The masterpieces of the literature are filled with humor. The farce came into existence early in Spain and is still popular. Even a mordant satirist like Mariano José de Larra cannot resist a joke occasionally.

4. Dignity and honor are strong, often exaggerated, concepts in the Spaniard, and his sense of personal worth has been felt in his literature. It is especially noticeable in the seventeenth-century drama, but is also in evidence in the romantic period and later in the drama of Echegaray and other postromantic writers. The loss of it, or rather the frustration arising from his inability to maintain this noble concept in a highly competitive world, has been portrayed by the writers of the modern generation. But if the Spaniard insists on respect for his own person, he is just as quick to grant it to his fellow man. His politeness, generosity, courtesy, and his feeling of social equality, all an outgrowth of his sense of personal dignity, coupled with his natural affability, make him one of the most pleasant persons in the world.

El Cid: A Spanish Hero Sets a Pattern for the Future

Rodrigo Diaz de Vivar, known as El Cid, is perhaps the best known Spanish hero. Before he died in about 1100 A.D., he developed as a model Christian warrior. From his native Burgos, he fought against both Christian and Moorish kings. He conquered and ruled over Valencia many years. His deeds during the reconquest of Spain from the Moors earned him a place in history. Spaniards who came to America recalled his career and admired him. El Cid is part of the historical tradition of Spanish-speaking peoples, including Mexicans. His view, that life should be lived in a heroic manner, is part of Mexican-American culture.

The following selection from *The Poem of the Cid* by Lesley Byrd Simpson shows the great admiration in which El Cid was held by his contemporaries and perhaps explains why, even after nearly 900 years, he remains Spain's most enduring hero.

A Selection from The Cid

Into Burgos rode My Cid, sixty lances in his company, and men and women ran out to see him. The citizens of Burgos, sorely weeping, stood at their windows, and each one made the same lament:

"God, what a worthy vassal, had he but a worthy lord!"

Gladly would they have sheltered him, but none dared, so fearful they of the great wrath of Don Alfonso the King, for his edict had come that day to Burgos, well guarded and strongly sealed with the royal seal, commanding that none give shelter to My Cid Ruy Díaz, and that he who did so would surely lose his goods, his eyes besides, his body even, and his soul! All Christian people with grief were stricken; all fled the presence of My Cid and no one dared bespeak him. To his lodging rode the

Campeador, but its door was locked in fear of King Alfonso and only by force could he have opened it. The men of My Cid shouted, but those within refused to answer. My Cid spurred forward and gave the door a mighty kick, but the door, well barred, held fast. Then up there came a little girl of nine and stood before him.

"O Campeador," cried she, "who in a happy hour girded on your sword, last night the King's edict came, well guarded and strongly sealed, forbidding us to help you. So we dare not open our doors to you for any price, nor yet give you shelter, for we should lose our goods and houses, our eyes besides. O Cid, nothing would you gain by our destruction, and may our Lord God look after you with His holy strength!"

Thus spoke the little girl and went back to her house.

Now did My Cid perceive he might expect no mercy from the King. So he left the door and spurred through Burgos to St. Mary's Church, and there alighted and fell upon his knees and prayed from his heart. His prayer finished, he mounted again and rode out St. Mary's Gate across the Arlanzón, and there upon a sandy spot, not far from Burgos, he pitched his tent and loosed his horse.

Thus My Cid, he who in a happy hour girded on his sword, seeing that no one would receive him, make his camp upon the sand, his goodly company about him. My Cid camped as in a wilderness, for it was forbidden him to buy his provender in the town of Burgos, and none dared sell him the smallest morsel that could be bought for money. But Martín Antolínez, that sturdy son of Burgos, got bread and wine for My Cid and his men. He bought it not, but gave of his own and supplied them well. My Cid, the excellent Campeador, was pleased with him, as were all his men.

Then up spoke Martín Antolínez. Hear now what he said:

"O Campeador, born in a happy hour, let us tarry here tonight, but tomorrow let us leave, for I shall be denounced for having served you, and the wrath of King Alfonso will be upon me. If I survive at your side, late or soon the King will want me for a friend. If he does not, well, I would not give a fig for what I leave behind."

My Cid, he who in a happy hour girded on his sword, thus made reply:

"Martín Antolínez, a sturdy lance you are! Your wages shall be doubled if I live! But now my gold is spent and all my silver. Well you know I have not wherewith to pay my company. Since I may not have it for the asking, I will take it. With your help I will make two coffers, which we will fill with sand to make them heavy and cover them with tooled leather, the leather red, the nails well guilded. Go then speedily to Raquel and Vidas and tell them this: that it is forbidden me to buy in Burgos, for the King has banished me; that I cannot bring my treasure with me, for it is heavy; and that I wish to pawn it at its just value. Let them bear it away by night, lest some Christian sees it. And may our Lord God and all His saints be judges of me, for what I do, I do because I must and can do no other."

Martín Antolínez rode swiftly through Burgos to the citadel and there asked urgently for Raquel and Vidas. These two were counting up their gains when Martín Antolínez, the prudent one, entered.

"Where are you, Raquel and Vidas, my dear friends?" cried he. "I would have a private word with you."

The three withdrew.

"And now, Raquel and Vidas," said Don Martín, "give me your solemn word that neither to Christian nor to Moor will you betray me, and I shall make you rich forever and you will never be in want again. Know, then, that when the Campeador went to collect the tribute he seized treasure in vast amount and kept for himself whatever was of value, and for this he was denounced. He has two coffers filled with gold fine-wrought. The King has banished him, as well you know, and he has abandoned his estates, his palaces and houses. He cannot bring the coffers with him, for he would be discovered. So the Campeador will leave them in your hands and you will lend him a just sum for them. Take the coffers and put them safely by, and give me your solemn word that in all the coming year you will not open them."

Raquel and Vidas communed together:

"We stand to make a profit in this business. Well we know he brought a great treasure back from Moorish lands. Ah, he sleeps not quietly who guards his money! Let us take these coffers, then and put them safely by where they will not be found."

"But tell us now," they said to Don Martín, "what will My Cid be pleased to get for them and what usury will he pay?"

Martín Antolínez, like the prudent man he was, thus made reply:

"My Cid will accept what is just. Little will he ask if his treasure is safe. From all parts the disinherited are coming to join him and he will need six hundred marks to pay them."

"That we will give him gladly," said Raquel and Vidas. . . .

"Take the coffers quickly now," said Martín Antolínez. "Take them, Raquel and Vidas, and put them safely by. I will go with you and bring the money, for My Cid must be off before cockcrow."

Ah, you should have seen their joy when they tried to lift the coffers! They cannot get them upon their backs, although they are strong men both! Raquel and Vidas are happy men, for they will be rich so long as they both shall live! . . .

Raquel and Vidas withdrew apart and said:

"Let us reward him well for bringing us this business."

"Martín Antolínez," they said to him, "famed son of Burgos, well have you earned a present! Take now this rich skin and this good cloth and with them make yourself doublet and hose. Take these thirty marks besides—you well deserve them. This is just, for you were the mediator of our contract."

Don Martín thanked them and took the money, then bade them farewell and rode forth from Burgos across the Arlanzón and came to the tent of him who in a happy hour was born. My Cid received him with open arms.

"Martín Antolínez, my faithful vassal!" he cried.

"You have returned! May I see the day when I can reward you!"

"Good news, O Campeador!" said Martín Antolínez. "Good news! You have your six-hundred marks and I my thirty! Order your tent struck and let us go in haste, and let cockcrow find us in San Pedro de Cardeña, where we shall see your noble wife. But make our stay there brief and let us leave the kingdom, as needs must, for our time grows short."

He spoke and the tent was struck, and My Cid and his men mounted in all haste. My Cid turned his horse's head toward St. Mary's Church and raised his right hand and crossed himself, praying:

"I thank Thee, O God, Lord of heaven and earth! O glorious St. Mary, lend me Thy strength! Now must I depart from Castile, for the King loves me not, and I know not whether I shall return in all the days of my life. Help me, Glorious One, in my exile! Help and succor me both day and night! If thou do so, and fortune favor me, good and beautiful gifts shall I bring Thee for thy altar. And I further promise I shall have a thousand masses sung in praise of Thee." . . .

The cocks were loudly crowing and day was breaking when the good Campeador came to San Pedro. Abbot Don Sancho, that excellent Christian, was saying matins, and Doña Ximena, with her the five noble ladies of her household, was thus praying to St. Peter and Our Lord:

"O Thou who rulest all, help Thou My Cid the Campeador!"

My Cid knocks. The news travels fast! God, how happy is Abbot Don Sancho! All run to the courtyard with lamps and torches to welcome him who in a happy hour was born.

"Thank God that you have come!" cried Abbot Don Sancho. "O Cid, this is your house!"

"I thank you, Sir Abbot," answered My Cid. "I am in your debt; but I shall tarry only to feed myself and men, for I must leave the country. Take these fifty marks, which I shall double if I live, for I would put the monastery to no pennyworth of expense. Receive besides these hundred marks for the service of Doña Ximena and her daughters and ladies-in-waiting this year. Cherish these daughters of mine, Abbot Don Sancho! I commend them to you. Serve them and my wife with all loving-kindness, and if this sum should not suffice, let them lack for nothing, I beseech you. For each mark you spend in their behalf four will I give the monastery."

The Abbot willingly agreed.

And now behold Doña Ximena who comes to My Cid, her daughters in the arms of their nurses. Doña Ximena kneels before the Campeador, sorely weeping, and would kiss his hands.

"O Campeador," she cried, "born in a happy hour, grant me now this boon! You are banished from the land by the work of wicked men. A boon, My Cid of the noble beard! Behold me here before you with your daughters, babies still, few in days, and these my ladies who serve me. You are leaving me and we must part in life. For St. Mary's love tell us what we must do!"

He of the noble beard held out his hands to his daughters and pressed them to his heart, for he loved them much. He wept and sighed heavily, saying:

"Ah, Doña Ximena, my noble wife, I love you as I love my soul! We must part in life; I go and you remain. May it please God and St. Mary that I may yet give these my daughters in marriage with my own hands and that I have the good fortune to live yet a little while in which to serve you, my honest wife!"

In San Pedro de Cardeña a great feast is spread for the Campeador and the bells ring out.

In Castile the banishment of My Cid the Campeador is everywhere proclaimed, and some abandon their houses, others their estates, to join him. That very day a hundred and fifteen knights gather at the bridge of Arlanzón and ask where My Cid the Campeador may be. Martín Antolínez meets them there and they set out for San Pedro de Cardeña, where he is who in a happy hour was born.

My Cid heard that his company had increased, and mounted and went forth to meet them. When he saw them he smiled again, and all came up to kiss his hands. My Cid spoke joyfully:

"I pray God Our Heavenly Father that, before I die, I may reward you who have left your houses and estates for me! What you lose thereby you shall regain twofold!"

My Cid was happy to see his company increase, and all shared his happiness.

Know you now that six days of his term have passed and three remain, no more. The King has commended that My Cid be watched and that if he be taken in the land after his term he escape not for gold or silver.

The day is done and night is falling. My Cid gathers his knights about him and speaks to them:

"Listen, my barons, and be not afflicted by what you shall hear. I have little money, but of what there is you shall have your share. Hear now what you must do. In the morning at cockcrow you will have your horses saddled. The good sword, since we plan to take Castejón by surprise, do you remain in the rear with a hundred men of our company, while I take two hundred and ride ahead. With God's help and your good luck we shall take much booty." . . .

The people of Castejón arise and open their gates and go forth to tend their fields. All have now left, their gates are wide, and few remain in Castejón. The people are scattered without.

The Campeador then leaves his ambush and makes for the gate. The guards see him coming and abandon it in fear. My Cid Ruy Díaz, bare sword in hand, then attacks and slays some fifteen Moors who oppose him. He takes Castejón and all its gold and silver. His knights bring up the booty and leave it with My Cid. They value it not at all.

Behold now the two hundred of the van and three, how they boldly ride and sack the countryside. Minaya's standard reaches Alcalá. They bring their booty up the Henares by Guadalajara. Great are the spoils: many flocks of sheep and herds of cattle, and clothing and other riches. Minaya's standard holds firm and none dares attack his rear. Laden with spoils the company returns. Behold them once again in Castejón, where the Campeador awaits them. My Cid leaves the castle to its guard and marches forth with all his men. He greets Minaya, embracing him:

"Is it you, Alvar Fáñez, my stout lance? Where I send you there would I expect such deeds! Let us heap together all our spoils and of all our gains I will give you the fifth part, Minaya, if you will accept it."

"Much do I thank you, illustrious Campeador!" replied Alvar Fáñez. "The Castilian Alfonso himself would be happy to have this fifth you offer me! But I yield it to you; you owe me nothing. Before God on high I vow that until I am sated with fighting Moors on the field of battle, mounted on my good horse, thrusting with my lance and striking with my sword, their blood dripping from my elbow down, in the presence of My Cid Ruy Díaz, the renowned Battler, I shall take from you not a cursed penny! When with my help you shall have won something of worth, very well, but the rest, lo, it is yours!" . . .

EL NUEVO MUNDO—TWO CULTURES COMBINE IN NEW SPAIN

Spain opened a New World to European eyes in 1492. Under Queen Isabella of Castille and her successors, Spain took on the job of conquering, Christianizing, and developing the New World.

After a generation of bloody conquest, Spain began to develop the New World along Spanish lines. For the most part, she was successful. Even when she failed, it was a failure that can be explained in the light of the gigantic task Spain undertook. Mexico today reflects both Spain's successes and her failures; so, too, do Mexican Americans.

Second Letter from Cortés to the King of Spain

History has produced few people like Hernán Cortés. Like other great men, Cortés balanced a respect for law and a readiness to use extra-legal means to gain his objective. Cortés defied royal authorities in Cuba when he undertook the expedition to Mexico—technically he was an outlaw. He also assumed civil and military authority after landing in Mexico by the will of an assembly he convened of all the men with him. In calling this Spanish version of a town hall or constitutional convention, he was appealing to ancient Spanish customs. After the troops with him declared him their commander, all he needed was to gain recognition of the King for his authority granted by the "people." Cortés felt compelled to justify his defiance of the Governor of Cuba and sought royal recognition for his authority in his first letter to the King.

The second letter of Cortés to the King was written about a year after the first. Many revealing things about the man and his time emerge in this document. Soon after it reached Spain, a German printer living in Seville obtained a copy and it was published in 1522.

The Second Dispatch from Cortés

Very Great and Powerful and Very Catholic Prince, Most Invincible Emperor, Our Lord. On the sixteenth of July, 1519, I sent a ship to Your Royal Highness with a very long and detailed account of everything which had happened here from the time of my arrival. This account was taken by Alonzo Hernandez Puertocarreo and Francisco de Montejo, procurators of the Rica Villa de la Vera Cruz which I had founded in the name of Your Royal Highness. Since then I have had no word of the ship or the procurators. Nor have I had the means or the opportunity to send you further reports. There have been no ships and I myself have been occupied with the conquest and pacification of the country. It pains me that you should not be better informed of this country, for it is no less worthy of your Emperorship than is Germany, of which by the grace of God Your Sacred Majesty already bears the title.

In the present account, I am compelled to leave out certain information such as the precise names of cities, towns and provinces which have offered their allegiance to Your Royal Highness. In a recent misfortune, of which I shall write fully in this letter, I lost all my papers including the official agreements I had made with the natives of this country.

In my last letter, Most Excellent Prince, I told you of all the cities and towns which I had conquered for you. I also mentioned that the natives of this country had told me about a great lord called Montezuma, who lived, according to their computation of distances, about ninety or a hundred leagues from the port where I had disembarked. Trusting in the greatness of God and the power of Your Royal name, I decided to go and see him, wherever he might be, and I vowed that I would have him prisoner or dead or subject to Your Majesty.

With this determination I left the city of Cempoal, which I had named Seville, on the sixteenth of August, with fifteen horsemen and three hundred foot soldiers, all equipped for war as best I could.

I left behind in Vera Cruz two horsemen and one hundred and fifty men engaged in completing a fort. The province of Cempoal and the neighboring mountain region with some fifty thousand warriors in fifty towns and forts were all well pacified. According to my information, they had only recently been made subjects of Montezuma. When they learned from me of Your Highness's great power, they asked to become vassals of Your Royal Majesty, and to be my friends. They begged me to protect them against Montezuma, who held them subject by force and tyranny and took away their sons to sacrifice them to their idols. Today they are very firm in their loyalties to the service of Your Highness, and I believe they will remain so, not only to escape from Montezuma's tyranny but also because I have always treated them well. For the greater security of those who remained at Vera Cruz I brought with me some of their chiefs and some of their people, and they have been quite useful to me on the road. . . .

Everything ever created on land and sea of which Montezuma has ever heard was imitated in gold and silver and precious stones, and feather-work, with such perfection that they seemed almost real. He gave me a large number for Your Highness, besides others which he ordered to be made in gold, and for which I furnished the designs, such as images, crucifixes, medals, jewelry of small value, and many others of our things which I had them copy. We received one hundred odd marks of silver, and for your royal fifth, I had the natives cast large and small plates, porringers, cups, and spoons, all of which they executed as perfectly as we could make them comprehend our descriptions.

Besides these, Montezuma gave me a large quantity of stuffs. Considering it was cotton and not silk, there was nothing like it in the whole world, for texture, colors and handiwork. . . .

The great city of Temixtitan is built on the salt lake, and from the mainland to the city is a distance of two leagues, from any side from which you enter. It has four approaches by means of artificial causeways, two cavalry lances in width. The city is as large as Seville or Cordova. The principal streets are very broad and straight; some of these are one half land and the other half water on which they go about in canoes. All the streets have openings at regular intervals, to let the water flow from one to the other. At all these openings, some of which are very broad, there are bridges, very large, strong, and well constructed. Over many of them ten horsemen can ride abreast. I saw that if the inhabitants wished to try any treachery against us, they had plenty of opportunity, because, by raising the bridges at the exits and entrances, they could stop us from ever reaching land, and in that way starve us. Therefore, as soon as I entered the city, I made great haste to build four brigantines, which, whenever we might wish, could take three hundred men and the horses to land. . . .

Each kind of merchandise is sold in its respective street, and they do not mix the different kinds of merchandise so that they preserve perfect order. Everything is sold by a kind of measure, and, until now, we have not seen anything sold by weight.

In this square there is a very large building, like a Court of Justice, where there are always ten or twelve persons sitting as judges, and delivering their decisions upon all cases which arise in the markets. There are other persons who go about continually among the people, observing what is sold, and the measures used in selling, and they break those which are dishonest.

This great city contains many mosques, or houses for idols, very beautiful edifices situated in the different precincts. The principal ones house the priests of the religious orders. All these priests dress in black and never cut or comb their hair from the time they enter the religious order until they leave it. The sons of all the principal families are placed in these religious orders at the age of seven or eight years and remain till they are ready for marriage. This applies more frequently to the firstborn who inherit the property. They have no access to women, who are not allowed to enter the religious houses; they abstain from eating certain dishes, particularly at certain times of the year.

There is one principal mosque which no human tongue can describe. It is so large that within the high wall which surrounds it a village of five hundred houses could easily be built. All around it are very handsome buildings with large rooms and galleries where the priests are lodged. There are as many as forty very high and well-built towers, the largest having fifty steps to reach the top; the principal one is higher than the tower of the chief church in Seville. I have never seen anything so well built. The masonry inside the chapels where they keep their idols is carved with figures, and the wood work is all wrought with designs of monsters and other shapes. These towers are places of burial for the chiefs, and each one of their chapels is dedicated to a particular idol. Within this great mosque, there are three halls in which stand the principal idols, figures of marvellous grandeur. Inside these halls there are other chapels, entered by very small doors, and which have no light. These house more images and figures of idols, and only the priests may enter them.

I overturned the idols in which these people believe the most and rolled them down the stairs. Then I had those chapels cleansed, for they were full of blood from the sacrifices; and I set up images of Our Lady and other Saints in them. This disturbed Montezuma and the natives a good deal, and they told me not to do it. They said that if it became known, the people would rise against me, as they believed that these idols gave them all their temporal goods. If the people allowed them to be ill-treated, they would be angered and give nothing, and would take away the fruits of the soil and cause the people to die of want. I made them understand by the interpreters how deceived they were in putting their hope in idols made of unclean things by their own hands. I told them that they should know there was but one God, the Universal Lord of all, who had created the heavens and earth and all things, and them, and us, who were without beginning and immortal; that they should adore Him and believe in Him and not in any creature or thing. All of them, especially Montezuma, answered that they had already told me they were not natives of this country and that it was a long time since their forefathers had come to it. Therefore, they had left their native land, while I, who had arrived only recently, should know better than they what they should believe, and if I would explain to them, they would accept what I told them as being for the best. Montezuma and many chiefs of the city remained with me until the idols were taken away, the chapels cleansed, and the images put up, and they all wore happy faces. I forbade them to sacrifice human beings to their idols, as they were accustomed, for besides its being very hateful to God, Your Majesty had also prohibited it by your laws and commanded that those who killed should be put to death. They abolished it, and in all the time I remained in the city I never again saw them sacrifice any human creature. . . .

So far, we have not learned the extent of Montezuma's kingdom, but everywhere within two hundred leagues of this capital, wherever he sent his messengers, they were heeded, although there were some provinces in these countries with which he was at war. From what I have learned, I judge that his territories were as large as Spain, for he sent messengers to Puntunchan beyond the river of Grijalba ordering the natives of a city called Cumatan to give themselves as vassals to Your Majesty. That is a distance of two hundred thirty leagues from the great city. . . .

There is so much similarity between this country and Spain, that it seemed to me the most suitable name for this country would be New Spain of the Ocean Sea, and thus in the name of Your Majesty I have christened it. I humbly supplicate Your Highness to approve of this and order that it be so called.

Although badly expressed, I have written to Your Majesty the truth about everything that has happened here. By my other dispatch which goes with this one, I entreat Your Royal Excellency to send a trustworthy person to make an investigation of everything I have told you, to give full credence to what I have written. In this dispatch too, I humbly implore you to grant this request which I shall consider a very particular favor.

Very High and Most Excellent Prince, may God, Our Lord, preserve the life and the very royal person and the very powerful state of Your Sacred Majesty, and augment it for a long time with the increase of many greater kingdoms and dominions, as your royal heart may desire. From the town of Segura de la Frontera, of this New Spain, on the 30th October, 1520. Your Sacred Majesty's very humble servant and vassal, who kisses the very royal feet and hands of Your Highness.

Hernán Cortés

The Aztec Account of the Conquest of Mexico

Generally history is the account of the victor. Those who lost are not usually in a position to place their interpretation before a large audience, and official documents and books usually reflect the views of those who were victorious. However, in this selection we have a rare account of one of the conquered. The Aztec account of the conquest, translated from the Nahuatl, covers events from the arrival on the beach of the Spaniards through the fall of the great capital. Other accounts may be found in time, but it is not likely. Therefore this reading from *The Broken Spears* by Miguel Leon-Portilla has great value. Notes that explain details in the Nahuatl text have been included.

The Messengers' Journeys

MOTECUHZOMA INSTRUCTS HIS MESSENGERS

Motecuhzoma then gave orders to Pinotl of Cuetlaxtlan and to other officials. He said to them: "Give out this order: a watch is to be kept along all the shores at Nauhtla, Tuztlan, Mictlancuauhtla, wherever the strangers appear." The officials left at once and gave orders for the watch to be kept.

The year 13-Rabbit now approached its end. And when it was about to end, they appeared, they were seen again. The report of their coming was brought to Motecuhzoma, who immediately sent our messengers. It was as if he thought the new arrival was our prince Quetzalcoatl.

This is what he felt in his heart: He has appeared! He has come back! He will come here, to the palace of his throne and canopy, for that is what he promised when he departed!

Motecuhzoma sent five messengers to greet the strangers and to bring them gifts. . . .

He said to them: "Come forward, my jaguar knights, come forward. It is said that our lord has returned to this land. Go to meet him. Go to hear him. Listen well to what he tells you; listen and remember."

Then Motecuhzoma gave the messengers his final orders. He said to them: "Go now, without delay. Do reverence to our lord the god. Say to him: 'Your deputy, Motecuhzoma, has sent us to you. Here are the presents with which he welcomes you home to Mexico.'" . . .

MOTECUHZOMA AWAITS WORD FROM THE MESSENGERS

While the messengers were away, Motecuhzoma could neither sleep nor eat, and no one could speak with him. He thought that everything he did was in vain, and he sighed almost every moment. He was lost in despair, in the deepest gloom and sorrow. Nothing could comfort him, nothing could calm him, nothing could give him any pleasure.

He said: "What will happen to us? Who will outlive it? Ah, in other times I was contented, but now I have death in my heart! My heart burns and suffers, as if it were drowned in spices. . . ! But will our Lord come here?"

Then he gave orders to the watchmen, to the men who guarded the palace: "Tell me, even if I am sleeping: 'The messengers have come back from the sea.'" But when they went to tell him he immediately said: "They are not to report to me here. I will receive them in the House of the Serpent. Tell them to go there." And he gave this order: "Two captives are to be painted in chalk."

The messengers went to the House of the Serpent, and Motecuhzoma arrived. The two captives were then sacrificed before his eyes: their breasts were torn open, and the messengers were sprinkled with their blood. This was done because the messengers had completed a difficult mission: they had seen the gods, their eyes had looked on their faces. They had even conversed with the gods!

When the sacrifice was finished, the messengers reported to the king. They told him how they had made the journey, and what they had seen, and what food the strangers ate. Motecuhzoma was astonished and terrified by their report, and the description of the strangers' food astonished him above all else.

He was also terrified to learn how the cannon roared, how its noise resounded, how it caused one to faint and grow deaf. The messengers told him: "A thing like a ball of stone comes out of its entrails: it comes out shooting sparks and raining fire. The smoke that comes out with it has a pestilent odor, like that of rotten mud. This odor penetrates even to the brain and causes the greatest discomfort. If the cannon is aimed against a mountain, the mountain splits and cracks open. If it is aimed against a tree, it shatters the tree into splinters. This is a most unnatural sight, as if the tree had exploded from within."

The messengers also said: "Their trappings and arms are all made of iron. They dress in iron; their bows are iron; their shields are iron, their spears are iron; their deer carry them on their backs wherever they wish to go. These deer, our lord, are as tall as the roof of a house.

"The strangers' bodies are completely covered, so that only their faces can be seen. The skin is white, as if it were made of lime. They have yellow hair, though some of them have black. Their beards are long and yellow, and their moustaches are also yellow. Their hair is curly, with very fine strands.

"As for their food, it is like human food. It is large and white, and not heavy. It is something like straw, but with the taste of cornstalk, of the pith of a cornstalk. It is a little sweet, as if it were flavored with honey; it tastes of honey, it is sweet-tasting food.

"Their dogs are enormous, with flat ears and long, dangling tongues. The color of their eyes is a burning yellow; their eyes flash fire and shoot off sparks. Their bellies are hollow, their flanks long and narrow. They are tireless and very powerful. They bound here and there, panting, with their tongues hanging out. And they are spotted like an ocelot."

When Motecuhzoma heard this report, he was filled with terror. It was as if his heart had fainted, as if it had shriveled. It was as if he were conquered by despair.

MOTECUHZOMA GOES OUT TO MEET CORTÉS

The Spaniards arrived in Xoloco, near the entrance to Tenochtitlan. That was the end of the march, for they had reached their goal.

Motecuhzoma now arrayed himself in his finery, preparing to go out to meet them. The other great princes also adorned their persons, as did the nobles and their chieftains and knights. They all went out together to meet the strangers.

They brought trays heaped with the finest flowers —the flower that resembles a shield; the flower shaped like a heart; in the center, the flower with the sweetest aroma; and the fragrant yellow flower, the most precious of all. They also brought garlands of flowers, and ornaments for the breast, and necklaces of gold, necklaces hung with rich stones, necklaces fashioned in the petatillo style.

Thus Motecuhzoma went out to meet them, there in Huitzillan. He presented many gifts to the Captain and his commanders, those who had come to make war. He showered gifts upon them and hung flowers around their necks; he gave them necklaces of flowers and bands of flowers to adorn their breasts; he set garlands of flowers upon their heads. Then he hung the gold necklaces around their necks and gave them presents of every sort as gifts of welcome.

When Motecuhzoma had given necklaces to each one, Cortés asked him: "Are you Motecuhzoma? Are you the king? Is it true that you are the king Motecuhzoma?"

And the king said: "Yes, I am Motecuhzoma." Then he stood up to welcome Cortés; he came forward, bowed his head low and addressed him in these words: "Our lord, you are weary. The journey has tired you, but now you have arrived on the earth. You have come to your city, Mexico. You have come here to sit on your throne, to sit under its canopy.

"The kings who have gone before, your representatives, guarded it and preserved it for your coming. . . .

"This was foretold by the kings who governed your city, and now it has taken place. You have come back to us; you have come down from the sky. Rest now, and take possession of your royal houses. Welcome to your land, my lords."

When Motecuhzoma had finished, La Malinche translated his address into Spanish so that the Captain could understand it. Cortés replied in his strange and savage tongue, speaking first to La Malinche: "Tell Motecuhzoma that we are his friends. There is nothing to fear. We have wanted to see him for a long time, and now we have seen his face and heard his words. Tell him that we love him well and that our hearts are contented."

Then he said to Motecuhzoma: "We have come to your house in Mexico as friends. There is nothing to fear."

La Malinche translated this speech and the Spaniards grasped Motecuhzoma's hands and patted his back to show their affection for him. . . .

Editor's Note

Some of the Aztecs attacked the Spanish guests. Montezuma was confused and appeared weak. Some Aztecs criticized their Emperor for helping the strangers. The Emperor died from wounds inflicted by rocks when Aztecs protested against Montezuma's efforts to stop the attacks on Spaniards. Before long, Cortés decided to flee the capital and during the night of July 1, 1520, about 450 Spaniards died retreating from Mexico City to the shoreline over the causeways. After "la Noche Triste,"

Cortés and the survivors were given shelter by the Tlaxcalan Indians who hated Aztecs.

After months of preparation, the Spaniards and many thousands of Indian allies attacked Mexico City with a desire to destroy it. After a terrible siege, Cuahtemoc and the valiant defenders were overcome.

THE SIEGE OF TENOCHTITLAN

When the Spaniards left Tenochtitlan, the Aztecs thought they had departed for good and would never return. Therefore they repaired and decorated the temple of their god, sweeping it clean and throwing out all the dirt and wreckage.

Then the eighth month arrived, and the Aztecs celebrated it as always. They adorned the impersonators of the gods, all those who played the part of gods in the ceremonies, decking them with necklaces and turquoise masks and dressing them in the sacred clothing. This clothing was made of quetzal feathers, eagle feathers and yellow parrot feathers. The finery of the gods was in the care of the great princes.

THE PLAGUE RAVAGES THE CITY

While the Spaniards were in Tlaxcala, a great plague broke out here in Tenochtitlan. It began to spread during the thirteenth month and lasted for seventy days, striking everywhere in the city and killing a vast number of our people. Sores errupted on our faces, our breasts, our bellies; we were covered with agonizing sores from head to foot.

The illness was so dreadful that no one could walk or move. The sick were so utterly helpless that they could only lie on their beds like corpses, unable to move their limbs or even their heads. They could not lie face down or roll from one side to the other. If they did move their bodies, they screamed with pain.

A great many died from this plague, and many others died of hunger. They could not get up to search for food, and everyone else was too sick to care for them, so they starved to death in their beds.

Some people came down with a milder form of the disease, they suffered less than the others and made a good recovery. But they could not escape entirely. Their looks were ravaged, for wherever a sore broke out, it gouged an ugly pockmark in the skins. And a few of the survivors were left completely blind.

The first cases were reported in Cuatlan. By the time the danger was recognized, the plague was so well established that nothing could halt it, and eventually it spread all the way to Chalco. Then its virulence diminished considerably, though there were isolated cases for many months after. The first victims were stricken during the fiesta of Teotlecco, and the faces of our warriors were not clean and free of sores until the fiesta of Panquetzaliztli.

THE FIGHTING IS RENEWED

The Spaniards made ready to attack us, and the war broke out again. They assembled their forces in Cuepopan and Cozcacuahco. A vast number of our warriors were killed by their metal darts. Their ships sailed to Texopan, and the battle there lasted three days. When they had forced us to retreat, they entered the Sacred Patio, where there was a four day batttle. Then they reached Yacacolco.

The Tlatelolcas set up three racks of heads in three different places. The first rack was in the Sacred Patio of Tlilancalco (Black House), where we strung up the heads of our lords the Spaniards. The second was in Acacolco, where we strung up Spanish heads and the heads of two of their horses. The third was in Zacatla, in front of the temple of the earth-goddess Cihuacoatl, where we strung up the heads of Tlaxcaltccas.

The women of Tlatlclolco joined in the fighting. They struck at the enemy and shot arrows at them; they tucked up their skirts and dressed in the regalia of war.

The Spaniards forced us to retreat. Then they occupied the marketplace. The Tlatclolcas—the Jaguar Knights, the Eagle Knights, the great warriors—were defeated, and this was the end of the battle. It had lasted five days, and two thousand Tlatclolcas were killed in action. During the battle, the Spaniards set up a canopy for the Captain in the market place. They also mounted a catapult on the temple platform.

And all these misfortunes befell us. We saw them and wondered at them; we suffered this unhappy fate.

> Broken spears lie in the roads;
>   We have torn our hair in our grief.
> The houses are roofless now, and their walls
>   are red with blood. . . .

When we had meat, we ate it almost raw. It was scarcely on the fire before we snatched it and gobbled it down.

They set a price on all of us: on the young men, the priests, the boys and girls. The price of a poor man was only two handfuls of corn, or ten cakes made from mosses or twenty cakes of salty couchgrass. Gold, jade, rich cloths, quetzal feathers—everything that once was precious was now considered worthless.

The captains delivered several prisoners of war to Cuauhtemoc to be sacrificed. He performed the sacrifices in person, cutting them open with a stone knife.

Soon after this, the Spaniards brought Xochitl the Acolnahuacatl, whose house was in Tenochtitlan, to the market place in Tlatclolco. They gripped him by both arms as they brought him there. They kept him with them for twenty days and then let him go. They also brought in a cannon, which they set up in the place where incense was sold.

The Tlatclolcas ran forward to surround Xochitl. They were led by the captain from Huitznahuac, who was a Huasteco. Xochitl was placed under guard in the Temple of the Woman in Axocotzinco.

As soon as the Spaniards had set Xochitl loose in the market place, they stopped attacking us. There was no more fighting, and no prisoners were taken.

Three of the great Chiefs said to Cuauhtemoc: "Our prince, the Spaniards have sent us one of the magistrates Xochital the Acolnahuacatl. It is said that he has a message for you."

Cuauhtemoc asked them: "What is your advice?"

The chiefs all began to shout at once: "Let the message be brought here! We have made auguries with paper and with incense! The captain who seized Xochitl should bring us the message!"

The captain was sent to question Xochitl in the Temple of the Woman. Xochitl said: "The 'god' and La Malinche send word to Cuauhtemoc and the other princes that there is no hope for them. Have they no pity on the little children, the old men, the old women? What more can they do? Everything is settled.

"You are to deliver women with light skins, corn, chickens, eggs and tortillas. This is your last chance. The people of Tenochtitlan must choose whether to surrender or to be destroyed."

The captain reported this message to Cuauhtemoc and the lords of Tlatclolco. The lords deliberated among themselves: "What do you think about this? What are we to do?"

THE CITY FALLS

Cuauhtemoc said to the fortune tellers: "Please come forward. What do you see in your books?"

One of the priests replied: "My prince, hear the truth that we tell you. In only four days we shall have completed the period of eighty days. It may be the will of Huitzilopochtli that nothing further shall happen to us. Let us wait until these four days have passed."

But then the fighting broke out again. The captain of Huitznahuac—the same Huasteco who had bought in Xochitl—renewed the struggle. The enemy forced us to retreat to Amaxac. When they also attacked us there, the general flight began. The lake was full of people, and the roads leading to the mainland were all crowded.

Thus the people of Tenochtitlan and Tlatlolco gave up the struggle and abandoned the city. We all gathered in Amaxac. We had no shields and no macanas; we had nothing to eat and no shelter. And it rained all night.

Cuauhtemoc was taken to Cortes along with

three other princes. The Captain was accompanied by Pedro de Alvarado and La Malinche.

When the princes were made captives, the people began to leave, searching for a place to stay. Everyone was in tatters, and the women's thighs were almost naked. The Christians searched all the refugees. They even opened the women's skirts and blouses and felt everywhere: their ears, their breasts, their hair. Our people scattered in all directions. They went to neighboring villages and huddled in corners in the houses of strangers. . . .

The lords of Tlatclolco went to Cuauhtitlan. Even the greatest captains and warriors left in tatters. The women had only old rags to cover their heads, and they had patched together their blouses out of many-colored scraps. The chiefs were grief-stricken and mourned to one another: "We have been defeated a second time!"

Whites and Indians Form a New People in Mexico

Only Spain among European empires made a formal statement that Indians were equal to whites in the eyes of God and under the nation's law. Spain took on the responsibility of protecting and Christianizing natives in Spanish territories of the New World. There was no legal separation of races that hindered intermarriage, so many Spaniards married Indians and their descendants become known as the *Mestizos*.

In this selection from *The Rise of the Spanish American Empire*, Salvador de Madariaga tells us how the Spaniards reached their decision about integrating Indians after a heated debate that affected all of Spain. In time, Blacks were accepted on a similar basis. Slavery for Indians was soon eliminated, but freedom for Blacks was much longer in coming. Spaniards were encouraged to free slaves as a Christian duty, and thus many Blacks were gradually freed.

Although Orientals, Europeans, and Blacks mixed freely in Mexico, Indians and Spaniards came to be the major components of the new Mexican, and many Mexican Americans today proudly proclaim heritage from both.

A New People in Mexico

This empire earnestly endeavoured from the very first to justify itself on a basis of principle. In 1494, the Queen submitted to a committee of jurists and theologians the question whether the Indians should or could be reduced to slavery. The committee declared them free. At the request of King Ferdinand, the chief crown jurist, Palacios Rubios, examined the rights of Spaniards in the Indies, and he took as his starting point the freedom of the natives. . . .

He was convinced that the Indians were free by nature and that the Spaniards had no right to deprive them of their property. He admitted, however, that all pre-existing political sovereignties were cancelled by the Christian Conquest, and that the Indians were unable to govern themselves. Thus, Palacios Rubios stands at the origin of the two schools of thought which are to develop later in Spain; and while Sepúlveda, the imperialist, will avail himself of his arguments, Las Casas, the evangelist, will sing his praise. He was strict on the principle the war had to be just; on which he drafted the formal statement which Spanish captains were required to read to the Indians before any warlike operation could be initiated against them. Starting from the fact that all men are brothers as sons of Adam and Eve, the statement imparts to the Indians the news that the world has been divided between the Kings of Castille and of Portugal by the Pope, as direct representative of the Lord, so that the Indians may be converted to the faith, and summons them to listen to the Word. This document, quaint and naive as it was, and provoking as it did the mirth of many a soldier, proves nevertheless the earnestness with which the question of principle was tackled by the Spanish Crown.

It is well-known that Isabel sent back to Santo Domingo a number of Indians whom Colón—

against her repeated orders—had seized as slaves. Las Casas raised the issue plainly before the King's conscience, notably in 1519, in the presence of the monarch himself, assisted by Diego Colón, son and heir of the admiral. Las Casas was a converted conqueror and settler. He was shocked to see the doctrine that it was right to go to war in order to spread the faith put forward in a book, *De justis bellie causis apud indos,* published by the King's chronicler, Dr. Juan de Sepúlveda. The indefatigable apostle of the Indians found powerful support in the famous Melchor Cano, one of the professors of theology in Salamanca, while other churchmen (the Archibishop of Tarragone one of them) sided with Sepúlveda. Charles V took the matter in dead earnest and called together a "Congregation" of jurists and theologians at Valladolid to decide whether it was legitimate for the Spaniards "to wage wars known as conquests" against the Indians "without their having committed fresh guilty acts other than those of their infidelity." Another eminent theologian, Domingo Soto, drew up for the Congregation a summary of the two opposing views. The reasons Dr. Sepúlveda put forward to justify armed force against the Indians were: (i) The gravity of their crimes and particularly their idolatry and other sins "against nature"; (ii) The rudeness of their minds as of people servile and barbarous by nature, and therefore bound to serve those of a more elegant mind, such as the Spaniards; (iii) For the sake of the faith, since their subjection will make it more convenient and expeditious to preach the faith to them and to persuade them; Because they do harm to each other, killing each other and sometimes eating each other. The Congregation took Las Casas' view. The merit of this decision was not exclusively due to Las Casas. Many members, eminent in themselves as personal thinkers, were powerfully influenced by the outstanding genius of the age, Francisco de Vitoria, whose immortal lessons known as De Indis, taught in 1532, established the right of the Indians to their territories and laws and denied to the Spaniards any right to be in the Indies at all, other than that of

every man peacefully to go and trade everywhere and the duty of every Christian to convert the heathen. Vitoria was then at the height of his powers, a leader of legal and theological thought recognized by all Christiandom, respected by Erasmus, repeatedly consulted by Charles V in personal letters on the affairs of the Indies. His authority, both scientific and moral, was as deeply felt in the Congregation of Valladolid as it was later in the Council of Trent. The conclusions of the Congregation of Valladolid conformed to his teachings, established the freedom of the Indians and were the basis of Spanish policy in the Indies for the next three centuries, as well as the chief inspiration of the Laws of the Indies.

Spain, therefore, confronted with an entirely original historical situation, reacted as a state, first almost instinctively, then deliberately, in a Christian and generous way; she recognized the human problem involved, examined it intelligently and objectively in the light of the highest principles, and officially adopted the most Christian and enlightened attitude towards the population of the New World. . . .

Save in the Antilles, where the native race had gradually disappeared during the first years of the Spanish conquest, the Indians were preserved in the whole New World by the combined efforts of church and state; indeed, the New World kingdoms were conceived on the basis that both whites and natives were vassals of the King and equally entitled to the King's protection. The Spaniards felt no repugnance to mating with Indian women, and, moreover, during the first years of the exploration and conquest, the number of women who sailed over was very small; a *mestizo* population soon began to appear in the New World. These *mestizos* were inevitably destined to be the prototype and the symbol of the new kingdom of the Indies. . . .

The Expedition Into New Mexico of Don Juan de Oñate

The Spanish crown (after the death of the Catholic monarchs, Ferdinand and Isabella) could not finance the numerous expeditions around the world. Gradually many types of joint financial ventures developed to stimulate investments by groups and individuals in cooperation with the crown. The ingenuity of Spanish government in the Indies remains largely overlooked.

The colonizing expedition of Oñate was the product of private enterprise in partnership with the crown. The documents in this selection from *Don Juan de Oñate, Colonizer of New Mexico, 1595–1628* by George P. Hammond and Agapito Rey describe essential features of the contract between Oñate and his King: the men and supplies Oñate promised to gather at his expense, the supplies and weapons of each soldier were supplied by the King and the act of taking possession of New Mexico was in his name.

The superior arms, horses, and domesticated animals of the Spaniards were important to the conquest of the unknown territory. The Indians used bows and arrows as their main weapons. But they soon learned to use geography and cunning by encouraging Spaniards to wander far into the deserts, with false tales of riches over the horizon.

Contract of Don Juan de Oñate for the Discovery and Conquest of New Mexico

I, Don Juan de Oñate, resident of the city of Zacatecas in the Kingdom of New Galicia, state that, having offered to serve his majesty and your lordship in the pacification of New Mexico and on any other occasions that might arise, continuing in this respect what I have been doing for more than twenty years in fighting and pacifying the Chichimecas and Guachichiles Indians and other nations in the Kingdoms of New Galicia and New Zizcaya, at my own expense—emulating my father, Christobal de Oñate, who, as captain general in the Kingdom of New Galicia, conquered, pacified, and settled the greater portion of it at his own cost, in which he spent a large part of his estate, as your lordship knows and as is common knowledge, and in which he followed in the footsteps of his fore-

fathers, who, as knights and gentlemen, always devoted themselves to the service of the royal crown of Castile—your lordship was pleased to honor me by accepting my offer and ordering me to enter the said province in pursuit of Captain Francisco de Leyva Bonilla and his followers in order that they might be arrested and punished, as their excesses deserve, they having set out against the order and command of your lordship and contrary to the special prohibition of his majesty, this without taking into consideration the great inconveniences that would necessarily result by disturbing and abusing the natives and making their pacification and conversion more difficult later, for the main purpose that must prevail—which his majesty favors and you lordship not any less so—is this conversion (which depends on avoiding such excesses); and since we might in one single effort punish the culprits and serve God our Lord and his majesty in the said conversion and pacification, I again offer your lordship my services for the discovery, pacification, and conversion of the said provinces of New Mexico.

I beg your lordship to favor me by accepting my offer and to choose me to carry it out, for which I propose the following:

OFFER OF DON JUAN DE OÑATE FOR THE CONQUEST

First, I offer to take at least two hundred men, furnished with everything necessary, including provisions sufficient to reach the settlements and even more, this all at my cost and that of the soldiers, his majesty not being obligated to pay them any wages besides what I may willingly give from my estate. Further:

Fifteen hundred pesos in flour and maize.
Five hundred pesos in wheat for sowing.
Five hundred pesos in jerked beef.
One thousand head of cattle.
Three thousand sheep.
One thousand rams.
One thousand goats.
One hundred head of black cattle.
One hundred and fifty colts.

One hundred and fifty mares.

Two pairs of bellows with equipment for the blacksmith's trade.

Four pairs of bellows for mines, in case there should be any.

Two thousand pesos in iron for horseshoes, with the necessary nails, five hundred pesos of this sum to be in extra nails.

Five hundred pesos in footgear.

Five hundred pesos in medicines.

Six hundred pesos in iron tools such as plowshares, bars, picks, wedges, hoes, sledge hammers, adzes, axes, augers, chisels, saws, and sickles.

Six hundred pesos in unmanufactured iron.

Five hundred pesos in articles to trade and to use as gifts for the Indians.

Two hundred pesos in paper.

Five hundred pesos in frieze and sackcloth.

Twenty carts provided with oxen and everything necessary.

All of these things I offer to take in addition to supplies and food for the soldiers in the amount needed until the settlements are reached and which shall not be used on the way except in case of extreme need. If it should be desirable to replace some of the above goods with others more necessary, provided that it is for the same amount of money, this may be done if it conforms to this statement.

Further, I offer to take the following for my personal outfit:

Twenty-five horses.

Twenty-five harnessed mules.

Two coaches with mules.

Two carts with iron-rimmed wheels and mules.

Six cavalry saddles (*sillas estradiotas*).

Six riding saddles (*sillas jinetas*).

Six leather shields.

Six lances.

Twelve halberds.

Six coats of mail.

Six cuisses.

Six helmets with beavers.

Six sets of horse armor.

Six harquebuses.

Six swords and daggers.

Two complete corselets.

Two heavy fighting saddles (*sillas de armas*).

Six buckskin jackets.

All of which I will have assembled at the town of Santa Bárbara, which is the last place in the conquered territory, as soon as possible, trying to have it by the end of March, 1596.

DECLARATIONS OF THE SOLDIERS

Francisco Vazquez: Articles taken by Francisco Vazquez, soldier, to serve his majesty on the expedition to New Mexico:

One harquebus and sword.

Two coats of mail.

Some small breastplates.

A short jacket of mail (*jaco*).

One cuisse, with helmet and beaver.

Some horse armor.

One mule.

Two *jineta* saddles.

All the aforesaid is mine and I am taking it for the purpose declared, and I so swear in due legal manner.

In the valley of San Bartolomé, Santa Bárbara, December 7, 1597, in the presence of the commissary general, Françisco Vázquez, soldier, made the above declaration under oath. The commissary general accepted this statement and affixed his rubric. Françisco Vázquez, Jaime Fernández. Juan Medel: Record of what I, Juan Medel, soldier, am taking on the expedition to New Mexico to serve his majesty:

One cart with five oxen.

Twelve horses.

One coat of mail, beaver, and cuisses of mail.

One harquebus.

One buckskin jacket.

One hooked blade (*dalle*).

Two *jineta* saddles.

One sword.

All of this is mine, and I so swear in the name of God in due legal manner. The above does not include my personal clothes. Juan Medel. . . .

Be it known to all present, or who may come later, how I, Don Juan de Oñate, governor, captain general, and *adelantado* of New Mexico, of its kingdoms and provinces, and those adjacent and neighboring, discoverer, settler, and pacifier of them and of the said kingdoms, for the king our lord, state: that by virtue of the appointment and title which his majesty now confers upon me as governor, captain general, and *adelantado,* not counting greater honors promised me by virtue of his royal ordinances and two royal *cedulas,* two other modifying *cedulas,* and chapters of letters from the king our lord, dated April 2 of this past year, 1597, in which, in spite of competition from other persons, his majesty approves of the choice made of my person and qualifications, ratifying and continuing my appointment. And having come now in search of the said kingdoms and provinces with my head officials, captains, *alféreces,* soldiers, and men of peace and war to settle and pacify, and with a great assemblage of necessary equipment such as wagons, carts, carriages, horses, oxen, sheep, and other livestock, and many married people, so I find myself this day with my entire army, with more people than I led out of Santa Bárbara, camped at the bank of the river called Del Norte at a place close to and neighboring upon the first settlements of New Mexico. Through these settlements there passes a road for carts, wide and level, that I have opened, after marching close to one hundred leagues over uninhabited country, so that it may be traveled without difficulty.

California Missions and their Military Protection

Accounts of the missions in California have either ignored or belittled them or romanticized them beyond reality. The missions are an important part of the religious and cultural heritage of the entire Southwest, not just California. They stand today as evidence of the early expeditions of the Mexicans and Spanish into what is now the United States.

From the heart of Mexico men and women pushed north to build outposts of Christian and Spanish civilization. The missions in Alta California (Upper California) were at the end of the earth at the time the United States was about to be born. A handful of soldiers and a few other men held California for the King of Spain. The costs of her empire weakened Spain. This account from the *Writings Of Junípero Serra* edited by Antoine Tibesar, O.F.M. shows the small returns Spaniards gained for risking their lives in the service of God and their King. This selection is used through the courtesy of the Academy of American Franciscan History.

A Letter from Junípero Serra

Hail Jesus, Mary, Joseph!

Most Excellent Sir:

Fray Junípero Serra of the Order of Friars Minor of our Seraphic Father Saint Francis, Apostolic Preacher of the College de Propaganda Fide of San Fernando of this Court of Mexico, President of the missions to the heathens of the Ports of Monterey and San Diego, and the intervening country:

Respectfully heeding what Your Excellency graciously commands and orders, in the letter dated the thirteenth of the present month, by means of Your Excellency's governmental secretariat, comprising the resolutions adopted at the meeting of the Most Illustrious Junta de Guerra, y Real Hacienda, which was convened and presided over by Your Excellency, and was pleased to take action on the petitions which I presented on March 13 of this year, concerning matters pertaining to the missions of Monterey and their dependencies belonging to this Apostolic College, namely:

That I should report, with all possible brevity, on the reduction that could be made in the number of soldiers which I requested for these new establishments, under number 10 of my said memorandum, since the number I propose there seemed to be too great.

However, as regards the individual escorts for each of the missions, following the proposals as laid down, at the present time little reduction could be made. As for the total of a hundred soldiers that I asked for, a considerable number could be taken away, if you are ready to defer, till a more suitable time, the plan we have for additional foundations. The number, as I clearly expressed in my written proposals, was in regard to the missions already founded, as well as in reference to those yet to be founded—and for the Royal Presidio besides. But, as regards the establishments that already exist, I say without any hesitation that a little more than sixty soldiers would suffice.

Now if Your Excellency desires to gain the merit and glory, in the sight of God, that by your orders the San Buenaventura Mission be founded, an undertaking which for years—and my heart is sad at the thought—has been postponed, while the Court at Madrid considers it as well established; and that by means of it, the Most Holy Name of Jesus Christ be made known to that vast multitude of gentiles living along the Santa Barbara Channel, as well as to the islands opposite, you could leave the rest of the foundations for a more opportune time; and thus as many as twenty might be deducted from the aforementioned number. That would leave us with eighty. These—and it is a suggestion I am offering to Your Excellency—might be divided in the following manner:

For the Royal Presidio of San Carlos de Monterey, soldiers	15
For the Mission of the same San Carlos on the Carmel	7
For the Mission of the same San Carlos	10
For the Mission of San Luis Obispo	10
For the Mission of San Gabriel	10
For the Mission and Port of San Diego	13
For the Mission of San Buenaventura	15
Total number of soldiers	80

Also two cannons like those carried on ships for salutes, similar to those at San Diego Mission.

This number might be sufficient for the present, and for the future. When later new foundations are made, the number may be reduced in the older foundations. I leave the whole matter in Your Excellency's hands.

I have nothing further to suggest on the subject.

Concerning the spiritual side: My said mission, when I left it, at the end of August, had about thirty Christians, not counting various babies who had winged their flight to God; most of the said Christians were baptized during the first year, because, in the second year, finding ourselves unable to give them food and keep them with us, we baptized very few, except when necessity demanded. Of these some absented themselves for days and even weeks, and when recalled, or without being recalled, they came back to the mission, they gave as their excuse the need to search for food. The cows' milk which we gave them appeared to them to be insufficient. And although we had no proper answer to make to their complaints, it hurt us all the same. They came back to us from the gentiles so changed that we could hardly recognize them. That is why we did not wish to increase the number, till a more suitable time.

Since my departure, the Fathers I left there write saying they have performed some more Baptisms, but I do not give any figure; some marriages also. And so of Christian Indian souls in that place, I should imagine there must be about forty, or thereabouts. Besides, they add that they have under instruction almost the whole of the *ranchería* close at hand, who, impatient of delay, declare that they want to be Christians, even though they do not get anything to eat.

To conclude: Most Excellent Sir, the missions, as is clear from what has been said, are still tender plants, and have made little headway, because they are as yet new, and also because they lacked the means. Then, too, every step they have made forward, or even hoped to make, has been to the accompaniment of contradictions and obstructions. But, without being at all prejudiced in the matter, I can certainly give Your Excellency the assurance that, on the part of the religious, both as regards the temporal and spiritual progress, no time has been wasted; and what little has been accomplished, to anyone who knows or may come to know how they did it, it will appear, and very rightly, a very great deal. How devotedly the religious have worked, and continue to work, God alone knows; but for us, that is sufficient.

I may further add this: if Your Excellency will kindly order proper measures to be taken—as indeed you are now doing—and remove hindrances, I take the future as a witness that before long, with the help of God, the outlook will be totally changed. That certainty, together with the longing I am bound to entertain to see such vast countries incorporated into the fold of our Holy Mother Church, and subjected to the Crown of our Catholic and most pious Monarch, whom God keep, has been the one and only reason of my laborious journey here. This I consider more each day as time well spent, since I have experienced so many favors from your Excellency. Your good will, added to your great piety and zeal, provides the crowning touch to the success of this great enterprise. And thus I hope, and will continue to pray that Our Lord God may grant Your Excellency the crown likewise of glory.

From this Apostolic College de Propaganda Fide de San Fernando de Mexico, May 21, 1773.

Most Excellent Sir.

Kissing the hand of Your Excellency,

Your most affectionate and devoted servant and chaplain, who holds you in the greatest respect, etc.,

Fray Junípero Serra

Report on Missions in the Southwest About 1776

Spain's mission in America has been described as "God, Glory and Gold." Her dedication to God's work has received less attention in history than her quest for gold and glory, but a more enlightened study of history will reveal great efforts on the part of Spain to take God's word to all living creatures in her realm. Among Spain's soldiers of God, the secular and regular clergy assumed the most important role and represented different forms of religious devotion. Gradually, the secular clergy (priests) in charge of ordinary church affairs gained domination over the friars and nuns from the many religious orders. Among these, Franciscans and Jesuits often took on tasks which other clergymen would not.

Father Garcés, a Franciscan friar, made five long journeys into Sonora, Arizona, and California between 1768 and 1781. His fifth journey (entrada, or entry) during 1775–1776 gives us a picture of life there at the time the United States was gaining independence. This portion of his journal describes travels that few men could survive in view of the distances and geography.

A Report from Francisco Garcés

ON THE EQUIPMENT OF THE MISSIONS

Since the first time that I was at San Gabriel, and saw the neediness of those missions, I have been pondering the means there may be to equip those of the Rio Colorado, when these shall come to be founded and the presidio that is proposed, inasmuch as always have I found difficulty enough. Leaving now to whomsoever may undertake to do it, to think up a better plan, I will speak my mind. By sea and by land I find that these establishments can be equipped, the country being pacified as I expect it to be, in view of the special providences which give themselves to this end. The route may be that which I indicated above: from Chihuahua to Janos, San Bernardino, Santa Cruz, Rio Gila, thence down river to the Yumas, if not to the (proposed) Presidio de la Asumpcion and to the Rio de Santa Maria down to the Colorado. But, considering that this road, taken from (the city of) Mexico, is of more than of 600 leagues; that there are encountered some difficulties thereon; that there may occur in the future some disturbance among the intermediate nations; and lastly (considering) the very great expense necessarily incurred in equipping missions and presidios by this route; I have pondered the other (way) by sea. This may be by the Golfo de Californias . . .

In view of that which the first Espanoles did; of that which the next ones left undone; and of that which is now beginning to be done; I cannot do less than thank God. The first Espanoles commenced to catechise in Sinaloa, and made discoveries unto the coast of the sea at the Canal, in connection with the settlements that they called Quevira—those which some of their successors held to be supposititious but which in these times seem to us probably, since in view of the houses of Moqui there is no reason to deny the others. I see that for a century has the faith been planted in these provinces, and that nothing prospered in those most propitious times when there were no enemies, and when his Majesty had no other expenses on these frontiers than the Presidio de Janos. For the Espanoles having lapsed from that primal fervor of conquest of souls for God and of provinces for their sovereign, when was alluring them the manageability of so many vicinities, I persuade myself that God permitted to infuriate itself more and more every day the Apache nation, until not only was pursuit impeded and rendered impracticable, but also were devastated our lands, we becoming obliged to spend immense sums in war defensive, and therein to sacrifice many lives. If that which has been expended in contending against the Apache from the beginning of his hostilities, or better say since God took him for an instrument to punish our sins, had been employed in new establishments, where would not now be raised the standard of the holy cross? In how many provinces as yet unknown would not now be obeyed the name of the catholic monarch? Thank God that it seems that in our times revives that antique Spanish spirit of discovering and possessing new lands, sacrificing in this enterprise lives and moneys for the acquisition of the precious pearls that are souls. Within a short time have we seen discovered anew the coasts of

the Mar del Sur to the far-famed and never-so-well praised Puerto de San Francisco, where there is rendered already worship to the great God, and this is pushed with sacred intrepidity still further up the coast. I see the grand providences which have given and still give themselves to the end that we may be able to penetrate further inland. I believe firmly that God must help us and that he must domesticate the nations most ferocious, if we oblige him, aggregating to his church so many thousands of souls as I say in the Diary are available for that purpose and who are awaiting us with open arms. When I have heard tell that the king our lord, in his royal cedulas of the new reglamento, expresses himself in these or some such words: "As one of the things that most occupy my royal attenton is the conversion of the gentiles, I command to my viceroy that he give me notice if there be any nation or nations who wish to flock to our religion"—I say, that when I have heard these expressions I have persuaded myself that his majesty must have an especial complacency at the sight of so many as I enumerate in this Diary, who, having been questioned and examined in this particular, have manifested desires to receive the catechism, and to submit themselves to his royal dominion; as also do I persuade myself that the desires which his majesty manifests will be carried into effect, even though for this it may be necessary to increase the royal costs. All of us who have the good fortune to be vassals of such a great king have learned his royal disposition to desire rather souls for God than moneys for his exchequer; inasmuch as there is no doubt it will redound to his greater glory in this world and in the other, opening the gates of heaven to so many souls, even though there remain few millions in the royal coffers. I conclude with lively hope thus: The king our lord wills. The king our lord is able. Soon the king our lord will do that which is at once so sacred and suitable a thing. Amen.

I protest that in all which I say in the Diary and in the Reflections thereupon nothing else moves me but the glory and honor of God, nor do I intend to prejudice the opinion of any one. I have told with Christian candor what I have learned, communicating without invidiousness what I have seen, heard, and experienced, which perhaps may serve to throw some light upon the decisions which the superior government may wish to make. Well do I recognize that my shortcomings, and the many faults and errors that I have committed in this and other entradas that I have made into gentiledom may be in part or perhaps altogether such as never have been seen hitherto; but I have consolation that the way is open to be able to enter to reap the harvest, and that if it be not gathered now it will be simply because no laborers are sent.

In this Diary will be found many defects, but I confess that all are unavoidable. If there be found any discrepancy between the Diary and the map in number of leagues, points of the compass, and observations for latitude, I advise that always must the map prevail; for it has been drawn since the Diary was written, and pains have been taken to make some corrections, though none of much consequence, and for this purpose the map was made in my presence. The figures which were promised to be put upon it to show each day's journey have since been omitted, there being so many.—Tubutáma and January 3, of 1777. Fray Francisco Garcés

A Census of Spanish Texas in 1783

As American independence approached, Spain continued its efforts to hold and expand its northern frontier against all odds. The pueblos and missions held on with little, if any, growth in population and physical development. Throughout the Spanish colonial period, pueblos and missions displayed Spanish concern for good urban planning, health, and a beautiful location.

Spaniards were keepers of accurate records, and made many studies of geography, plants, resources, and Indian medicine. Their principal interest, however, was people. The annual census of the Province of Texas for the year 1783 reveals much about the types of people and where they lived. (See the chart on the opposite page.)

Province of Texas

Statement that manifests the number of vassals and inhabitants which the King has in this province, with distinction as to class, condition and race of all the persons of both sexes, including the children.

Names of the Populations	Men	Women	Boys	Girls	Male Slaves	Female Slaves
Presidio of San Antonio de Béxar and Village of San Fernando	331	311	321	264	8	13
Mission of:						
San José	41	31	26	25		
San Juan Capistrano	53	26	13	7		
San Francisco de la Espada	32	28	30	6		
Nuestra Señora de la Concepción	32	29	18	8		
San Antonio de Valero	49	35	36	29		
Presidio of La Bahía del Espíritu Santo	193	147	68	45	1	
Mission of La Bahía del Espíritu Santo	75	66	33	40		
Mission of Nuestra Señora del Rosario						
Town of Nuestra Señora del Pilar de los Nacogdoches	129	104	52	50	8	6
Totals of the present year	935	777	597	474	17	19
Totals for last year	947	786	597	474	17	19
Decrease	12	9				
General summary:						
Of Spaniards	488	373	376	340		
Of Indians	290	241	70	76		
Of Mestizos	43	38	32	12		
Of Mulattos [de Color Quebrado]	114	125	119	46		
Of Slaves					17	19
Totals	935	777	597	474	17	19
General summary:						
Of secular ecclesiastics	3					
Of regular clergy	8					
Of those married	655	655				
Of widows and widowers	61	122				
Of single persons	208					
Totals	935	777	597	474	17	19

Royal Presidio of San Antonio de Béxar, December 31, 1783.

2

SOME HIGHLIGHTS IN MEXICAN HISTORY

The empires of Portugal and Spain split up when about twenty new American nations broke away from their mother countries, as the United States had broken away from England. Mexico was one of the many new nations formed early in the 19th century. Never before had so many new countries been formed in such a short time (about 1810 to 1830).

Republican forms of government established by constitutions followed a pattern set by the United States. Some features of government were copied from England and others from revolutionary France. In all this movement towards nationhood, the will of the people became the most important goal. Representative constitutional government in Mexico did not realize its goals of equality and justice at the start. The Mexican people suffered many wrongs at the hands of unjust leaders and the loss of territory to the Texans and the United States. Later, the French imposed an empire on Mexico for several years. From the 1870's to 1910, General Porfirio Díaz ruled Mexico with an iron hand.

Mexicans discovered new strength and ideals during the great Revolution of 1910. A new Mexico emerged into modern times. Its progress in government, peace, education, and the arts was copied by many new nations formed in the 20th century.

The readings in this section illustrate some major ideas and events that made Mexico a unique nation and people. The selections suggest some of the problems and possibilities for the future that lie within the mixture of Europeans, Africans, Asians, and Indians that blend to form the Mexican of today.

REPUBLICS REPLACE MONARCHIES IN AMERICA

Mexico and the United States emerged as independent nations in a very similar way. Each was formed as a revolutionary society that struggled against a monarchy for freedom.

Mexicans were profoundly affected by the U.S. Declaration of Independence and the Revolutionary War. Soon after the Declaration of Independence appeared, Spanish colonists in Mexico read it and were inspired by its statements of the rights of man and its justification for revolt against the injustices of a foreign monarch.

Less than a half century later, Mexico, too, was an independent nation. Efforts toward freedom had started in 1810, but it was not until 1821 that Mexico actually became independent from Spain.

The Mexican movement for independence differed from the American one because traditions and political conditions differed. Moreover, the extent of the Mexican republic was vast, stretching from Central America to Texas and northwest to the border between California and Oregon. Mexico tried to establish republicanism and to populate this vast area. In this effort, it encouraged immigrants from the United States, as well as from other lands.

Miguel Hidalgo as Seen by a Contemporary Mexican Historian

In many respects Mexican independence was more troublesome for descendants than that in the United States. Mexican independence was gained in several stages, some of which were anti-democratic, and only after many years. The first formal movement for independence began with the revolt of Father Miguel Hidalgo. His movement failed, but it served to usher in a new era during which independence did finally come.

Lucas Alamán was opposed to the revolution that freed Mexico, although he tried to help the new republic. Alamán gives us an interesting picture of Father Hidalgo, who started the revolution in 1810. Although Hidalgo was captured and executed in less than a year, the revolution's first period lasted until 1815.

Although he was a Spaniard, Father Hidalgo grew to hate Spanish injustices and took the side of the poor and uneducated, especially the Indians. Thousands of Indians rallied behind his banner of *la Virgen de Guadalupe* (the Virgin Mary of Guadalupe) whom he worshipped as the patron of the Indians. The fighting between the Spaniards and the Indians was bloody. The royal troops finally reestablished order by 1815.

Hidalgo: Torchbearer of the Revolution

Miguel Hidalgo (1753–1811), the scholarly white-haired priest of the town of Dolores and onetime rector of the college of San Nicolás at Valladolid, hardly seemed fitted by background and disposition to head a revolution. It was Hidalgo, nevertheless, who overcame the waverings of his associates when their conspiracy was discovered, and who transformed what had been planned as an upper-class creole revolt into a rising of the masses. Alamán, historian and bitter enemy of the revolution—who knew Hidalgo in the peaceful years before the great upheaval—describes the curate of Dolores.

Don Miguel Hidalgo, being neither austere in his morals nor very orthodox in his opinions, did not concern himself with the spiritual administration of his parish, which he had turned over, together with half the income of his curacy, to a priest named Don Francisco Iglesias. Knowing French—a rather rare accomplishment at that period, especially among churchmen—he formed a taste for technical and scientific books and zealously promoted various agricultural and industrial projects in his parish. He considerably furthered viticulture, and today that whole region produces abundant harvests of grapes; he also encouraged the planting of mulberry trees for the raising of silkworms. In Dolores eighty-four trees planted by him are still standing, in the spot called "the mulberry trees of Hidalgo," as well as the channels that he had dug for irrigating the entire plantation. He established a brickyard, constructed troughs for tanning hides, and promoted a variety of other enterprises.

All this, plus the fact that he was not only generous but lavish in money matters, had won him the high regard of his parishioners—especially the Indians, whose languages he had mastered. It also gained him the esteem of all who took a sincere interest in the advancement of the country, men like Abad y Queipo, the bishop-elect of Michoacán and Riaño, the intendant of Guanajuato. It seems, however, that he had little basic knowledge of the industries which he fostered, and even less of that systematic spirit which one must have to make substantial progress with them. . . .

He was very fond of music, and not only had it taught to the Indians of his parish, where he formed an orchestra, but borrowed the orchestra of the provincial battalion of Guanajuato for the frequent parties that he gave in his home. Since his residence was a short distance from Guanajuato, he often visited the capital and stayed there for long periods of time. This gave me an opportunity to see him and to know him. He was fairly tall and stoop-shouldered, of dark complexion and quick green eyes; his head bent a little over his chest and was covered by sparse gray hair, for he was more than sixty years old. He was vigorous, though neither swift in his movements; short of speech in ordinary conversation but animated in academic style when the argument grew warm. He was careless in dress, wearing only such garb as small town curates commonly wore in those days.

THE STORMING OF THE GRANARY IN GUANAJUATO, 1810

A little before twelve a numerous rabble of Indians—a few armed with rifles, the majority with lances, clubs, slings, and bows and arrows—appeared in sight on the causeway of Our Lady of Guadalupe, which leads into the city from the Marfil road. The vanguard of this group passed over the bridge of the same name as the causeway and arrived in front of the barricade at the foot of Mendizabal Hill. Don Gilberto de Riaño, to whom his father had entrusted command of that spot as the most dangerous one, ordered them to stop in the name of the king; as the multitude continued to advance, he gave the order to fire. A number of Indians were killed, and the rest retreated precipitately. On the causeway, a native of Guanajuato told them they should go to Cuarto Hill, and he himself led them there.

Meanwhile Hidalgo's other foot soldiers, amounting to some 20,000 Indians, joined by the miners and the common people of Guanajuato, occupied the heights and all the houses fronting on the granary. The soldiers from Celaya, armed with rifles, took up positions there, while a cavalry corps of some 2,000 men, composed of dragoons of the regiment de la reina, and country people armed with lances, with Hidalgo at their head, ascended the road called de la yerbabuena as far as the place known as "the racetracks" and from there descended to the city. Hidalgo stopped at the barracks of the cavalry regiment del principe, where he remained during the action. The column continued its march across the whole city, finally halting at the street de Belen. In their march the soldiery looted a candy store and released from jail all prisoners of both sexes, numbering between 300 and 400 persons, among them criminals guilty of grave offenses. The male prisoners were impressed into the insurgent ranks for the attack on the granary. . . .

The taking of the granary of Granaditas was entirely the work of the populace of Guanajuato, joined by the numerous gangs of Indians led by Hidalgo. Hidalgo and his lieutenants could do no more than lead their people to the hills and begin the attack. Once it was begun, it was impossible to give any orders, since there was no one to receive orders and carry them out; there was no order in that confused mob, and no subordinate officers to direct it. The Indians throwing themselves with extraordinary bravery into the first military action they had ever seen, could not turn back, for the mob pressing upon those who went in front, compelled them to advance and instantly took the space left by the fallen. The resistance of the defenders, though courageous, lacked all order and plan, owing to the early death of the intendant, and the early end of the action must be attributed to this, for by four in the afternoon everything was over.

The Mexican Constitution of 1824

Mexico established a republican government which combined features of the government of the United States and Spanish legal tradition. Some liberties guaranteeed in the U.S. Bill of Rights were included in the Mexican Constitution. Many other Latin American countries adopted constitutions modeled, in part, on the United States example.

By 1830, it had become clear that a federal governmental system was difficult to implement in Mexico. The rights of states as against the federal government were not clear. Many individuals and groups placed national loyalty below their own selfish interests. Thus, areas like California, New Mexico, and Texas lost interest in preserving the Mexican union. A fine constitution could not preserve the nation without the support of the people.

The Constitution of the Mexican United States

The Supreme Executive Power, provisionally appointed by the general sovereign Congress of the Nation, to all who shall see these presents, Know and Understand, That the same Congress has decreed and sanctioned the following:

THE FEDERAL CONSTITUTION OF THE UNITED MEXICAN STATES

In the name of God, all powerful, author and supreme legislator of society. The general constituent Congress of the Mexican Nation, in the discharge of the duties confided to them by their constituents, in order to establish and fix its political Independence, establish and confirm its Liberty, and promote its prosperity and glory, decree as follows:

CONSTITUTION OF THE UNITED MEXICAN STATES

Title 1st. Only Section.—Of the Mexican Nation, its Territory and Religion.

Article 1. The Mexican Nation, is forever free and independent of the Spanish government, and every other power.

2. Its Territory consists of that which was formerly called the vice-royalty of New-Spain that styled the captain generalship of Tucaton, that of the commandant generalship formerly called the Internal Provinces of East and West, and that of Lower and Upper California, with the lands annexed, and adjacent lands in both seas. By a constitutional law, a demarkation of the limits of the Federation will be made as soon as circumstances will permit.

3. The Religion of the Mexican-Nation, is, and will be perpetually, the Roman Catholic Apostolic. The Nation will protect it by wise and just laws, and prohibit the exercise of any other whatever.

Title 2nd. Only Section.—Form of Government of the Nation, of its integral parts and division of Supreme Power.

4. The Mexican Nation adopts for its Government, the form of Republican representative, popular Federal.

5. The parts of this Federation, are the States and Territories as follows:—The state of the Chiapas, Chiuahua, Coahuila and Texas, Durango, Guanajuato, Mexico, Michoacan, New Leon, Oajaca, Puebla de los Angeles, Quctaro, San Luis Potosi, Sinora and Sinaloa, Tobasco, Tumaulipas, Vera Cruz, Xalisco, Yucatan Zacatecas, the Territory of Upper California, Lower California, Colima and Santa Fe of New Mexico—a constitutional law shall fix the character of Tlaxcala.

6. The supreme power of the Federation will be divided for its exercises, in Legislative, Executive, and Judicial. . . .

171. The Articles of this Constitution and the Constitutional Act which establishes the Liberty and Independence of the Mexican Nation, its Religion, form of Government, Liberty of the Press, and division of the Supreme Powers of the Federation, and of the States, can never be reformed. . . .

Given in Mexico, 4th October, 1821, fourth year of Independence, third of Liberty, and second of the Federation.

Signed by the members of Congress and the Supreme Executive Power.

The Constitution of the State of Coahuila and Texas, 1827

The history of the United States has been one of territorial expansion. In this respect Mexico has been losing territory ever since it was formed. At the outset the Republic of Mexico claimed the lands formerly part of the Viceroyalty of New Spain, which included part of present Central America. States' rights were great under the Constitution of 1824, and some states opted for separation. To some extent the desire of the people of Coahuila for a division into two states was within the legal tradition of Mexico. Already some parts of the Republic of Mexico had broken away to form Central American republics of their own.

The Mexican Republic granted wide local authority to each state in the union. The portions below of the 1827 Constitution in Coahuila and Texas show how laws in Mexico helped define and protect individual liberties. Slavery was abolished in this constitution and public education was ordered in all pueblos. This development was cut short by events that culminated in war. Texas broke away from Mexico in 1836 and formed the Republic of Texas. The southern part of Coahuila remained as part of Mexico.

Some Articles of the Constitution of the State of Coahuila and Texas

In the name of the omnipotent God, author and Supreme Legislator of the universe, The Constitutive Congress of the State of Coahuila and Texas, desiring to comply with the will of the people their Constituents, and for the purpose of duly fulfilling the grand and magnificent object of promoting the glory and prosperity of the same State, decree, for its administration and government, the following: . . .

Art. 6. The Territory of the State, embraces those Provinces formerly known under the name of the Provinces of Coahuila and Texas. . . .

Art. 9. The Roman Catholic Apostolic Religion is the Religion of the State. The State protects it by wise and just laws, and prohibits the exercise of any other.

Art. 10. The State will regulate all the expenses necessary to the preserving of this Religion, according to the Concordates which the nation will celebrate with the Apostolical Seal, and to have the laws which the said Nation will pass concerning the exercise of the Patronato in the whole confederation.

Art. 11. Every man who inhabits the territory of the State, although he may be but a traveller, enjoys the imprescriptible rights of Liberty, Security, Property and Equality, and it is the duty of the said State, to preserve and protect by wise and equitable laws, these universal rights of men.

Art. 12. The State is also obliged to protect all its inhabitants, in the exercise of that right which they have, of writing, printing and publishing freely, their political ideas and opinions, without the necessity of any examination, revision or censure, anterior to the publication, under the restrictions and responsibility (sic) established, or which may hereafter be established by the general laws on that subject.

Art. 13. From and after the promulgation of this Constitution in the principal town of each District, nobody can be born a slave, and the introduction of slaves under any pretext after six months from said publication is prohibited. . . .

Art. 22. The exercise of these rights (of citizenship) is suspended: . . . fifthly, for not having any employment, office, or known means of living; sixthly, for not knowing how to read or write: but this disposition shall take effect only after the year 1850, and with respect to those who then may enter upon the exercise of the rights of Citizens. . . .

Art. 145. In the chief town of each department of the State, there shall be a functionary, in whose charge the political government of the same shall be placed, and he shall be called, Chief of Police of the department.

Art. 146. In order to be chief of police of a department, one must be a citizen in the exercise of his rights, of twenty-five years of age, a citizen of the State and a resident in it for three years, one of which immediately before his election.

Art. 147. The governor, on the proposition of three of the councillors (sic), together with the petition of the ayuntamientos of each department, shall nominate the chiefs of departments, except that of the capital.

Art. 148. The chiefs of the departments shall be immediately subject to the governor of the State. . . .

Art. 155. The duty of the ayuntamientos is to watch over the interior government of the pueblos of the State, and to this end each pueblo that heretofore possessed one, shall continue to do so.

Art. 156. In those pueblos which have no ayuntamiento, and which have a right to one, there shall be one; and they cannot avoid having them in the chief towns of the district, no matter what may be their population, nor in those pueblos which by themselves or with the neighboring one, amount to one thousand souls, unless these latter be joined to some other municipality. . . .

Art. 159. The ayuntamientos, shall be composed of the Alcalde or Alcaldes, Snydic or Snydics and Regidors, the number of whom shall be settled by the regulations already mentioned.

Art. 160. In order to be a member of the ayuntamiento one must be a citizen in the exercise of his rights, of the age of twenty-five years, or if married, of the age of twenty-one, a resident of the district to which the ayuntamiento belongs, and have three years of residence in it, and one of them immediately before the election, have some capital or trade, by which he can make a living and know how to read and write. . . .

Art. 164. The members of the ayuntamiento shall be nominated through the medium of electoral municipal assemblies. . . .

Art. 215. In all the pueblos of the State there shall be a competent number of elementary schools, in which youth shall be taught reading, writing, and arithmetic, the catechism of the Christian religion, a brief and plain explanation of this constitution and the general constitution of the Republic, the rights and duties of men in society, and whatever may be conducive to the best education of youth.

Art. 216. In proper places also, in proportion as circumstances permit it, there shall be established for those branches of education most necessary to public instruction, the sciences and arts useful to the State, and the above mentioned constitution shall likewise be explained with the greatest attention.

Art. 217. The method of education shall be uniform all through the State, and to this end Congress shall, in order to facilitate it, form a general plan of public instruction, and shall regulate by means of statutes and laws, every thing appertaining to this very important business. . . .

Art. 224. In the following Congress, the alterations, reformations or repeals proposed, shall be discussed, and should they be approved of, they shall immediately be published as constitutional articles. . . .

Given in Saltillo, on the 11th March, 1827
Santiago del Valle, president—
Juan Vincente Campos, vice president—.

A FOREIGN EMPEROR, A LIBERAL PRESIDENT, A DICTATOR, AND ANOTHER REVOLUTION

Between the early 1860's and the Revolution of 1910, Mexico was ruled by Emperor Maximilian, Benito Pablo Juárez, a liberal reform-minded president, and Porfirio Díaz, a general who seized power.

When Juárez was elected president in 1861, he found his country in serious financial difficulty, so he immediately stopped payments on loans his predecessors had obtained from European countries. The French, to whom Mexico was indebted, used his action as an excuse to invade Mexico and install Maximilian, an Austrian archduke, as emperor.

Juárez was a leader in the fight for freedom, and when the French were finally expelled in 1866, he was again elected president.

A few years after Juárez died in 1872, Porfirio Díaz, a Mexican Army general, seized power and ruled until he was ousted in 1910.

Mexico's history until recently is more representative of the world in general than of the United States. With such a complex history, it is not surprising, then, that Mexicans are a complex people who do not agree on who or what they are. Even their language is not uniform. Spanish is the language of the upper classes or educated people, but is not a universal tongue. The other major languages are Mexican (or Aztec or Nahuatl), Maya, Mixtecan, Zapotecan, and Otomí. The problem of national self-identity was increased by political leaders like President Carranza, who tried to "Americanize" Mexico at the expense of Mexican and Indian culture and traditions.

It should not surprise anyone that many Mexican Americans share this problem of self-identity. Most peoples and even nations share this riddle. As a land formed by immigrants, Americans can understand the experience of Mexico to a great extent.

President Benito Juárez and the United States Try To Expel France from Mexico

Within one man's lifetime, Mexico suffered a disastrous defeat at the hands of the United States (1846–48), and then France imposed an Austrian emperor over Mexico. At the city of Puebla, on May 5, 1862, Mexican patriots won a great victory over the French invaders. Later overwhelmed, Mexican patriots never surrendered. The United States was busy with its Civil War and Mexico fought alone against French troops and Emperor Maximilian. After the War Between the States ended, the United States increased its pressure on France to leave Mexico.

Mexican patriots did not trust United States desires to expel France in view of American desires for expanding its territory. Juárez reflected the mixed feelings of Mexican patriots in 1865 as they saw U.S. troops mass along their border. The French government was impressed with the American pressures. In view of Maximilian's failure to gain popular support, France pulled out its troops in 1866. Soon after, the Empire of Maximilian in Mexico fell.

The following selection is from *Viva Juárez* by Charles A. Smart.

Two Men, Two Women, and Destiny

In watching and comparing Juárez and Maximilian, doña Margarita and Charlotte, and others, as they were caught up in the tides of history, we need not commit the common error of assuming that these great forces were above and beyond the decisions and control, and hence the responsibility, of individual human beings. Millions of unknown persons in North America and Europe were deciding what they wanted most, and it was their decisions and actions, and not inhuman laws or powers, that determined the results that constituted destiny.

One tide of history came from the north. Even before the Union victory and the death of Lincoln, enough Americans in the North were sufficiently irritated and humiliated by the presence on the continent of an empire supported by the French army to arouse their congressmen, and so indirectly to make it possible for Generals Grant, Sheridan, and John M. Schofield, acting just within the limits of their authority, to take steps towards the Mexican border. In May, 1865, after various schemes of an American auxiliary force to go to the aid of the Mexican Republic had come to nothing because of the prudent reserve of Lincoln and Juarez, General Sheridan was sent by President Johnson to the border, and in time his well-armed force grew to the formidable number of 100,000 men. While Gwin, Maury, Magruder, and other ex-Confederates were busying themselves within the Empire, this force just beyond the Rio Bravo undoubtedly had more influence on Bazaine and Maximilian. Whenever there were rumors of imperial advances to the north, more American soldiers appeared at El Paso, and although he rebuked General Sedgwick for meddling in the cauldron at Matamoros, Sheridan relieved himself by staging demonstrations all along the border, and by "condemning" large supplies of arms and ammunition, leaving them conveniently beside the river, and then making sure that the Mexican republicans knew that he had done so.

Seward had a broader view than the eager generals, whose pressure on the civil government was becoming troublesome, and he pulled a trick from his sleeve by sending General Schofield on a futile mission to France. Then in a long series of communications of various kinds, notable among which were those of September 6, 1865, December 16, 1865, and February 12, 1866, he slowly drew the velvet glove from the steel fist. On the last date he declared, in reply to French fictions and evasions, "that the proceedings in Mexico were regarded in the United States as having been taken without the authority, and prosecuted against the will and opinions of the Mexican people; that the United States had not seen any satisfactory evidence that the people of Mexico had spoken and called into being or accepted the so-called empire, and that the withdrawal of the French troops were deemed necessary to allow such a proceeding to be taken." He concluded with a virtual ultimatum: "We shall be gratified when the Emperor shall give to us . . . definite information of the time when French military operations may be expected to cease in Mexico."

President Johnson had made a similar statement on December 4, 1865, and Juárez's comment on it deserves study: "I said in my last that we were entirely in agreement in judging the message of Mr. Johnson in relation to the cause of Mexico. He said what he had to say, and that harms us in no respect. On the contrary, what he said surprised me agreeably, because I was hoping for very little or nothing. I have never had illusions with regard to the open aid that that nation could give us. I know that the rich and the powerful do not feel or try to alleviate the miseries of the poor. The former fear and respect each other and are not able to break lances in the quarrels of the weak or against the injustices with which they are oppressed. This is and has been the way of the world. Only those who do not recognize it deceive themselves. Instead of complaining, Mexicans must redouble their efforts to free themselves from their tyrants. Thus they will be worthy to be free and respected, for thus they will owe their glory to their own efforts and will not, like miserable slaves, need others to think, work, and speak for them. It may happen occasionally that the powerful will find it advantageous to defend a poor, oppressed people, but they will do that for their own interest and gain. The weak can never have any sure hope in that outcome. This could happen in our present situation; only for that reason may Napoleon withdraw his forces, no matter how many troops he has sent and kept on sending, only to withdraw them, if his fear of the United States, or his other interests, or more probably both, counsel him to do so. His plan may be to reinforce his troops in order to make as advantageous a bargain as he can with the power that he fears and respects because it is strong. We shall see. We shall continue our defense as though we were self-sufficient."

Porfirio Díaz Rules Mexico for a Generation

For about thirty years after the death of Juárez, one man dominated Mexico. Although Don Porfirio Díaz, the new leader, was from a background like that of Juárez, he imposed a very different stamp upon Mexico than the justice under the rule of law which Juárez championed.

Díaz used cunning and bloody force to maintain a dictatorship dedicated to peace and order, as well as material prosperity. Foreign ideas and investments entered Mexico and she became known around the world. Most Mexicans did not gain much, because Díaz favored the rich and educated. He spent little for public education, so few poor people could join the ranks of the happy upper class.

No one expected the Díaz government to fall in 1910, or that a rich man like Francisco Madero would be the instrument to start the Mexican revolution. Madero and a few friends argued for modest reforms, but others drew to his side and demanded a social revolution instead. Within several months, a dictatorship of some thirty years came to an end, and a new revolutionary period began.

This selection about the rule of Díaz is from *Many Mexicos* by Lesley Byrd Simpson.

Mexico Under Porfirio Díaz

The legend of Don Porfirio is full of magic. In all Mexico there is only one Don Porfirio. His name evokes the nostalgic longings of the disinherited who, since the Revolution of 1910, have been looking back on the Age of Don Porfirio much as Lot's wife looked back on Sodom and Gomorrah. The good old days of Don Porfirio have become a kind of cult, not limited by any means to the ex-nobility for the present: devotees of the God of Industrialization recognize in Don Porfirio the prophet who showed them the way to the Promised Land—which makes *porfirismo* a much less prickly subject to attack than *juarismo*. For everyone of late feels kindly toward Don Porfirio, although his most ardent admirers, naturally, continue to be those who hope that some day another Strong Hand will take over and run the country more to their heart's desire. It is one of the many charming inconsistencies of Mexico that Porfirio Díaz, the military caudillo and bitter enemy of Juárez, should have succeeded the Lawgiver of Oaxaca and ruled Mexico for a third of a century as an irresponsible despot, under the cloak of the liberal Constitution that Juárez and his devoted company had fought so long to establish.

Sebastián Lerdo de Tejado, the immediate successor of Juárez, was an able and vigorous man, but he lacked something, and I suspect it was the symbolic value of Juárez: Juárez the Indian, Juárez the high priest of Law and Justice. Who but Don Benito could have gone unguarded through the back country for ten years, alone in his battered black carriage, trusting to the exquisite courtesy of his own people? Lerdo de Tejada continued the policies of his late chief, and he even succeeded in appeasing most of the caudillos who had "pronounced" for Díaz; that is, all but Díaz himself, who retired to a sugar farm in Vera Cruz and bided his time. . . .

Porfirio Díaz had the virtues of a great barbarian, and he needed them. The lesser caudillos who had elevated him had to be kept quiet, and they had to be kept harmless. Unlike Juárez, Don Porfirio was not so naive as to expect his military chieftains to put their country's welfare before their personal fortunes. Their new master had the cunning of a Cesare Borgia. He gave his generals little jobs and restored them to their rightful place at the public trough; he kept them apart and played them off against each other; he split the army into small units and scattered them about the country; but he did not trust it. For his immediate use in terrorizing dissenters he organized a private army of thugs, whom he called his *bravi* and who could be counted on to wreck newspapers and remove suspected opponents in their own way. The police, of course, could never track down the criminals.

The nation was suffering from its endemic plague of banditry. Don Porfirio's solution was to set up a national gendarmerie called the Rurales, recruited from the gunmen of the cities and from among the bandits themselves. They were given showy uniforms, good salaries, and the power to shoot on sight, and no questions asked. Into their capable hands was placed the task of making Mexico safe for Don Porfirio and his friends. Troublesome Indian caciques, striking workmen, indiscreet speakers and writers, and honest bandits disappeared into the noisome dungeons of the fearful old Belén Penitentiary, or were shot "while attempting to escape," an effective device known as the Ley Fuga. In the course of a few years Mexico became the best policed country in the world. It was ruled by martial law, without courts, and the Rurales loved to shoot. . . .

As the years rolled by and Mexico lay quiet in her straitjacket, foreign capital was encouraged to come in; manufactures and agriculture flourished; railroads pushed their way south from the border; American miners reopened the ancient reales de minas of the Spaniards, and smelters began to belch their yellow fumes into the desert air. Silver, gold, copper, lead, and zinc flowed north to feed the rapidly expanding commerce and industry of the United States; and coffee, sugar, bananas, and henequen found a ready market abroad. In 1893, Don Porfirio's brilliant Minister of Finance, José Ives Limantour, funded the public debt at a reasonable rate of interest and balanced the national budget. Mexico was solvent! This feat was so close to being a miracle that Don Porfirio was hailed everywhere as the "Coming Man." Grumblers were quiet for once, or, if they had anything to say, they said it to themselves. For many years Mexico saw not a single pronunciamiento, and the Pax Porfiriana was a blessing that his country could appreciate meaningfully. . . .

The clergy awoke from their long nightmare and discovered that religion and the liberal dictatorship of Don Porfirio were not necessarily incompatible. The offensive laws of Juárez's day were discreetly ignored; religious schools and thinly disguised nunneries appeared; and should there be trouble the pious Doña Carmen Díaz could be counted on to patch things up with Don Porfirio, who was an indulgent husband. The ranks of the clergy were swelled by Spanish, French, and Italian priests, until by the end of the regime they numbered some five thousand, against the pitiful five hundred of the dark days of Juárez. Only the native clergy grumbled.

Don Porfirio had the intelligence to surround himself with able men, his cientificos, a brilliant group of lawyers and economists, headed by Limantour, worshipers at the new and glittering shrine of Science and Progress. They honestly believed that a dictatorship was the only possible government for their backward country, and they did their utmost to force modernity upon it. . . .

The cientificos were cultivated men, and along with its material improvements they thought their capital should have its cultural ornaments as well. They encouraged letters of an innocuous kind, mostly perfumed imitations of the French, but no subversive nonsense. Poetry, the novel, the theater, all flourished in Mexico City in Don Porfirio's reign, but they were remote from the life of the country and are now hardly more than literary curiosities. . . .

Beyond question the material and even the cultural advancement of Mexico during the dictatorship of Don Porfirio was very great; so many miles of railroads, so many millions of dollars invested in this and that, so many years of peace and order, eighty millions of pesos in the treasury. It may even be true that Díaz was a superior kind of benevolent despot. It may also be true that some sort of military dictatorship was inevitable after the frightful chaos of the mid-century, and that if Don Porfirio had not taken over, Mexico would have been torn to pieces by the rival caudillos whom he so effectively checkmated. Otherwise, the price of the Pax Porfiriana was too high. . . .

The year 1910 was the year of the Great Centennial, celebrating the hundredth anniversary of Miguel Hidalgo's Grito de Dolores and the birth of Independence. It was also meant to advertise to the world the triumph of progress and porfirismo. The irony of the double program was almost too heavy to be ignored, but it was ignored. Like a plant whose roots have been cut off, the Golden Age of Don Porfirio threw out its last spray of blossoms with the Centennial, and died. The century died as it had begun, in bloodshed. . . .

The fall of Don Porfirio was as inevitable as it was unplanned. . . .

The Mexican Constitution of 1917

For many Mexican Americans *la Revolution* in Mexico in 1910 has an appeal that exceeds the American Revolution of 1776. Perhaps because it took place during this century, the Mexican Revolution is more relevant to contemporary Mexican Americans. A central part of the Revolution was the Constitution of 1917.

Under the dictatorship of General Porfirio Díaz, material and social progress stagnated for the majority of the population. In 1910, a revolution started to gain modest goals. Before long Mexico caught on fire with demands for justice, peace, and land. The early revolutionary leaders like Emiliano Zapata, Francisco Madero, Alvaro Obregón, and Pancho Villa were in time overshadowed by Venustiano Carranza. Under his leadership the Constitution of 1917 was formed as a great document of this century.

This selection from *The Ejido: Mexico's Way Out* by Eyler N. Simpson describes the events and major new features of the Constitution of 1917.

A Constitution That Combined Tradition and Reform

The Constitution of 1917 has been justly recognized as one of the most important social documents of modern times. The ideas embodied therein, to be sure, were not entirely new nor extremely radical; on the contrary, the conceptions regarding property and the rights of labor had long been commonplace in the western world and many of them were to be found on the statute books of other countries. What gives the Mexican constitution its general importance is the number and variety of advanced social and economic doctrines brought together in one place and set down as the basic law of a country. Mexico, in theory at any rate, achieved at one bound what many other countries have been struggling step by step to obtain. The particular importance of the constitution derives from the fact that whatever their source, or however familiar they may have been in other parts of the world, many of the ideas written into the 1917 constitution were, so far as Mexico was concerned, both novel and radical. The framework of the 1917 constitution is essentially the same as that of 1857. The political structure of the government—with such characteristic democratic features as the separation of powers between the executive, legislative and judicial branches; universal suffrage; periodical elections with a president as the highest executive officer, and so forth—is the same under the Constitution of 1917 as it was before. The Constitution of 1857 was not destroyed; nor was it, strictly speaking, reformed. It was added to. The additions, however, were of such a nature as to shift the whole emphasis and meaning of the document. . . .

DETAILS OF ARTICLE TWENTY SEVEN

1. The Nature of Property

a. Private title to lands and waters is not "original" but results from an act of the Nation.

The ownership of lands and waters comprised within the limits of the national territory is vested originally in the Nation, which has had, and has, the right to transmit title thereof to private persons, thereby constituting private property. (Par. 1.)

b. In constituting private property the Nation reserves the right to impose certain limitations in the public interest:

The Nation shall have at all times the right to impose on private property such limitations as the public interest may demand, as well as the right to

regulate the development of natural resources, which are susceptible of appropriation, in order to conserve them and equitably to distribute the public wealth. For this purpose necessary measures shall be taken (1) to divide large landed estates; (2) to develop small landed holdings; (3) to establish new centers of rural population with such lands and waters as may be indispensable to them; (4) to encourage agriculture and to prevent the destruction of natural resources, and (5) to protect property from damage detrimental to society. (Par. 3)

c. The power of the Nation to expropriate private property is restricted.

Private property shall not be expropriated except for reasons of public utility and by means of (mediante) indemnification. (Par. 2)

d. The liability of the Nation in cases of expropriation is strictly limited:

The Federal and State laws shall determine within their respective jurisdictions those cases in which the occupation of private property shall be considered of public utility; and in accordance with the said laws the administrative authorities shall make the corresponding declaration. The amount fixed as compensation for the expropriated property (cosa) shall be based on the sum at which the said property shall be valued for fiscal purposes in the cadastral or revenue offices, whether this value be that manifested by the owner or merely impliedly accepted by reason of the payment of his taxes on such a basis, to which there shall be added ten percent. The increased value which the property in question may have acquired through improvements made subsequent to the date of the fixing of the fiscal value shall be the only matter subject to expert opinion and to judicial determination. The same procedure shall be observed in respect to objects whose value is not recorded in the revenue offices. (Par. 8)

e. The Nation's ownership of waters and minerals is direct and imprescriptible; only the "right of exploitation" of the Nation's waters and subsoil may be conceded to private parties—and that only on the condition that the resources be regularly developed and the right legally exercised:

In the Nation is vested direct ownership of all minerals or substances which in veins, layers, masses, or beds constitute deposits whose nature is different from the components of the land, such as minerals from which metals and metaloids used for industrial purposes are extracted; beds of precious stones, rock salt and salt lakes formed directly by marine waters; products derived from the decomposition of rocks, when their exploitation requires underground work; phosphates which may be used for fertilizers; solid mineral fuels; petroleum and all hydrocarbons—solid, liquid or gaseous. (Par. 4) . . .

2. *Legal Entities Having the Right to Hold Private Property and the Nature of their Rights*

a. Legal capacity to acquire ownership of lands and waters is not a "uniform" capacity automatically bestowed upon all and sundry alike. On the contrary, certain individuals and corporate entities may not hold property at all while the rights of other individuals and corporations are definitely limited, to wit:

(1) Mexicans vs. foreigners.

Only Mexicans by birth or naturalization and Mexican companies have the right to acquire ownership in lands, waters and their appurtenances, or to obtain concessions to develop mines, waters or mineral fuels in the Republic of Mexico. The Nation may grant the same right to foreigners, provided they agree . . . to be considered Mexicans in respect to such property, and accordingly not to invoke the protection of their Governments in respect to the same . . . Within a zone of 100 kilometers from the frontiers, and of 50 kilometers from the seacoast, no foreigner shall under any conditions acquire direct ownership of lands and waters. (Par. 7; fr. I.)

(2) Religious institutions.

The religious institutions known as churches, irrespective of creed, shall in no case have legal capacity to acquire, hold or administer real prop-

erty or loans as may be at present held by the said religious institutions, either on their own behalf or through third parties, shall vest in the Nation. . . . (Par. 7; fr. II.)

(3) Charitable institutions, schools, etc.

Public and private charitable institutions for the sick and needy, for scientific research, or for the diffusion of knowledge, mutual aid societies or organizations formed for any other lawful purpose shall in no case acquire, hold or administer loans made on real property, unless the mortgage terms do not exceed ten years. . . . (Par. 7; fr. III.)

(4) Commercial stock companies.

Commercial stock companies shall not acquire, hold or administer rural properties . . . (Par. 7; fr. IV.)

(5) Banks.

Banks duly organized under the laws governing institutions of credit may make mortgage loans on rural and urban property in accordance with the provisions of the said laws, but they may not own nor administer more real property than that absolutely necessary for their direct purposes. (Par. 7; fr. V.)

(6) Communal groups.

Properties held in common by co-owners (conduenazgos), settlements (rancherias), towns (pueblos), congregations (congregaciones), tribes and other bodies of population which, as a matter of fact or law, conserve their communal character, shall have legal capacity to enjoy in common the waters, woods and lands belonging to them, or which may have been or shall be restored to them according to the law of January 6, 1915, until such time as the manner of making the division of the lands shall be determined by law. (Par. 7; fr. VI.)

3. *Principles and Procedures for the Solution of the Agrarian Problem*

In addition to reaffirming and strengthening the provisions of the Constitution of 1857 designed to prevent the Church from monopolizing rural property, to forbidding commercial stock companies from holding or administering rural property and to reestablishing the rights of villages to hold and enjoy property in their corporate capacity—all of which represent more or less negative contributions to the solution of the agrarian problem—Article 27 also sets up a body of positive principles and procedures designed to rectify the inequalities in the distribution of rural property. These may be classified under three heads: (a) the creation by restoration or by outright grant of village lands (ejidos); (b) the recovery of national lands and waters illegally alienated or held "in prejudice of the public interest"; and (c) the destruction of latifundia through limitations on the extent of private holdings. In general the federal government is charged with carrying out that part of the agrarian program concerning ejidos and the recovery of national lands while the states are entrusted with the duty of forcing the dissolution of large landed estates.

a. Villages which have been deprived of their lands shall have these lands restored to them according to the provisions of the law of January 6, 1915:

All proceedings, findings, decisions and all operations of demarcation, concession, composition, judgment, compromise, alienation, or auction which may have deprived co-owners, settlements, towns, congregations, tribes and other bodies of population still existing since the law of June 25, 1856, of the whole or a part of their lands, woods and waters, are declared null and void; all findings, resolutions and operations which may subsequently take place and produce the same effects shall likewise be null and void. Consequently all lands, forests and waters of which the above-mentioned communities may have been deprived shall be restored to them according to the decree of January 6, 1915, which shall remain in force as a constitutional law. In case the adjudication of lands, by way of restitution be not legal in the terms of the said decree, which adjudication has been requested by any of the above entities, these lands shall nevertheless be given to them by way of grant (dotacion), and they shall in no event fail to receive such as they may need. Only such lands, title to which may have

been acquired in the divisions made by virtue of the said law of June 25, 1856, or such as may be held in undisputed ownership for more than ten years are excepted from the provision of nullity, provided their area does not exceed 50 hectares. Any excess over this area shall be returned to the community, and the owner shall be indemnified. All laws of restitution enacted by virtue of this provision shall be immediately carried into effect by the administrative authorities. Only members of the community shall have the right in the lands destined to be divided, and the rights to these lands shall be inalienable so long as they remain undivided; the same provision shall govern the right of ownership after the division has been made. (Par. 9) . . .

A Ministry of Education is Founded to Transform the Soul of Mexico

Educators throughout Latin America know about the work of José Vasconcelos. His ideas and accomplishments go far to explain the high reputation in which public education in Mexico is held in many developing nations. Mexico offers much to others who are in a similar social situation. Vasconcelos could deal with the world of ideas and also with the world of politics.

This one man left his mark on Mexican education. Vasconcelos established the Ministry of Education and took over control of the University of Mexico. He directed the University and the Ministry to start a modern era of education after the Revolution of 1910. Vasconcelos was a man who expressed his opinions on many matters and tried to change conditions around him. He admired much about life in the United States; however, he felt Mexican culture was superior in several ways. He opposed Mexican political figures, like President Venustiano Corranza, who tried to "Americanize" Mexico. Vasconcelos spoke out in defense of Mexican life and its Indians. He had a definite plan to raise academic standards. He wanted to shape graduates who loved Mexico and who would be devoted to the new revolutionary and democratic society. The following selection was written by Vasconcelos.

Development of the Ministry of Education

The great papers had ridiculed Madero, considering him weak, and they deserted Obregón when he represented the highest interests of the country. Afterward, when he went over to the Plan, and served as a gendarme to Calles, they fawned upon him to the point of masochism.

Unexpectedly, Calles offered his resignation from the Carranza cabinet and left for Sonora. One or two months after his entry into the State, all the local forces had risen against Carranza, and Calles came to be in command of the troops, Military Commandant, or what have you, of the whole region.

To me they later gave a Ministry, or in better words, allowed me to violate the Constitution of Querétaro in order to create a Ministry of Education which was the only glory of the Revolution, but which Calles destroyed with fury and handed over to pickpockets; this story does not belong in the present volume, but it is not superfluous to call attention to it. I have few pages left in which to complete the present volume, and I shall limit myself to what I have planned; I shall tell how my return to Mexico and my entry into the new government were accomplished.

The friendly presence of Antonio Villarreal woke me one morning. "This money," he said, "is from the treasury of the State of Sonora, and it is to help you join the movement."

I pocketed the money and said jokingly to Villarreal, "Tell them that they still have to give me public satisfaction and a special car to take me from the border to the capital."

A few days later I received a telegram; they asked urgently for a proclamation drawn up and signed by me, to distribute among the troops in Sonora for the purpose of explaining the change of front to them and justifying it. I drew it up and sent it by telegraph. It was reproduced all over the State. Poor fellows, they had to use an exile in order to speak to their own people, since what they had to tell them was the opposite of what they had been preaching during the six miserable years of Carranza rule. Discredited before the bar of public opinion by their servile attitude toward Carranza, the Obregónists relied on the word of revolutionary veterans like us, provisionally and until they could give us a kick and go back to their old tricks, that is, to despotism, political assassination, abuse, theft, · and submission to the Plan.

A few weeks later, when Villarreal and I reached Mexico City by way of Monterrey, General Obregón was waiting for us in the station. And it was that very morning, in the special car that brought us to the capital, that we learned of the assassination of Carranza.

Adolfo de la Huerta arrived. With his habitual generosity he opened his arms to me, gave me a place at the table of Chapultepec, took me hither and yon with him on official visits. Always with him was Miguel Alessio, who now began to act as Private Secretary to the President. And it was Miguel who reminded him in my presence, "Well, why don't you sign it and give Vasco an office, so he can take charge of the University?" Turning to me, he added, "Adolfo agrees that the Ministry of Education ought to be reestablished."

I was obsessed with the idea of the University as a base on which to create the Ministry which would perhaps transform the soul of Mexico.

De la Huerta sent for me. "Pepe, I didn't know you were a Catholic!" he said.

"Well, now you know it; but Catholic or not, if I am to carry on in Education, the Protestants have got to get out of there, for they have carried out a foreign policy; but since this is making difficulties for you, I have come to give you my resignation."

De la Huerta then conducted himself with perfect loyalty as a friend and with firmness as an official. "Don't ever tell me that again! Go and do what you like!"

In the various schools of the University, even if it meant sacrificing old fellow students and friends, I tried to appoint as Directors men who would know how to demand something of professors and students. I persecuted and tried to exile the type of Director they had had in the chaotic periods: the director who is always smiling at the students, flattering them, raising their grades, so that the poor kids won't lose a year's work. In the case of the "poor kids" who don't deserve to pass because of their incompetence or laziness, you are doing them a real favor if you drop them from the rolls so that they can quickly get to work, according to their aptitudes. And the level of the school rises too.

While we were still discussing in the Rectory of the University a law that would create a Federal Ministry, we were already beginning as a Ministry. I invited many exiles and absent scholars, from the United States and Europe, capable of making an important contribution to the great impetus that the work had gained. With complete impartiality we opened the doors to merit, and he was my best friend who worked hardest at the common task.

Soon you could feel that something serious was beginning in the country. There were some who compared our pulse to that of a vibrating dynamo, from which energy pours. Since then many a fool has called himself "dynamic"; the adjective made a hit; but it is not enough to move; you must know where you are going.

3

COLLISION OF CULTURES
IN THE WEST

By the time Mexico gained its independence from Spain, there was a westward movement in the United States that seemed destined to eventually cause conflict between the two countries. In 1803, President Thomas Jefferson had extended the western boundary of the United States far across the Mississippi River by purchasing Louisiana, a vast territory that now makes up much of the American mid-West. Settlers began pouring into the new territory, and some proposed extending the boundaries even farther west.

The new nation of Mexico embraced all of the territory that is now the Southwestern United States, and some Americans began to view parts of Mexico as a possibility for territorial expansion. By the early 1840's, many considered a United States that extended from the Atlantic to the Pacific as inevitable. Mexico, of course, stood in the way of such a plan.

A clash between the two countries finally came when the United States declared war against Mexico in 1846. At the end of the war, Mexico had lost vast territories.

Readings in this unit will help explain the formation of an Anglo-American culture that embraced ideas and attitudes which brought about a direct confrontation with Mexico. When the United States and Mexico collided, the former gained a great victory that sparked new progress and great wealth. Mexico suffered a great defeat and loss of confidence among its peoples. The fate of the two peoples have been affected greatly ever since.

Mexican Americans in the United States thus have a special history. This experience has been a handicap for the most part. Anglo and Mexican Americans may view the war differently because one group represents the victor and the other the loser. Such different attitudes can cause tensions between groups, even long after a conflict has ended. The war between the neighbor nations has affected history deeply. How it affects the future remains to be seen, and a better understanding of the past can help direct the course of the future.

HOW ANGLO-AMERICAN CULTURE DEVELOPED

There are many ways to explain why peoples and nations differ. Among these are climate, race, religion, economics, chance, God's will, or the influence of history. Most of these forces may act in combinations that change from time to time. In any case, nations differ even when their people come from the same general stock. Thus, Americans developed a different style of life that was evident even before 1776 and which set them apart from others, such as Englishmen, Frenchmen, and Spaniards.

One of the early characteristics of the new American man was his desire to spread out across the continent, although he left much empty space behind him. The westward movement into the Mississippi Valley and across the plains brought Anglo Americans into contact with Spaniards and later with Mexicans.

American confidence in its new institutions led many to a feeling of superiority over other peoples. More and more Americans came to believe that it was their destiny to occupy and govern lands from sea to sea, as well as beyond. It was unavoidable that the two sister republics of Mexico and the United States confront each other as aggressive Americans pushed back Indians in their westward expansion into Spanish and Mexican lands.

The Majority and Minorities in Young America as Seen by a French Observer

Alexis de Tocqueville was one of the best interpreters of the American character in the early days of the republic. Writing during the 1830's, he observed an interesting contest between individualism and democratic ideas among Americans, on the one hand, and the overpowering force of the majority, on the other. The all-powerful majority imposed its will over minorities as they made relatively weak appearances in political and other matters.

Frontier life altered American ideas, which stemmed primarily from Northern European, and especially English and Protestant customs. When Mexicans came face-to-face with Americans, a new situation occurred. The history and traditions of both peoples influenced their reactions to each other.

The following selection by de Tocqueville and many of his other observations are still widely read by historians and other scholars in their attempt to understand early Americans.

Democratic Social Condition of the Anglo Americans

THE STRIKING CHARACTERISTIC OF THE SOCIAL CONDITION OF THE ANGLO-AMERICANS IS ITS ESSENTIAL DEMOCRACY

The social condition of the Americans is eminently democratic; this was its character at the foundation of the colonies, and it is still more strongly marked at the present day.

Great equality existed among the emigrants who settled on the shores of New England. Even the germs of aristocracy were never planted in that part of the Union. The only influence which was obtained there was that of intellect; the people were used to reverence certain names as the emblems of knowledge and virtue. . . .

This picture, which may, perhaps, be thought to be overcharged, still gives a very imperfect idea of what is taking place in the new States of the West and Southwest. At the end of the last century, a few bold adventurers began to penetrate into the valley of the Mississippi; and the mass of the population very soon began to move in that direction: communities unheard of till then suddenly appeared in the desert. States whose names were not in existence a few years before, claimed their place in the American Union; and in the Western settlements we may behold democracy arrived at its utmost limits. In these states, founded offhand, and as it were by chance, the inhabitants are but of yesterday. Scarcely known to one another, the nearest neighbors are ignorant of each other's history. In this part of the American continent, therefore, the population has escaped the influence not only of great names and great wealth, but even of the natural aristocracy of knowledge and virtue. None are there able to wield that respectable power which men willingly grant to the remembrance of a life spent in doing good before their eyes. The new States of the West are already inhabited; but society has no existence among them. . . .

THE GREATEST DANGERS OF THE AMERICAN REPUBLICS PROCEED FROM THE OMNIPOTENCE OF THE MAJORITY

It is important not to confound stability with force, or the greatness of a thing with its duration. In democratic republics, the power which directs society is not stable; for it often changes hands, and assumes a new direction. But, whichever way it turns, its force is almost irresistible. The governments of the American republics appear to me to be as much centralized as those of the absolute monarchies of Europe, and more energetic than they are. I do not, therefore, imagine that they will perish from weakness.

If ever the free institutions of America are destroyed, that even may be attributed to the omnipotence of the majority, which may at some future time urge the minorities to desperation, and oblige them to have recourse to physical force. Anarchy will then be the result, but it will have been brought about by despotism.

THE PROFESSION OF THE LAW SERVES TO COUNTERPOISE THE DEMOCRACY

In visiting the Americans and studying their laws, we perceive that the authority they have intrusted to members of the legal profession, and the influence which these individuals exercise in the government, is the most powerful existing security against the excesses of democracy. . . . Men who have made a special study of the laws derive from this occupation certain habits of order, a taste for formalities, and a kind of instinctive regard for the regular connection of ideas, which naturally render them very hostile to the revolutionary spirit and the unreflecting passions of the multitude. . . .

The Santa Fe Trade: Mutual Interests of Anglos and Mexicans

A series of revolts by the 1840's made it clear that young Mexico did not have a government supported by its people. Conflicts raged over religion, politics, economics, and race. Each regime in Mexico City undid the previous legislation and provoked new civil outbreaks. Such turmoil led some states or regions to despair and they sought new ways to serve their narrow interests at the expense of the nation. Contraband trade in California and New Mexico was symptomatic of a gradual loss of confidence in Mexico on the part of key members of its society.

Commercial interests drove Mexicans to trade with Anglo Americans, even though it was forbidden under Mexican law. Contraband trade flourished because it met a real need. James J. Webb's personal account illustrates this reality. This selection offers an example of the early cultural conflicts which led Mexicans and Anglo Americans to dislike each other. By this time the Republic of Texas had been formed and tension was high in the region.

The Santa Fe Trade

The next day was spent in greasing up and making repairs, cooking, and resting teams, preparatory to entering the *jornada*, or journey of fifty miles without water, and by the couriers who go ahead to Santa Fe to make arrangements for renting stores and bargaining about introduction of goods, and duties to be paid.

The duties charged by Governor Armijo for several years previously had been five hundred dollars per wagon load, and many goods contraband under the Mexican tariff were admitted by him and no examination made. This was the foundation of the Santa Fe trade, and the only advantage gained by introducing goods by the overland route for Chihuahua and the interior states of Mexico. . . .

As our whole interests were not under the protection of law, but subject to the will of one man, and being recognized and confessed contrabandists, it was necessary for the traders to start early and take a long and rapid journey ahead and see how the land lay. Colonel Owens being the leading merchant in Independence and having control of the outfitting trade for Mexicans as well as Americans, and Governor Armijo having sent a train to "the States" for goods for several years, felt safe to remain with the train and depend upon reports of other traders of any change of rulers or rates of duty. . . .

During the winter of 1844 and 1845 Armijo visited Santa Fe, and occupied a little house, one room of which was occupied by B. Pruett as a store. The door between the store and the room of Governor Armijo was one of the old-fashioned affairs, swinging upon a stud, or post, fitted into holes in the upper and lower doorsills, thus swinging without iron hinges or latch and of course leaving large cracks [on] each side. Governor Martinez made a formal call upon him [Armijo] and Pruett had the curiosity to listen to the conversation. After the usual formalities and while partaking of their wine, Governor Armijo asked Governor Martinez why General Santa Anna had superseded him in the office of governor, and stated in justification of his course how he had maintained the government in New Mexico without calling on the National treasury for aid.

"Well," replied Martinez, "Santa Anna told me he wanted, and would make, a change here. The administration of affairs had become exceedingly corrupt. There had been stealing in every department, from the governor to the lowest subordinate officer."

"True," said Armijo, "the custom-house officers have no doubt stolen. They demand fees and perquisites from the merchants introducing goods to which they are not legally entitled. And my secretary also avails himself of his opportunities. I have also stolen a good deal by permitting this indirect and illegal trade. And in fact, if you call it stealing, I have been stealing all my official life and have got the money in my pocket to show for it. But I don't see how he has mended matters by sending you here, for I know your history and have known your course for years. You, poor devil, have been stealing all your life, and today haven't got a dollar. Which is the smartest man, and which is the best fitted to administer an economical government in New Mexico?" . . .

American Sectional Interests Foster American Commercial Expansion

Senator Thomas Hart Benton from Missouri was an early champion of American commercial expansion to the Southwest. He had a low opinion of the new Mexican republic to the south, but he persuaded Congress and President James Monroe to finance the survey of a road from Missouri to the Mexican border. This road would favor U.S. commerce. Economic interests clearly moved the United States flag southwestward.

The selection that follows is a statement Senator Benton made to the U.S. Senate in 1825 in support of his bill to survey the road.

Statement by Senator Benton, 1825, on Profits of and U.S. Interest in Santa Fe Trade: U.S. Bill to Survey Road

And now on January 3, 1825, almost a year having gone into education of his constituency, state colleagues, and fellow congressmen, Senator Benton rose in the Senate and stated that he had received a paper which he took the liberty of presenting. It was a statement of facts in relation to the origin, present state, and future prospects of trade and intercourse between the valley of the Mississippi and the internal provinces of Mexico. The reporter of Congressional Debates missed nothing of the true spirit of the great man and caught the rhetorical phrases as they fell from his lips:

"Intending, for a year past, to bring this subject before the Senate, and to claim for it a share of the national protection, Mr. B. said that he had felt the necessity of resting his demand upon a solid foundation of facts. With this view, he had addressed himself, during the last summer to many inhabitants of Missouri, who had been personally engaged in the trade; among others, to Mr. Augustus Storrs, late of New Hampshire, a gentleman of character and intelligence, every way capable of relating things as he saw them, and incapable of relating them otherwise. This gentleman had been one of a caravan of eighty persons, one hundred and fifty-six horses, and twenty-three wagons and carriages, which had made the expedition from Missouri to Santa Fe (of New Mexico) in the months of May and June last. His account was full of interest and novelty. It sounded like romance to hear of caravans of men, horses, and wagons traversing with their merchandise the vast plain which lies between the Mississippi and the Rio del Norte. The story seemed better adapted to Asia than to North America. But, romantic as it might seem, the reality had already exceeded the visions of the wildest imagination. The journey to New Mexico, but lately deemed a chimerical project, had become an affair of ordinary occurrence. Santa Fe, but lately the Ultima Thule of American enterprise, was now considered as a stage only in the progress, or rather, a new point of departure to our invincible citizens. Instead of turning back from that point, the caravans broke up there, and the sub-divisions branched off in different directions, in search of new theaters for their enterprise. Some proceeded down the river to the Passo del Norte; some to the mines of Chi-

huahua and Durango, in the province of New Biscay; some to Sonora and Sinatoa (sic) on the Gulf of California; and some, seeking new lines of communication with the Pacific, had undertaken to descend the Western slopes of our continent, through the unexplored regions of the Multnomah and Buenaventura. The fruit of these enterprises for the present amounted to $190,000 in gold and silver bullion and coin, and precious furs; a sum considerable in itself, in the commerce of an infant State, but chiefly deserving a statesman's notice as an earnest of what might be expected from a regulated and protected trade. The principal article given in exchange is that of which we have the greatest abundance, and which has the peculiar advantage of making the circuit of the Union before it departs from the territories of the republic—cotton—which grows in the South; is manufactured in the North, and exported from the West. . . .

To make a long story short, the bill authorizing a road to the Mexican boundary seemed to be undergoing a metamorphosis into one authorizing a road to be surveyed and marked to the Mexican settlements. The Mexican government should be asked to cooperate, though Benton well knew, as he told the Senate, that he expected no cooperation—the people were too ignorant. "We are not to expect anything more from them than the privilege to mark out the way."

On March 3, just before James Monroe stepped out of the White House to make way for John Quincy Adams, he affixed his signature to the bill and it became a law. It provided $10,000 for surveying and marking the road—little enough, one thinks, to make what Senator Benton called "a highway between nations"—and $20,000 for treating with the Indians for a right of way.

Manifest Destiny: Typical Arguments for American Territorial Expansion

Manifest destiny became, early in the 1840's, an expression of the desire for American acquisition of Texas, California, other parts of the Southwest, and Oregon. Some Americans believed that it was the destiny of the United States to acquire all of Mexico and Central America, if not more. Manifest destiny developed into a mixture of ambition for more land and greater power, based on the belief in the superiority of North Americans over other Americans. Some believed it was actually an obligation to impose American society, culture, and political control over less fortunate peoples. This mixture of ambition and idealism became a powerful force in American life for a long time.

In the selection that follows, the comments that several prominent Americans made on manifest destiny not long before the War with Mexico are quoted. While some Americans opposed expansion into the territories of other nations, the comments quoted are generally rather typical of the American attitude at the time.

Comments on Manifest Destiny

RALPH WALDO EMERSON

Gentlemen, the development of our American resources, the extension to the utmost of the commercial system, and the appearance of new moral causes which are to modify the state, are giving an aspect of greatness to the Future, which the imagination fears to open. One thing is plain for all men of common sense and common conscience, that here, here in America, is the home of man. After all the deductions which are to be made for our pitiful and most unworthy politics, which stake every gravest national question on the silly die, whether James or whether Jonathan shall sit in the chair and hold the purse, after all the deduction is made for our frivolities and insanities, there still remains an organic simplicity and liberty, which, when it loses its balance redresses itself presently, which offers opportunity to the human mind not known in any other region. . . .

JOHN L. O'SULLIVAN

The American people having derived their origin from many other nations, and the Declaration of National Independence being entirely based on the great principle of human equality, those facts demonstrate at once our disconnected position as regards any other nation; that we have, in reality, but little connection with the past history of any of them, and still less with all antiquity, its glories, or its crimes. On the contrary, our national birth was the beginning of a new history, the formation and progress of an untried political system, which separates us from the past and connects us with the future only; and so far as regards the entire development of the natural rights of man, in moral, political, and national life, we may confidently assume that our country is destined to be the great nation of futurity. . . .

CHARLES WILKES

The situation of Upper California will cause its separation from Mexico before many years. The country between it and Mexico can never be anything but a barren waste, which precludes all intercourse except that by sea, always more or less interrupted by the course of the winds, and the unhealthfulness of the lower or seaport towns of Mexico. It is very probable that this country will become united with Oregon, with which it will perhaps form a state that is destined to control the destinies of the Pacific. This future state is admirably situated to become a powerful maritime nation, with two of the finest ports in the world—that within the straits of Juan de Fuca and San Francisco. These two regions have, in fact, within themselves every thing to make them increase, and keep up an intercourse with the whole of Polynesia, as well as the countries of South America on the one side, and China, the Philippines, New Holland, and New Zealand, on the other. Among the latter, before many years, may be included Japan. Such various climates will furnish the materials for a beneficial interchange of products, and an intercourse that must, in time, become immense; while this western coast, enjoying a climate in many respects superior to any other in the Pacific, possessed as it must be by the Anglo-Norman race, and having none to enter into rivalry with it but the indolent inhabitants of warm climates, is evidently destined to fill a large space in the world's future history. . . .

LEWIS C. LEVIN

I will not fatigue the House by an examination of the title under which we claim to hold the Oregon territory. I consider that question settled on principles too broad and deep to be now doubted by the most infatuated advocate of foreign usurpation. On this point learning, statesmanship, and eloquences have exhausted their resources, and left no candid mind free from the conviction of the justice of our claim, and the insolence of the foreign pretension that attempts to invalidate it.

Am I asked on what I found this principle of inherent and pre-existent right? I answer, on the genius of American institutions—on the spirit of republicanism, that permits not the contaminating proximity of monarchies upon the soil that we have consecrated to the rights of man, and the sublime machinery of the sovereign power of the people; on the eternal laws of God, which have given the earth to man for a habitation, and told him that the natural boundaries to a country only terminate where oceans intervene, and contiguity is obstructed by some formidable obstacle which separates nations and marks out their native home as distinctly as if drawn by the lines of military art. Natural boundaries and the genius of a people always harmonize. As their limits are expansive, so will their enterprise be boundless and their spirit swelling. . . .

To establish valid title to Oregon, on the part of Great Britain, she must show—first, title by discovery, acquired by treaty; second, actual settlement as a permanent abode by the subjects of her kingdom; third, contiguity. Now, England can show not even one of these titles. On our part we exhibit them all. First, discovery by Capt. Gray, of Boston; second, acquired by treaties with France and Spain from 42° up to 54° 40′; third, by actual settlement; and, fourth, by contiguity. A complete chain of valid title. . . .

JOHN QUINCY ADAMS

Sir, there has been so much said on the question of title in this case, that I believe it would be a waste of time for me to say anything more about it, unless I refer to a little book you have there upon your table, which you sometimes employ to administer a solemn oath to every member of this House to support the Constitution of the United States. If you have it, be so good as to pass it to the Clerk, and I will ask him to read what I conceive to be the foundation of our title.

If the Clerk will be so good as to read the 26th, 27th, and 28th verses of the 1st chapter of Genesis, the committee will see what I consider to be the foundation of the title of the United States. . . .

We claim that country—for what? To make the wilderness blossom as the rose, to establish laws, to increase, multiply, and subdue the earth, which we are commanded to do by the first behest of God Almighty. That is what we claim it for. She claims to keep it open for navigation, for her hunters to hunt wild beasts; as well as of the savage nations. There is the difference between our claims. . . .

U.S. AND MEXICAN INTERESTS COLLIDE

The history of Mexican Americans as a minority group in the United States dates from the treaty that ended the Mexican-American War. All former citizens of Mexico who chose to stay in lands that were taken by the United States became Mexican Americans. Formerly the majority, they now became a minority and lost power they had once held.

War between the United States and Mexico would have been difficult to avoid. In Mexico, Americans were looked down upon and feared because of their aggressive behavior. Many Americans wanted to expand the U.S. borders and believed that Mexico stood in the way of the country's destiny. People of goodwill in both countries became so emotional over the issues that a peaceful negotiation of the major differences that divided the two nations would probably have been impossible.

The conflict between Mexico and the United States was extended over many years in distinct stages: (1) In the first stage, some American immigrants in northern Coahuila (Texas) tried to gain a separate state within the Mexican republic formed in 1824. When this effort failed, secession from Mexico gained popularity among American Mexicans in Texas. In 1836, the Republic of Texas was formed and the American Mexicans fought to achieve independence. (2) During the second stage in this drama (1836–1846) several nations argued over the future of Texas. Mexico wanted Texas back. The U.S. government showed an early interest in annexing Texas, but opposition of some U.S. leaders delayed action. Texas leaders desired annexation to the United States, but were opposed to waiting very long. England and France desired alliances with a separate Texan nation to form a barrier to U.S. expansion southward. (3) U.S. annexation of Texas provided the spark for a war both nations were willing to fight. The United States had complicated plans in action before 1846. European powers expected Mexico to win easily because of its large armies and great leaders. However, the Mexican Republic had been divided by civil war since 1828, and some of its leaders used their armies to fight each other, rather than the invaders. Others held back. Some, like the President himself, General Antonio López de Santa Anna, were charged by Mexican opponents with co-operating with the U.S. government to cut up Mexico. Mexico was soon over-whelmed by the invasion of American troops from several directions.

Within the new American lands, Mexican Americans were generally viewed with hostility by Anglo Americans. The war produced a bitter heritage. An understanding of the Mexican-American War from these selections sheds light on American history generally, as well as on the way Mexican Americans as a group came about.

Texas Declares Its Independence from Mexico

American Mexicans in Texas decided to separate from Mexico because they believed that their interests would be better served as a separate nation. Although American Texans helped Mexico separate from Spain, most later wanted Texas annexed to the United States. Many people in the United States, including some high government officials, encouraged the Texans to gain independence and offered hopes for annexation. With encouragement from Washington, Texas declared independence in March, 1836. Among the fifty-six signers of this declaration, there are only three Spanish names.

In 1836, the Mexican government had been reorganized in a conservative and centralized manner in order to restrict local autonomy. Thus, the new policies of Mexico were opposed to the interests of Texans. President Santa Anna promised to punish the Texans and restore rigid control from Mexico City. The stage was set for a show-down. The Constitution of Texas was formed two weeks after the Texas Declaration of Independence. It closely followed the U.S. Constitution, but provided for only one state in the Republic of Texas. These documents were actions that provoked a Mexican response to preserve itself, and war followed.

Some Provisions of the Texas Declaration of Independence March 2, 1836

THE DECLARATION OF INDEPENDENCE Made by the Delegates of The People of Texas in General Convention, at Washington, on March 2nd, 1836.

When a government has ceased to protect the lives, liberty and property of the people, from whom its legitimate powers are derived, and for the advancement of whose happiness it was instituted; and so far from being a guarantee for their inestimable and inalienable rights, becomes an instrument in the hands of evil rulers for their suppression. When the federal republican constitution of their country, which they have sworn to support, no longer has a substantial existence, and the whole nature of their government has been forcibly changed, without their consent, from a restricted federative republic, composed of sovereign states, to a consolidated central military despotism, in which every interest is disregarded but that of the army and the priesthood, both the eternal enemies of civil liberty, the ever ready minions of power, and the usual instruments of tyrants. When, long after the spirit of the constitution has departed, moderation is at length so far lost by those in power, that even the semblance of freedom is removed, and the forms themselves of the constitution discontinued, and so far from their petitions and remonstrances being regarded, the agents who bear them are thrown into dungeons, and mercenary armies sent forth to enforce a new government upon them at the point of the bayonet.

The Mexican government, by its colonization laws, invited and induced the Anglo-American population of Texas to colonize its wilderness under the pledged faith of a written constitution, that they should continue to enjoy that constitutional liberty and republican government to which they had been habituated in the land of their birth, the United States of America. . . .

In this expectation they have been cruelly disappointed, inasmuch as the Mexican nation has acquiesced to the late changes made in the government by General Antonio Lopez de Santa Anna, who, having overturned the constitution of his country, now offers, as the cruel alternative, either to abandon our homes, acquired by so many privations, or submit to the most intolerable of all tyranny, the combined despotism of the sword and the priesthood.

It hath sacrificed our welfare to the state of Coahuila, by which our interests have been continually depressed through a jealous and partial course of legislation, carried on at a far distant seat of government, by a hostile majority, in an unknown tongue, and this too, notwithstanding we have petitioned in the humblest terms for the establishment of a separate state government, and have, in accordance with the provisions of the national constitution, presented to the general congress a republican constitution, which was, without a just cause, contemptuously rejected. . . .

The necessity of self-preservation, therefore, now decrees our eternal political separation.

We, therefore, the delegates, with plenary powers, of the people of Texas, in solemn convention assembled, appealing to a candid world for the necessities of our condition, do hereby resolve and declare, that our political connection with the Mexican nation has forever ended, and that the people of Texas do now constitute a FREE, SOVEREIGN, AND INDEPENDENT REPUBLIC, and are fully invested with all the rights and attributes which properly belong to independent nations; and conscious of the rectitude of our intentions, we fearlessly and confidently commit the issue to the supreme Arbiter of the destinies of nations.

In witness whereof we have hereunto subscribed our names. . . .

Some Articles of the Constitution of the Republic of Texas
March 17, 1836

We, the people of Texas, in order to form a government, establish justice, ensure domestic tranquility, provide for the common defence and general welfare; and to secure the blessings of liberty to ourselves, and our posterity, do ordain and establish this constitution.

ARTICLE I.

Section 1. The powers of this government shall be divided into three departments, viz: legislative, executive, and judicial, which shall remain forever separate and distinct.

ARTICLE II.

Sec. 1. Congress shall have power to levy and collect taxes and imposts, excise and tonage duties; to borrow money on the faith, credit, and property of the government, to pay the debts and to provide for the common defence and general welfare of the republic.

Sec. 2. To regulate commerce, to coin money, to regulate the value thereof and of foreign coin, to fix the standard of weights and measures, but nothing but gold and silver shall be made a lawful tender.

Sec. 3. To establish post offices and post roads, to grant charters of incorporation, patents and copyrights, and secure to the authors and inventors the exclusive use thereof for a limited time.

Sec. 4. To declare war, grant letters of marque and reprisal, and to regulate captures.

Sec. 5. To provide and maintain an army and navy, and to make all laws and regulations necessary for their government.

Sec. 6. To call out the militia to execute the law, to suppress insurrections, and repel invasion.

Sec. 7. To make all laws which shall be deemed necessary and proper to carry into effect the foregoing express grants of power, and all other powers vested in the government of the republic, or in any officer or department thereof.

ARTICLE III.

Sec. 1. The executive authority of this government shall be vested in a chief magistrate, who shall be styled the president of the republic of Texas.

GENERAL PROVISIONS

Sec. 1. Laws shall be made to exclude from office, from the right of suffrage, and from serving on juries, those who shall hereafter be convicted of bribery, perjury, or other high crimes and misdemeanors. . . .

Sec. 6. All free white persons who shall emigrate to this republic, and who shall, after a residence of six months, make oath before some competent authority that he intends to reside permanently in the same, and shall swear to support this constitution, and that he will bear true allegience to the republic of Texas, shall be entitled to all the privileges of citizenship. . . .

Sec. 9. All persons of color who were slaves for life previous to their emigration to Texas, and who are now held in bondage, shall remain in the like state of servitude: provided, the said slave shall be the bona fide property of the person so holding said slave as aforesaid. Congress shall pass no laws to prohibit emigrants from bringing their slaves into the republic with them, and holding them by the same tenure by which such slaves were held in the United States; nor shall congress have power to emancipate slaves; nor shall any slaveholder be allowed to emancipate his or her slave or slaves without the consent of congress, unless he or she shall send his or her slave or slaves without the limits of the republic. No free person of African descent, either in whole or in part, shall be permitted to reside permanently in the republic, without the consent of congress; and the importation or admission of Africans or negroes into this republic, excepting from the United States of America, is forever prohibited, and declared to be piracy. . . .

And whereas many surveys and titles to lands have been made whilst most of the people of Texas were absent from home, serving in the campaign against Bexar, it is hereby declared that all the surveys and locations of land made since the act of the late consultation closing the land offices, and all titles to land made since that time, are, and shall be null and void.

And whereas the present unsettled state of the country and the general welfare of the people demand that the operations of the land office, and the whole land system shall be suspended until persons serving in the army can have a fair and equal chance with those remaining at home, to select and locate their lands, it is hereby declared, that no survey or title which may hereafter be made shall be valid, unless such survey or title shall be authorized by this convention, or some future congress of the republic. And with a view to the simplification of the land system, and the protection of the people and the government from litigation and fraud, a general land office shall be established, where all the land titles of the republic shall be registered, and the whole territory of the republic shall be sectionized, in a manner hereafter to be prescribed by law, which shall enable the officers of the government or any citizen, to ascertain with certainty the lands that are vacant, and those lands which may be covered with valid titles. . . .

The foregoing constitution was unanimously adopted by the delegates of Texas, in convention assembled, at the town of Washington, on the seventeenth day of March, in the year of our Lord one thousand eight hundred and thirty-six, and of the Independence of the Republic, the first year.

In witness whereof, we have hereunto subscribed our names. . . .

Encounter Between Sam Houston and President Santa Anna

The Battle of San Jacinto established the independence of the Texas Republic from Mexico. Before this, the execution of Texans by Mexican forces at the Alamo and Goliad had embittered the victorious Texan forces against Mexicans. The following selection points to the responsibility of Mexican officers for conduct that all Mexicans and Mexican Americans suffered for after Texan independence. Violence on both sides bred more violence, suspicion, and hostilities between Mexican Americans and Anglo Americans.

Conversations Between Houston and Santa Anna After His Capture

The Commander-in-Chief awoke the next morning after the battle of San Jacinto and asked, "Are we really victors, or is it only my dream?" He could hardly believe that the battle for Independence had been fought and won. Only seven Texans had lost their lives, and less than thirty had been wounded. Seven hundred soldiers had vanquished nearly three times their number. Six hundred and thirty had perished on the field of battle, and of their number were one general officer, four colonels, two lieutenant colonels, seven captains, and twelve lieutenants. Large numbers met their death in the morass and bayous. Two hundred and eighty were wounded and eight hundred taken prisoners.

Gen. Houston sent a detachment of men at ten o'clock in the morning to bury the slain. The troops returned and reported that decomposition had taken place so rapidly that it was impossible to execute the order. The Mexican prisoners accounted for the rapid decomposition, by resolving it, like the defeat of the previous day, into a malignant blast of destiny.

The Texans, meantime, during the day were scouring the prairie, bringing in prisoners. Such as had not been taken the day previous were crawling on their hands and knees through the grass, which was everywhere four or five feet high, endeavoring in this way to effect their escape.

The victors were diligently searching for Santa Anna, the Dictator, who had not been taken. "You will find the Hero of Tampico," said Gen. Houston, "if you find him at all, making his retreat on all fours, and he will be dressed as bad at least as a common soldier. Examine every man you find, closely."

About three o'clock in the afternoon, Lieutenant J.A. Sylvester, a volunteer from Cincinnati, Joel W. Robison, now of Fayette Co., John Thompson, and others were riding over the prairie. They espied a man making his way toward Vince's bridge. They pursued him, whereupon he fell down in the grass. Sylvester dashed on in the direction where he fell and his horse came very near trampling upon him. Disguised in a miserable rustic dress, wearing a skin cap, a round jacket, pantaloons of blue domestic cotton, and a pair of coarse soldier's shoes, he sprang to his feet, and without the slightest apparent surprise looked his captor full in the face. His countenance and manners showed that he belonged to a different class from that indicated by his coarse disguise. Beneath his common garb his victors espied a shirt of the finest linen cambric.

"You are an officer, I perceive, Sir?" said his captor, raising his cap politely. "No, soldier," was his reply. He then drew out a letter in Spanish addressed to Almonte. Seeing that there was no hope of escape, he inquired for Gen. Houston. As the party with the captured Santa Anna rode into the Texan camp past the Mexican prisoners, they cried out with the greatest surprise as they lifted their caps, and exclaimed, "El Presidente."

Numerous were the devices by which Houston maintained discipline over his brave, heroic, although too often wayward and reckless men. His methods were his own, and concealed in his own bosom. The belief became general that Houston was the only man in the world that could have kept the army in subjection, or achieved the independence of Texas, or preserved it after it was won. He treated his prisoner rather as a guest and a gentleman than as a captive, and exercised the keenest vigilance over his safety. His guard was so disposed at night as to include the marquee of Santa Anna, who slept on his camp bed with every comfort he could have had if he had been the victor, while nearby, on the earth, on his usual bed in camp, lay Houston, with no respite from the intense agony of his wound. About one inch above the ankle joint, the ball had entered, shattering the bone, and severing the muscles and arteries. Prostrated for months, he was worn down by fever and pain from this wound to the shadow of a man.

The morning after the capture, Santa Anna asked and obtained leave to see Gen. Houston. Elegantly dressed in citizen's garb, he presented himself, tendering a most respectful and cordial greeting to his host, inquiring kindly concerning his health and the condition of his wound. Houston was far differently clad. He wore a plain, old black coat, snuff colored pantaloons, a black velvet vest, a fur cap, a worn-out pair of boots, a scimitar of tried metal with a plated scabbard, a gift from Captain Joseph Bonnell, of Fort Jesup. The scimitar was hung about his person by buckskin thongs. Such was his armory and wardrobe. A stranger would have taken the captive for the victor. With his usual courtesy, the Texan commander received his prisoner, who proposed immediately negotiations for his liberty. From the beginning to the end of Santa Anna's capture, Houston was never alone with him a single moment. In accordance with this line of policy, he immediately sent for Gen. Rusk, the Secretary of War, and together they conversed some time with the prisoner. A proposition, written with pencil, was submitted by Santa Anna, which paper Gen. Rusk caused to be translated. The Mexican "President" was informed that no action could be taken on his proposals as Texas was ruled by a Constitutional Government, whose members had been sent for immediately after the battle. Santa Anna naturally desired to know where the Government was. An express had been dispatched to Galveston to the President, Hon. David G. Burnet, who was supposed to be in that place.

Santa Anna manifested perfect willingness to act with military men, and exhibited great aversion against any negotiations with civilians. Houston and Rusk, immovable in their determinations, would make no terms with Santa Anna, except to receive from him the Mexican troops, at least as far as Monterey. This order was tendered to Houston, without any intimation to Santa Anna that his life would be spared.

A Yankee's Opinion of Sam Houston Raises an Interesting Question

Much of Mexican-American history after 1848 was shaped in Texas. Thus, both Mexican-American and Anglo-American leaders of that time had an important role in shaping the future.

Sam Houston became President of the Republic of Texas and gave it leadership for several important years. Josiah Gregg, a longtime trader at Santa Fe and occasional resident in Mexico, saw the war between the United States and Mexico at close hand. His diary and letters reveal a low opinion of Houston. But they also add some interesting details about life in the Southwestern frontier area. An excerpt from his writings, entitled *Diary and Letters of Josiah Gregg: Southwestern Enterprises, 1840–1847,* edited by Maurice Garland Fulton, follows. The selection from Gregg's diary is used through the courtesy of the University of Oklahoma Press.

The Inauguration of Sam Houston, 1841

Mon. 13—Today Gen. Sam Houston was inaugurated president of the Republic of Texas. The audience consisted perhaps of about 1000 persons. He appeared on the stage in a linsey-wooley hunting shirt, and pantaloons, and an old wide brimmed white fur hat. I thought in this Gen. Houston demonstrated more vanity than if he had appeared in an ordinary cloth suit. He knew it would be much remarked, and thought it would be popular no doubt, with body of the people. General Burleson also appeared and was sworn in in his fancy Indian leathered hunting shirt—probably more for the purpose of being in unison with the president than for vanity—though Burleson was a hunter of the plainest raising and education.

But to return to Gen. Houston: After he was sworn in (by the speaker of the House) he delivered an inaugural address of some length, as it was said, entirely extempore, only some sketches of which were afterwards published. He did not demonstrate that extemporaneous eloquence, which I had expected to see and hear: indeed I could but pronounce the manner of his address rather dry and monotonous. A part of the substance did well enough; but he certainly would have done better not to have been his own eulogist—I should say he dwelt too much and unbecomingly on the merits of his former services and administration: of which the people generally do not speak near so favorably as he himself. Also he bore much too severely upon the maladministration of his predecessor—this he should have left for others to have censured.

Gen. Houston was elected by a heavy majority, and now seems quite the favorite of the people; but I fear this will be found to speak badly of the judgment and morals of his constituents. His morals and honest character, and general deportment through life will not, I fear, justify the favor he now seems to enjoy. His separating as he did from his family, and secluding himself amongst the Indians living a most degraded and dissolute savage life—his drunken and dissipated character ever since—all seem to hang over him without palliation; to say nothing of many imputations of his honesty, laid to his charge: therefore, I cannot augur well of his administration—but *nous verrons*.

Texas Makes Treaties with Foreign Powers

Between 1839 and 1842, the Republic of Texas negotiated treaties with France, Holland, and England to serve its commercial interests and assure protection in case the United States did not annex the new nation. Portions of the treaties below with France and England point to the world-wide consequences of the conflict between the U.S. and Mexico. Several European nations feared the growth of the United States and tried to strengthen Texas to stop American expansion southward. Texans, like President Houston, used European plans to pressure the U.S. into annexation. The Republic of Mexico grew more angry and desperate as more nations tried to impose their will over its people. The war in 1846–48 should be understood in the light of this complicated background.

Some Articles in
the Treaty with France
September 25, 1839

ARTICLE 1.

There shall be perpetual peace and amity between his Majesty the King of the French, his heirs and successors, on the one part, and the Republic of Texas, on the other part; and between the citizens of the two states, without exception of persons or of places. . . .

ARTICLE 3.

If it should happen that one of the two contracting parties be at war with any other power whatever, the other power shall prohibit their citizens from taking or holding commissions or letters of marque to cruise against the other, or to molest the commerce or property of her citizens.

ARTICLE 4.

The two contracting parties adopt in their mutual relations, the principle "that the flag covers the goods."

If one of the two parties remains neuter when the other may be at war with a third power, the goods covered by the neutral flag shall also be considered to be neutral, even if they should belong to the enemies of the other contracting party.

It is equally understood, that the neutrality of flag protects also the freedom of persons, and that the individuals belonging to a hostile power, who may be found on board a neutral vessel, shall not be made prisoners, unless they are actually engaged in the service of the enemy. . . .

ARTICLE 18.

The inhabitants of the French colonies, their property and ships, shall enjoy in Texas, and reciprocally the citizens of Texas, their property and ships shall enjoy in the French colonies, all the advantages which are or shall be granted to the most favored nation. . . .

Done at Paris, the twenty-fifth day of September, in the year of our Lord, one thousand eight hundred and thirty-nine.

J. PINCKNEY HENDERSON
MAL. DUC DE DALMATIE.

The November 14, 1840
Treaty with Great Britain

1. CONVENTION FOR BRITISH MEDIATION
WITH MEXICO
NOVEMBER 14, 1840
CONVENTION

Whereas Her Majesty the Queen of the United Kingdom of Great Britain and Ireland, being desirous of putting an end to the hostilities which still continue to be carried on between Mexico and Texas, has offered Her Mediation to the Contending Parties, with a view to bring about a pacification between them; and whereas the Republic of

Texas has accepted the mediation so offered; the Republic of Texas and Her Britannic Majesty have determined to settle, by means of a Convention, certain arrangements which will become necessary in the event of such pacification being effected, and have for this purpose . . . agreed upon and concluded the following Articles:

ARTICLE I.

The Republic of Texas agrees that if, by means of the Mediation of Her Britannic Majesty, an unlimited Truce shall be established between Mexico and Texas, within thirty days after this present Convention shall have been communicated to the Mexican Government by her Britannic Majesty's Mission at Mexico; and if, within Six Months from the day on which that communication shall have been so made, Mexico shall have concluded a Treaty of Peace with Texas, then and in such case the Republic of Texas will take upon itself a portion, amounting to One Million Pounds Sterling, of the Capital of the Foreign Debt contracted by the Republic of Mexico before the 1st of January, One thousand Eight Hundred and Thirty-Five.

ARTICLE II.

The manner in which the Capital of One Million Pounds Sterling of Foreign Debt, mentioned in the preceding Article, shall be transferred from the Republic of Mexico to the Republic of Texas, shall be settled hereafter by special Agreement between the Republic of Texas and the Republic of Mexico, under the Mediation of Her Britannic Majesty.

ARTICLE III.

The present Convention shall be ratified, and the Ratifications shall be exchanged at London, as soon as possible within the space of Nine Months from this date.

In witness whereof, the respective Plenipotentiaries have signed the same, and have affixed thereto the Seals of their Arms.

Done at London, the Fourteenth day of November, in the Year of our Lord One Thousand Eight Hundred and Forty.

J. HAMILTON
PALMERSTON

Was President Santa Anna a Traitor to Mexico?

Santa Anna is a source of much controversy. His supporters have written about his services to Mexico and his critics have claimed he was a fool, at best, and probably a traitor. Most Mexicans distrusted government officials during Santa Anna's time. In any case, the role of Santa Anna greatly affected both American and Mexican peoples.

This account from *Glory, God and Gold* by Paul I. Wellman, an American historian, is a clear accusation that Santa Anna and the United States government planned to take lands away from Mexico by force, if not legally through purchase. This reading suggests that war would have started somewhere else if not at Palo Alto in 1846.

Questions About Santa Anna's Loyalty to Mexico

War between the United States and Mexico was now a certainty. Santa Anna, twice dictator of that country, had again been overthrown and exiled in May, 1845, to Cuba, where he devoted himself to continual intrigue and graft. As a curious side note of the coming conflict, President Polk attempted— and almost succeeded—to conspire with this untrustworthy man to gain a bloodless victory over Mexico. Colonel Atocha, as "Unofficial envoy" from the exiled man, visited Polk and suggested certain sums of money—$30,000,000 to the nation and, say, $500,000—"to meet present purposes" for a certain personage from whom he could speak, who would, if he returned to power, conclude a peace at a show of force by the United States, ceding Texas and certain lands to the west of Texas.

Unfortunately the agent selected to arrange the negotiations, Captain A. Slidell Mackenzie of the

United States Navy, lacked discretion. He arrived at Havana with pomp and in full uniform, giving such publicity to the matter that, though Santa Anna was allowed to pass unmolested through the American naval cordon to Mexico—under the impression, apparently, that he would co-operate in the scheme he had himself instigated—he repudiated the matter in tones of such virtuous indignation that it served to reinstate him in the favor of the Mexican people. In December, 1846, Santa Anna once more was elected El Presidente, announcing that he would "punish the foreigners."

In the United States, meantime, a new slogan had been coined. Writing in the United States Magazine and Democratic Review for July-August 1845, John L. O'Sullivan spoke of "our manifest destiny to overspread the continent allotted by Providence for the free development of our yearly multiplying millions." . . .

After some preliminary maneuvers, including an unsuccessful effort made through John Slidell to purchase New Mexico, Arizona, and California for $30,000,000, General Zachary Taylor, who had landed with a force of United States troops at Corpus Christi, Texas, was ordered by President Polk to proceed to the Rio Grande.

Mexico recalled her minister from Washington and handed the American minister his passports. General Ampudia advanced toward the Rio Grande from the south, and sent a note to Taylor, politely inviting him to evacuate to Texas. General Taylor, equally polite, declined the invitation, saying he was in United States territory. When Ampudia displayed some hesitation as to what to do next, he was replaced by General Arista, with orders to fight.

Learning that two vessels with supplies for the Mexican army were about to enter the Rio Grande, Taylor ordered the river blockaded. Arista pronounced this an act of war and prepared to attack a newly built American fort, across the river from Matamoros, called Fort Taylor but later renamed Fort Brown (this was the beginning of Brownsville, Texas).

Mexican troops were thrown across the Rio Grande by Arista to cut communications between Taylor and his base of supplies at Point Isabel. On April 24, 1846, Captain Thornton and a company of dragoons who were reconnoitering this movement fell into an ambush by a superior force. After a loss of sixteen men killed and wounded, the whole company was captured save for Thornton himself, who escaped by a tremendous leap of his horse over a high hedge, in a storm of bullets.

First blood had been shed—and on Texas soil.

But Taylor, picking up reinforcements of Texas volunteers and United States marines from the fleet, hurried back to relieve the fort at the head of two thousand men. Arista still had the heavier battalions. With six thousand men he posted himself in a strong position at Palo Alto, about nine miles north of the beleaguered fort, where Taylor found him. Old Rough and Ready did not hesitate. . . .

The Battle of Palo Alto was significant as the first major engagement of the Mexican War.

War Threatens Santa Fe Trade

As the threat of war with Mexico increased, Senator Thomas H. Benton, of Missouri, and others feared that hostilities would cut off the Santa Fe trade.

Senator Benton conferred with President Polk, and the two men devised a policy which they hoped would prevent interruption of the valuable trade. The policy, which involved intrigues and high adventure by a young Santa Fe trader named James Magoffin, is described in the first reading.

The second reading is an excerpt from the diary of young Susan S. Magoffin, the trader's wife, who describes the trip to Mexico. Other entries in Mrs. Magoffin's diaries provide us with some of our best sources of information on early relations between Anglo Americans and Mexicans.

Such sources of information as the diary of Susan Magoffin, which apparently was not intended for publication, are extremely valuable to historians, for they often given an account of events that is not colored by political ideology.

American Traders Play a Role in the Peaceful Seizure of New Mexico

Foreword by Howard R. Lamar

Although the prospect of a conflict with Mexico was immensely popular with Missourians and with the entire population of the lower Mississippi Valley, it promised to affect the fortunes of the Santa Fe traders, many of whom were already on the trail by the time Congress had declared war. Not only did the conflict threaten to close the market, but the traders stood in danger of arrest and of losing their goods by confiscation. Thus while President Polk seemingly pursued a vigorous military policy to conquer and reduce Mexico, he also prayed for a small localized war which would avoid bloodshed in New Mexico, Chihuahua, and, if possible, the more distant province of California. At the same time he felt a small war would prevent the growth of "military reputations dangerous for the Presidency."

No one was more in agreement with this "small war" policy than Missouri's Senator Thomas H. Benton, one of Polk's chief advisers. It was Benton's fervent hope to avoid any interference in the New Mexican part of the trade through the twin devices of a peaceful occupation and a full assurance that all the rights and privileges of the local Mexican citizens would continue to be respected. To implement such a policy, Polk and Benton first sent Colonel George Howard to warn the traders already on the road that war existed and to wait until American troops could precede them into Mexico. Howard then went on to Taos and other border towns to create a favorable sentiment toward Americans. Orders were also given to stop any trains which might be carrying military supplies for the enemy. While these initial precautionary measures were being taken, Polk had appointed Colonel Stephen Watts Kearny, an army official long familiar with the Santa Fe Trail, to take some 1000 regular and volunteer troops rather grandly titled "The Army of the West" and carry out a bloodless occupation of New Mexico, Chihuahua, and California.

CHIHUAHUA AND CALIFORNIA.

The great care Polk and Benton took to prevent fighting was indicated both by the orders to Kearny and by the fact that the President invited the Catholic bishops of New York and St. Louis to the White House to ask their advice about the best means of placating the priests in New Mexico. Polk in particular was convinced—and correctly so—that the priests occupied such a dominant position in the lives and government of all Mexico that without their cooperation peaceful conquest of the border provinces could not possibly be accomplished. While the bishops promised to do all in their power to aid Polk, the President was still dissatisfied. What he wanted, Benton later reported, was a person of good character, preferably of the Roman religion and well known to the Mexicans, to precede the Army. At this point Senator Benton himself remembered James Magoffin, whom he had met in 1845. He wrote the trader to come to Washington post haste. On June 15, Benton brought Magoffin to the White House with the proposal that the experienced trader with his Mexican connections might be the ideal man to pave the way for the Army. In this first interview and a second one on June 17, 1846, Magoffin appears to have impressed the President so favorably that the latter wrote: "he is a very intelligent man and gave me much valuable information." As a result of the meetings Polk directed Secretary of War Marcy to instruct General Kearny to use Magoffin's services as part of his strategy.

From this point on, James Magoffin's life became a series of intrigues and high adventure. He had rushed to Washington in great haste upon the summons of Benton; now he rushed back to Missouri in order to set out across the plains in a buckboard in a race against time to catch Kearny. Both the caravan in which Susan and Samuel (James Magoffin's wife and brother) traveled and the main body of Kearny's Army of the West were so far ahead of James, however, that the brothers and the General did not meet until they all arrived at Bent's Fort on July 26. There, after consultation, Kearny appears to have fallen in with Magoffin's plans, for on August 1 he detailed Captain Philip St. George Cooke to take twelve men to accompany Magoffin to Santa Fe under a flag of truce and to negotiate with the Governor, General Manuel Armijo. When the small party arrived in the enemy capital twelve days later, Magoffin acted as if he were merely a merchant riding under Cooke's protection. But long after the guards and officials had gone to bed and left the Palace of the Governors in darkness, Magoffin brought Armijo, who was his cousin by marriage, to Cooke's chambers for secret conferences. They also held talks with Armijo's second in command, the able, hot-headed, patriotic Diego Archuleta. Exactly what arrangements were made between these men remains historical speculation. But it does appear that Magoffin first persuaded the already doubting Armijo not to resist Kearny, a decision which may or may not have been influenced by bribing the avaricious governor. Since Armijo's rule of New Mexico was notably harsh, arbitrary, and unpopular, it is quite likely that the governor so feared an internal uprising against his own regime when American troops appeared that he deemed flight the better part of valor.

Young Diego Archuleta, already in command of several thousand impatient troops who had gathered in Santa Fe along with many provincial priests and leaders to resist the Americans, proved more difficult to persuade. But Archuleta's own opposition seems to have collapsed when Magoffin—with what authority is not clear—assured the commander that Kearny was only interested in occupying New Mexico up to the east bank of the Rio Grande, and that the ambitious Archuleta might sieze the western half himself and become its governor.

What followed is well-known history. At the approach of the American troops Armijo fled into Mexico with a few regular soldiers while Archuleta finally agreed to disband the New Mexican volunteers. Late in the afternoon of August 18, Kearny after having marched over Raton Pass and occupied Las Vegas and San Miguel some days before, came through Apache Pass and entered Santa Fe. There a nervous acting governor, Juan Bautista Vigil y Alarid, turned over the province to the General, and the Stars and Stripes were raised in the dusty plaza. As couriers with proclamations rode out to every village along the Rio Grande to urge peaceful acceptance of the new order, many people congratulated Magoffin and Dr. Henry Connelly—another Santa Fe merchant who appears to have been privy to the negotiations with Armijo—for effecting the bloodless conquest. Magoffin himself wrote Secretary of War Marcy a detailed report of the peaceful occupation on August 26.

Travels in Mexico

My journal tells a story tonight different from what it has ever done before.

The curtain raises now with a new scene. This book of travels is ACT 2ND, literally and truly. From the city of New York to the Plains of Mexico, is a stride that I myself can scarcely realize. But now for a bit of my wonderful travels so far. . . .

Thursday, 11th. Now the Prairie life begins! We soon left "the settlements" this morning. Our mules travel well and we jogged on at a rapid pace till 10 o'clock, when we came up with the wagons. They were encamped just at the edge of the last woods. As we proceeded from this thick wood of oaks and scrubby underbrush, my eyes were unable to satiate their longing for a sight of the wide spreading plains. The hot sun, or rather the wind which blew pretty roughly, compelled me to seek shelter with my friends, the carriage and a thick veil. . . .

It is rather a new and novel sight to see *mi alma,* which he did today, mount a bare-back horse without a bridle, with only a halter, and ride through this deep water, with his feet drawn almost up to the horse's back after the manner of mill boys.

We nooned it on this side of the little stream.

A most delightful dinner we had, of *dos patos asado y frijoles cocido* (two roasted ducks and baked beans). It was a splendid dinner that, and many people in "the States" have set down to worse.

Thursday July 30th, 1846. Well this is my nineteenth birthday! And what? Why I feel rather strange, not surprised at its coming, nor to think that I am growing rather older, for that is the way of the human family, but this is it, I am sick! strange sensations in my head, my back and hips, I am obliged to lie down most of the time, and when I get up to hold my hand over my eyes. . . .

Susan goes on to tell about her interesting experiences on the trail to Santa Fe. She does not tell about the political intrigues of her husband, however.

Susan had a miscarriage on the Santa Fe trail and relates the difficulties that stemmed from little, or no medical attention on the frontier. Her observations of life, customs and conditions in Santa Fe shows how she liked Latin life, although other Americans disliked the culture there. Her interpretation offers us a female's view of life at that time.

The Bear Flag Revolt in California

The Bear Flag Revolt of June, 1846, began a process that separated California from Mexico. However, it is not clear that the revolt was planned to take place as it did. A number of American immigrants, charged with crimes by Mexican California authorities, decided to take revenge before they fled to U.S. territory. Some were aware of U.S. plans to seize California and used this idea to give dignity to their vague plans for revenge. Out of such mixed motives and unexpected events, California's history was greatly changed.

This reading offers one side of the story and passes harsh judgment on some of the participants such as John C. Fremont. This account by William B. Ide enhances his role as a leading figure in the Bear Flag revolt.

The Bear Flag Revolt

Just about sunrise on the 11th of June, '46, thirteen mounted men, armed with rifles and pistols, crossed the Sacramento River, a little below, or at the mouth of Feather River. Much time was spent in procuring fresh horses, and no accessions were made to our forces that day. We supped at Gordon's on Coche Creek, who gave us a bullock; but was too deeply interested in our enterprise to join our party just then. At night we groped our way over the mountain pass, and ere the sun had become oppressive, we were safely at the Rancho of Major Barnard. He, also, allowed us to kill and eat a fat bullock, but like the other bear friends, was too fond of the goods of this life, seriously to think of dying in defence (sic) of others.

Here or hereabouts were a considerable number of newly arrived emigrants, and the day was spent in obtaining recruits. Much time was spent in procuring as many as swelled our number to thirty-two; and on the 13th, at 11 P.M., sleep and drowsiness were on the point of delaying, if not defeating our enterprise. We were 36 miles from Sonoma. The sleepless energy of some aroused their companions by representing the danger of delay, and half an hour's debate turned the scale in favor of immediate action, and all put for Sonoma for dear life, as fast as our jaded horses could carry us, so, if possible, to arrive there by a rough path away from the traveled road, before the daylight gave notice of our approach.

And now, dear Sir, as it will be some little time before we get there, I will improve the time to state the views of the party as to the object of their intended visit.

It will be borne in mind that none of this party, save myself, were present when the sentiment of INDEPENDENCE was so heartily cheered in the camp under the Nevada mountains; nor was it reasonable to suppose that any of them were informed by any of Capt. Fremont's men, that his plan was to provoke an attack on Castro's camp, before he left for the States, to take along with him the offenders, to save them from certain destruction. It was known that Capt. F. possessed the unbounded confidence of those twelve men, and also that most of them desired to avail themselves of the opportunity for a safe return to the States, in the service of the United States, at $60 per month for the trip.

The subject of Independence was only talked of as an event that might occur; and no one of them seemed to understand that the taking of Sonoma formed any part of our errand there.

And, moreover, Capt. Fremont, who is allowed to be proverbially cautious and prudent, gave his directions—or rather "advice",—in such manner as to avoid legal testimony in any matter of interference in California politics, (which he invariably and solemnly disavowed) that it was impossible to prove, authoritatively from his responsibility for any line of conduct by our party; but every one (especially those of the "twelve"), seemed, as if by intuition, to understand that our only business was to capture and convey to Fremont's camp Gen. M.G. Vallejo, Don Salvadore Vallejo, Col. Prudshon, and Capt. Jacob P. Leese, if practicable, and if not, to drive off another band of horses, or commit any other act of violence, in its nature calculated to provoke pursuit and attack in the proper quarter.

Fully impressed with the importance of this mission of benevolence and goodwill towards the sleeping and unsuspecting gentlemen to whom we were about to pay our respects, we took timely precaution to swear certain of our number against the commission of violence against either of those gentlemen. This step was considered proper, as we were aware there were certain breathings of vengeance against some of them, in the minds of a few of our party.

It was known that Doct. Semple, who was an active and conspicuous leading man of the host, was in favor of Independence, instanter; but we knew of none willing to push the measure. Under these circumstances it was thought prudent not to broach the subject generally, until some crisis should call the principle into immediate action.

Thus circumstanced, we arrived at Sonoma; and after reconnoitering the place, and notifying our friends of our object in seizing the aforesaid gentlemen and having secured the captain of the guard whom we found a little way out of town, we surrounded the house of Gen. M.G. Vallejo just at daybreak, on the 14th. William Merritt, Doct. Semple, and Mr. Knight (who took wise care to have it understood on all hands that he was forced into the scrape as an interpreter), entered the house to secure their prisoners.

Jacob P. Leese, an American by birth, and brother-in-law of Gen. Vallejo, who lived nearby, was soon there, to soothe the fears, and otherwise as far as possible assist his friends. Doct. Salvadore was also found there, and Col. Prudshon was also soon arrested and brought there. After the first surprise had a little subsided, as no immediate violence was offered, the General's generous spirits gave proof of his usual hospitality—as the richest wines and brandies sparkled in the glasses, and those who had thus unceremoniously met soon became merry companions; more especially—the weary visitors.

While matters were going on thus happily in the house, the main force sat patiently guarding it without. They appeared to understand that they had performed all the duty required of them, and only waited that the said prisoners might be prepared and brought forth for their journey, and—waited still. The sun was climbing up the heavens an hour or more, and yet no man, nor voice, nor sound of violence came from the house to tell us of events within; patience was ill, and lingered ill. "Let us have a captain," said one—"a captain," said all. Capt. Grigsby was elected, and went immediately into the house. The men still sat upon their horses—patience grew faint; an hour became an age. "Oh! go into the house, Ide, and come out again and let us know what is going on there!" No sooner said than done. There sat Doct. S., just modifying a long string of articles of capitulation. There sat Merritt—his head fallen: there sat Knight, no longer able to interpret; and there sat the new made Capitan, as mute as the seat he sat upon. The bottles had well nigh vanquished the captors. The Articles of Capitulation were seized hastily, read and thrown down again, and the men outside were soon informed of their contents. Pardon us, dear Doctor—we will not make an exposition. It is sufficient to say, that by the rule of opposition, they gave motion and energy to the waiting mass, and all that was necessary was to direct the torrent and guide the storm.

No one hitherto in authority had thought of seizing the fortress, or disarming its guard. Capt. Grigsby was hastily called, and the men demanded of him that the prisoners should be immediately conveyed to the Sacramento valley. Capt. G. inquired, "What are the orders of Capt. Fremont in relation to these men?" Each man looked on his fellow, yet none spake. "But have you not got Capt. Fremont's name in black and white to authorize you in this you have done?" cried the enraged Captain —and immediately we demanded, that if there were anyone present who had orders from him, either written or verbal, he declare the same. All declared, one after another, that they had no such orders. Thereupon the Captain was briefly but particularly informed, that the people whom he knew had received from Gen. Castro, and others in authority, the most insolent indignities—had been, on pain of death, ordered to leave the country; and that they had resolved to take the redress of grievances into their own hands; that we could not claim the protection of any government on earth, and we alone responsible for our conduct; that— Here the Captain's "fears of doing wrong" overcame his patriotism, and he interrupted the speaker by saying, "Gentlemen, I have been deceived; I cannot go with you; I resign and back out of the scrape. I can take my family to the mountains as cheap as any of you" —and Doct. S. at that moment led him into the house. Disorder and confusion prevailed. One swore he would not stay to guard prisoners—another swore we would all have our throats cut—another called for fresh horses, and all were on the move—every man for himself; when the speaker (Mr. Ide) resumed his effort, raising his voice louder and more loud, as the men receded from the place, saying: "We need no horses; we want no horses. Saddle no horse for me. I can go to the Spaniards, and make free men of them. I will give myself to them. I will lay my bones here, before I will take upon myself the ignominy of commencing an honorable work, and then flee like cowards, like thieves, when no enemy is in sight. In vain will you say you had honorable motives! Who will believe it? Flee this day, and the longest life cannot wear off your disgrace! Choose ye! choose ye this day, what you will be! We are robbers, or we must be conquerors!"— and the speaker in despair turned his back upon his receding companions.

THE LAST WORD—NOW THE BATTLE!

With new hope they rallied around the desponding speaker—made him their Commander, their Chief; and his next words commanded the taking of the Fort. Joy lighted up every mind, and in a moment all was secured: 18 prisoners, 9 brass cannons, 250 stands of arms, and tons of copper, shot, and other public property, of the value of 10 or 1200 dollars, was seized and held in trust for the public benefit.

Arrangements were immediately made for putting the garrison in a complete state of defence. Tools suitable for fortification, and for supplying a well of water within our walls; and a liberal stock of provisions were procured on contract—pledging the public property now in possession for future payment. But that portion of our forces who still adhered to the "neutral conquest" plan, with the four gentlemen, the aforementioned prisoners at Sutter's Fort, were allowed to remain under the protection of Capt. Fremont, where every comfort was granted them that their situation allowed.

Thus and so was the "Independent Bear Flag Republic" inaugurated. Other circumstances might be given; but not to change its character. What dear friend of Capt. Fremont will hereafter claim that the taking of Sonoma, or the hoisting the Independent Flag, or any other act that grew out of the same, constituted any part of his plan for the conquest of California? If any of those twelve men who took the horses had had any idea that Fremont desired the seizure of the garrison, think you they would have sat on their horses more than two hours, within pistol shot of the Fort, and never thought of taking possession of it? Or think you that if Capt. F. had designed the capture and hoisting the Independent Flag, he would not have so instructed his three champions, who were the leaders of this force, up to the very moment of the recalling the scattering soldiers, and the appointment of the Commander by the people, who ordered taking the Garrison?

Next (if you will be pleased to exercise patience enough), we will consider the circumstances tending to its unexampled success, as we trace, step by step, its history to its first acquaintance with Capt. Fremont, and thence to its finale.

After the return of the three leaders of the party of the primitive plan of neutral conquest, and seven others had "left us alone in our glory," the said "Bear Flag"—made of plain cotton cloth, and ornamented with the red flannel of a shirt from the back of one of the men, and christened by the words "California Republic," in red-paint letters on both sides—was raised upon the standard where had floated on the breezes the Mexican flag aforetime. It was on the 14th of June, '46. Our number was twenty-four, all told. The mechanism of the flag was performed by Wm. Todd of Illinois. The grizzly bear was chosen as an emblem of strength and unyielding resistance.

American Pacific Squadron Seizes Ports of California and Establishes a New Government

Upon learning that war had broken out between Mexico and the United States, Commodore John Drake Sloat seized the vital harbor of Monterey on July 7, 1846. Sloat was acting on highly secret orders which the Secretary of the Navy had sent him about a year before. In the meantime, his ship had visited several ports in Mexico and California as guests, although Mexican authorities suspected U.S. ships of planning violence. In 1842, another American Commodore, Thomas Jones, had tried to seize Monterey for the United States. He apologized and left when he learned that the two nations were at peace.

Sloat reached California at a time when Mexican and American relations were not good. After his ships visited Monterey as guests for a few days,

Americans seized the harbor by force. Soon Sloat issued his proclamation.

The reading that follows is a vivid and interesting account of the incidents.

The Occupation of Monterey

SECRET DISPATCHES FROM SECRETARY OF THE NAVY, GEORGE BANCROFT TO COMMODORE SLOAT

The great distance of your squadron, and the difficulty of communicating with you, are the causes for issuing this order. The President hopes most earnestly that the peace of the two countries may not be disturbed. The object of the instructions is to possess you of the views of the government in the event of a declaration of war against the United States—an event which you are enjoined to do everything consistent with national honor on your part to avoid.

On July 12, 1846, Secretary Bancroft dispatched the following instructions to Sloat: . . . "the object of the United States under its rights as a belligerent nation, is to possess itself entirely of Upper California. . . . The object of the United States has reference to ultimate peace with Mexico; and if, the government expects, through your forces, to be found in actual possession of California."

On June 7, Commodore Sloat, having received more reliable reports of the outbreak of war, decided to act. Having earlier ordered several ships of his squadron to the California coast to await further instructions, he sailed for Monterey, arriving July 2. The next five days he spent preparing his landing forces for the occupation of the capital of California. Orders were issued to his two hundred and fifty-man landing party stressing the importance of cultivating the good opinion of the inhabitants, and adding that a conciliatory attitude was to be taken by all United States forces towards the Californians. On July 7, 1846, therefore, the troops under the command of Captain William Mervine landed and took possession of Monterey. At the nearby custom house the proclamation was read to the inhabitants and the standard of the United States hoisted amid three hearty cheers by the troops and foreigners present and a salute of twenty-one guns fired by all ships.

In the next several days the United States' flag was hoisted at San Francisco under the command of Captain John D. Montgomery and in Sonoma, Sacramento (Sutter's Fort), and San Jose. In each of these flag raising ceremonies the proclamation of Sloat was furnished and read to the people. Sloat's proclamation began by declaring that the state of war existing between the United States and Mexico was caused by the latter because of its invasion of United States territory. Sloat then continued:

"I declare to the inhabitants of California that, although I come in arms with a powerful force, I do not come among them as an enemy of California; on the contrary, I come as its best friend, and henceforth California will be a portion of the United States, and its peaceful inhabitants will enjoy the same rights and privileges as the citizens of any other portion of that territory, with all the rights and privileges they now enjoy, together with the privileges of choosing their own magistrates and other officers for the administration of justice among themselves; and the same protection will be extended to them as to any other state in the Union. They will also enjoy permanent government, under which life, property and the constitutional rights and lawful security to worship the Creator in the way most congenial to one's sense of duty, will be secured, which unfortunately the central government of Mexico cannot afford them, destroyed as her resources are by internal factions and corrupt officers, who create constant revolutions to promote their own interests and impress the people. . . .

"Such of the inhabitants of California, whether native or foreigners, as may not be disposed to accept the high privileges of citizenship and live peacefully under the government of the United States, will be allowed time to dispose of their property and to remove out of the country, if they choose, without any restrictions; or remain in it, observing strict neutrality. With full confidence in the honor and integrity of the inhabitants of the country, I invite the judges, alcaldes, and other civil magistrates to retain their offices, and to execute their functions as heretofore, that the public tranquility may not be disturbed; at least until the government of the territory can be more definitely arranged. All persons holding title to real estate, or in quiet possession of the lands under color of right, shall have these titles and rights guaranteed to them. All churches and property they contain in possession of the clergy of California shall continue in the same rights and possessions they now enjoy.

"All provisions and supplies of every kind furnished for the use of the United States ships and soldiers will be paid for at fair prices; and no private property will be taken for public use without just compensation at the moment."

The Treaty of Guadalupe Hidalgo

Legal conditions for Mexican Americans after 1848 were established by the peace treaty that ended the war between the U.S. and Mexico. Curiously enough, the terms pleased no one fully, for many in the United States wanted more Mexican territory, and Mexicans resented the loss of any part of their nation. Recently, the demands for justice by Mexican Americans in New Mexico and other states have made the 1848 treaty a source of controversy. Just what were the provisions of this treaty?

Provisions of the treaty, especially Article VIII, guaranteed certain protection to Mexican Americans. Actual practice did not always follow the treaty, which by legal tradition has the force of law in local courts. Mexican Americans have claimed that their rights were not fully protected in practice, although they were provided for in the treaty.

In recent years, several Mexican-American organizations have organized protests to dramatize the fact that their rights under the treaty have been violated.

Some Articles of the Treaty Establishing the Rio Grande as the Boundary Between Texas and Mexico, February 2, 1848

TREATY OF PEACE, FRIENDSHIP, LIMITS, AND SETTLEMENT BETWEEN THE UNITED STATES OF AMERICA AND THE MEXICAN REPUBLIC

ARTICLE I. There shall be firm and universal peace between the United States of America and the Mexican republic, and between their respective countries, territories, cities, towns and people, without exception of places or persons. . . .

ARTICLE V. The boundary line between the new Republics shall commence in the Gulf of Mexico, three leagues from land, opposite the mouth of the Rio Grande, otherwise called Rio Bravo del Norte, or opposite the mouth of its deepest branch, if it should have more than one branch emptying directly into the sea; from thence up the middle of that river, following the deepest channel, where it has more than one, to the point where it strikes the southern boundary of New Mexico; thence, westwardly, along the whole southern boundary of New Mexico (which runs north of the town called Paso) to its western termination; thence, northward, along the western line of New Mexico, until it intersects the branch of the River Gila; (or if it should not intersect any branch of that river, then to the point on the said line nearest to such branch, and thence in a direct line to the same;) thence down the middle of the said branch and of the said river, until it empties into the Rio Colorado; thence across the Rio Colorado, following the division line between Upper and Lower California, to the Pacific Ocean . . . And, in order to preclude all difficulty in tracing upon the ground the limit separating Upper from Lower California, it is agreed that the said limit, shall consist of a straight line drawn from the middle of the Rio Gila, where it united with the Colorado, to a point on the coast of the Pacific Ocean, distant one marine league due south of the southernmost point of the port of San Diego, . . .

ARTICLE VII. The River Gila, and the part of the Rio Bravo del Norte lying below the southern boundary of New Mexico, being, agreeably to the fifth article, divided in the middle between the two Republics, the navigation of the Gila and of the Bravo below said boundary shall be free and common to the vessels and citizens of both countries; and neither shall, without the consent of the other, construct any work that may impede or interrupt, in whole or in part, the exercise of this right; not even for favoring new methods of nagivation. . . .

ARTICLE VIII. Mexicans now established in territories previously belonging to Mexico, and which remain for the future within the limits of the United States, as defined by the present treaty, retaining the property which they possess in the said territories, or disposing thereof, and removing the proceeds wherever they please, without their being subjected, on this account, to any contribution, tax, or charge whatever.

Those who shall prefer to remain in the said territories may either retain the title and rights of Mexican citizens, or acquire those of citizens of the United States. But they shall be under the obligation to make their election within one year from the date of the exchange of ratifications of this treaty; and those who shall remain in the said territories after the expiration of that year without having declared their intention to retain the character of Mexicans, shall be considered to have elected to become citizens of the United States. . . .

In the said territories, property of every kind, now belonging to Mexicans not established there, shall be inviolably respected. The present owners, the heirs of these and all Mexicans who may hereafter acquire said property by contract, shall enjoy with respect to it, guarantee equally ample as if the same belonged to citizens of the United States.

ARTICLE XII. In consideration of the extension acquired by the boundaries of the United States, as defined in the fifth article of the present treaty, the Government of the United States engages to pay to that of the Mexican Republic the sum of fifteen millions of dollars. . . .

Article XIII. The United States engage, moreover, to assume and pay to the claimants all the amounts now due them, and those hereafter to become due, by reason of the claims already liquidated and decided against the Mexican Republic, under the conventions between the two republics severally concluded on the eleventh day of April, eighteen hundred and thirty-nine, and on the thirtieth day of January, eighteen hundred and forty-three; so that the Mexican Republic shall be absolutely exempt, for the future, from all expense whatever on account of the said claims.

Article XIV. The United States do furthermore discharge the Mexican Republic from all claims of citizens of the United States, not heretofore decided against the Mexican Government, which may have arisen previously to the date of the signature of this treaty; which discharge shall be final and perpetual, whether, the said claims be rejected or be allowed by the board of commissioners

provided for in the following article, and whatever shall be the total amount of those allowed.

Article XV. The United States, exonerating Mexico from all demands on accounts of the claims of their citizens mentioned in the preceding article, and considering them entirely and forever cancelled, whatever their amount may be, undertake to make satisfaction for the same, to an amount not exceeding three and one-quarter millions of dollars. . . .

Article XXIII. This treaty shall be ratified . . . and the ratifications shall be exchanged in the city of Washington, or at the seat of Government of Mexico, in four months from the date of the signature hereof, or sooner if practicable.

In faith whereof we, the respective plenipotentiaries, have signed this treaty of peace, friendship, limits, and settlement, and have hereunto affixed our seals respectively. Done in quintuplicate, at the city of Guadalupe Hidalgo, on the second day of February, in the year of our Lord, 1848.

N. P. Trist
Luis G. Cuevas
Bernardo Couto
Migl. Atristain

4

MEXICAN AMERICANS IN THE NEW AMERICAN WEST

When the Treaty with Guadalupe Hidalgo ended the war between Mexico and the United States Mexican Americans found themselves in the minority. In a rapid reversal of roles at mid-century, Anglo Americans became the majority, dominant group and Mexican Americans a new minority group. Within a decade, a new society, government, religion, and way of life replaced the Hispano-Mexican veneer that had been laid over Indian foundations for over three centuries.

Most Indians had resisted incorporation into Spanish and Mexican society by physical means, or by virtue of distances and difficulties Europeans had in controlling them. When Americans took over Mexican lands Indians faced a more formidable enemy, for Americans did not try to christianize, acculturate, or intermarry with Indians. Moreover, new weaponry and means of communication and transportation altered forever a certain balance which existed between Indians, Spaniards, and Mexicans. In the eyes of many Americans, Mexican Americans were hardly different from Indians.

Negroes have been an integral part of southwestern history since the arrival of Europeans. Intermarriage blended their history with that of Spaniards, Mexicans, and Indians. When Americans took over the region a different sort of Negro came with them, one with a background of Anglo culture and a clearly established racial status of inferiority that virtually precluded intermarriage. Life in Spanish or Mexican society was not a racial democracy, but certain religious, social, and cultural attitudes softened racism and offered considerable mobility to all groups. All of this changed after 1848.

The Southwest underwent a unique experience when people from all corners of the world were thrown together under difficult circumstances: a war had just ended, a new society had formed, and a frantic Gold Rush was on. Among the many minorities in the Southwest, Mexican Americans underwent a particularly difficult experience. The proximity of Mexico reminded everyone that they were remnants of a defeated nation. In the regions where they were predominant in numbers at the start and where they continued to play a major role in the economy, most Mexican Americans became isolated from the social and political mainstream of American life. Many Anglo Americans acted fairly, but most treated Mexican Americans as a conquered people.

The new society after 1848 rejected much of the Spanish and Mexican cultures that were deeply ingrained in the Southwest. However, valuable contributions survived from the Indians, Spaniards, and Mexicans as well as other groups such as Negroes and Orientals. New languages, ideas, customs, and institutions grew into prominence under Anglo Americans. The Southwest grew tremendously after 1848, due in great part to the stimulus of gold and silver. In time, however, agriculture became more profitable. Americans were inspired by the idea of progress, and Mexican Americans helped build the new American society as they spread out from the old pueblos and Mexican borderlands.

The new society in the West was modeled on that of the eastern seaboard. For the most part politics was dominated by Anglo Americans. Their laws, institutions, and customs favored them over minority groups. Segregation in housing, education, and social and religious life became common. Physical isolation made it difficult to overcome cultural differences in the new southwestern society.

Most Anglo and Mexican Americans judged each other as representatives of a group, rather than on the merits of the individual. Many Anglo Americans believed they were superior to minority groups like the Indian, Oriental, Negro, or Mexican. Because laws were administered by Anglos, Mexican Americans were forced to accept an inferior position in society and to make the best of it. Each group came to believe individuals of the other groups were all the same. With some exceptions, both Anglos and Mexican Americans grew accustomed to a double standard.

History has concentrated on the material and cultural progress associated with Anglo America and has given little attention to the cultural achievements of minority groups. After 1848 Mexican Americans formed a new culture as they sought a place in American society. These readings are only suggestive of developments in new Mexican American life after 1848.

The Rise of Nativism After 1848

Many Americans resented foreigners who came to the West as immigrants after gold was discovered in 1849. Opposition to foreigners, as well as to native Indians and Mexican Americans, to whom the western lands had originally belonged, led to laws restricting foreigners from working in the mines and prohibiting additional foreigners from immigrating.

Quite clearly, the glitter of gold moved good people to rise against newcomers who were competing for the same gold. The Anglo-American greed for gold was often disguised as patriotism—a weapon that could be used to strike out at foreigners. When other means failed, special taxes were imposed on foreigners. Many Americans treated newcomers from other countries as if they were inferior and dangerous.

The rise of nativism in the area of mining eventually also carried over to ranching, farming, politics, and social life.

The following essay on the beginning of nativism in California is from an article by Leonard Pitt in the *Pacific Historical Review*.

The Beginnings of Nativism in California

Josiah Royce deepened California's self-awareness when he explained that all gold rush disorders had been brought on by decent and moral Americans blinded and deranged by the glitter of gold. Those distresses, he wrote in 1886, arose when men of good character turned away from social responsibility and looked inward, toward their own selfish pursuits. Royce's generation had been weaned on the folklore of the prospectors and had preferred to believe that such turmoil as nativism was caused by "immoral" foreigners and "evil" Americans. Even though Royce reduced all social struggle to purely moral and racial issues (asserting, for example, that all foreigners were amoral rather than immoral) his book nonetheless had the merit of shocking California out of its complacency. . . .

For the Yankee, the normal discomforts of such a life was intensified immeasurably in 1849 by the sudden arrival of waves of Pacific immigrants— Mexicans, Chileans, Peruvians, Australians, and Pacific Islanders. By race and class this was an unusual immigration: except for the freebooting Australians, most were lowly bondsmen traveling in the company of their masters. These parties could swiftly set to work and outdig any couple of hundred independent prospectors. Sheer economic jealously, therefore, brought on the first Xenophobia and throughout 1849 the wildest rumors were circulated: organized "foreign capitalists" would pack off with four to nine million in gold and leave behind a scum of "degraded underlings" before the Yankees had a chance to get started; 10,000 Mexican miners "started up by the great capitalists and friends of Santa Anna" would seize California by force; 50,000 hungry, poor, and immoral wretches from Pacific countries would impoverish the state, for even now it had barely enough food to go around. . . .

The first attempt to cope with immigration was made by the army. In 1848, Oregon Yankees had clashed with naturalized native Californians but gold was still plentiful and after each side sustained a few bruises all ended well. Military Governor Richard B. Mason advised Washington that although some of the immigrants were obnoxious he saw no way to keep them out and was following an expedient policy of laissez-faire immigration. But his successor, General Persifor F. Smith, while traveling from Panama to California in January, 1849, was prevailed upon by a mass meeting of Yankees at the Isthmus port to discourage Pacific immigrants from crowding onto American ships. Smith issued a circular to all American consuls in Pacific ports declaring that in California he would "consider everyone, not a citizen of the United States who enters upon public land and digs for gold . . . a trespasser." Americans vowed solemnly to find the means of putting his policy into practice. . . .

Although Smith's pronouncement had "but little effect" in cutting down immigration at its sources, and although the army was impotent to impose that or any other edict in the mines, "some Yankees who had arrived by water" called a meeting at Sutter's Mill in April and were able to put teeth into the "doctrine of trespass." The crowd purged the neighborhood of all Chileans, Mexicans, and Peruvians —on the grounds that they had "no right" to occupy any claim. Many were chased to other diggings. Some sought relief in San Francisco but were set upon by a "patriotic" company of veterans called "The Hounds," later broken up by the town's first vigilance committee. In August and September the Hispanos were again systematically harrassed in the southern diggings (Mariposa, Stanislaus, and Tuolumne counties) and were forced to scamper to new mining sites, unless they could find employment with American protectors. General Smith's successor, Brigadier General Bennett Riley, rode out to the mines to investigate the trouble and announced to the miners that hereafter everybody would be regarded as a trespasser but that the federal government did not sanction any expulsions; to his superiors he reported that he was returning to a policy of laissez-faire—not as an expedient but as a positive measure for the good of the economy. . . .

Expulsionists had their day in the enforcement of the tax. A delegation representing 3,000 Frenchmen and Hispanos (out of a total of some 10,000 foreign-born in the neighborhood) declared to the collector of Tuolumne County that they could pay a tax of four or five dollars but were prepared to resist the "petty tyrants" who asked for twenty. The collector refused to compromise, and after obtaining the cooperation of the sheriff and local judge in prohibiting merchants from selling them any more goods, sent for a posse. From Mormon Gulch came 150 Mexican War veterans flourishing rifles and pistols, waving their old regimental colors, decked out in the remnants of their military uniforms and marching to the cadence of a battered bugle and drum. Sonora, normally a peaceful town, seethed with rumors of Mexican incendiarism, assassination, and massacre. In the hysteria one unfortunate Mexican who blundered into an argument with the sheriff was killed. By nightfall the town had "assumed the appearance of martial law.

The following day, 400 troopers toured the diggings, collecting the tax from the few miners who could afford it and chasing the others away. . . .

The patrol arrested the original troublemakers, two "hot-headed Frenchmen of the red republican order . . ."—then liquored up and headed for home. Five hundred Frenchmen shouting fiery slogans of 1848 rushed to Sonora vowing to defend their captured countrymen, but, on the assurance that the pair would be released rather than lynched, peaceably dispersed. Half the foreign-born population of Sonora had scattered and fully 10,000 had

fled from Columbia Camp which had been the most bustling spot in the southern mines, leaving behind a ghost town. Exclusionists had won a hands down victory in the battle later dubbed "The French Revolution." . . .

The Land Claims Issue After 1848

Almost all wealth comes originally from the land. Both before and after the gold rush, land ownership was very important. Wealth and power depended upon land ownership when farming and ranching became major sources of riches in several southwestern states. The settlement of land titles after the war with Mexico established conditions that determined economic opportunities for many years after. Conditions differed somewhat in Colorado, Texas, New Mexico, and California, but the same forces helped shape their development.

Many land owners during the Mexican period (1824–48) lost properties after 1848. Many owners sold their ranches and others lost them through violence. American laws governing ownership were a major reason for a great change in land ownership. These laws at the federal, state, and county levels of government have been the source of much controversy. Some feel the laws were fair, and others believe they discriminated against Mexican Americans.

In the following essay from *Readings in California History,* Paul W. Gates examines the issue.

Land Claims Issue

California and Kansas were the unwanted children, the wayward daughters, the creators of family discord in the American Union in the decade before the Civil War. Both were overwhelmed almost overnight by hordes of immigrants, many of a rough and turbulent character, who, in the face of government neglect, proceeded to create their own political institutions and to flout national law. California gained admission in 1850 after a bitter struggle but was denied major benefits that other states enjoyed. Kansas, the battleground of the

North and the South for six years, was kept out of the Union until 1860, and during that time it suffered under one of the worst sets of carpetbag officials ever to descend upon a community.

The failure to extend the federal land system to these communities and to survey the lands before settlers swarmed over them, to extinguish Indian titles in Kansas, and to settle speedily the validity of the land claims of the older residents in California, prevented the normal process of taking up and improving the land on the frontier from working as it did elsewhere. Because of this failure Kansas was wracked for nearly three years by raids and counterraids, by bushwhackers and jayhawkers. Their vendettas, night pillaging, arson, and assassinations were more related to conflicts over the jumping of claims, the location of the territorial capital, county seats, and other public institutions and railroad lines than they were to the conflict over slavery. California, niggardly treated by Congress in the matter of free homesteads, denied proper attention to its most pressing issues because of the slavery and sectional conflict in Washington, and distracted by the violence at the mines and squatters' hostility toward the large land claimants, seemed at times on the verge of social upheaval.

Congressional generosity in granting 640 acres to married settlers occupying land in Washington and Oregon on December 1, 1850, and 320 acres to immigrants arriving thereafter through 1855 was not extended to California. This was a clear break with past practice whereby residents of territories acquired by the United States, who were not possessed with land with foreign titles, were given homesteads of 400 to 600 acres. . . .

The vicious Spanish-Mexican system of granting lands by the mere will of some provincial governor or municipal chief without limitation as to area, or precise delineation of boundaries, here develops and matures its most pernicious fruits. Your title may be ever so good, and yet your farm may be taken from you by a new survey, proving that said title does not cover your tract, or covers it but partially. Hence, many refuse or neglect to improve the lands they occupy lest some title adverse to theirs be established, and they legally ousted, or compelled to pay heavily for their own improvements. And, in addition to the genuine Spanish or Mexican grants, which the government and the courts must confirm and uphold, there are fictitious and fraudulent grants—some of them only trumped up to be bought off, and often operating to create anarchy, and protract litigation between settlers and real owners. Then there are, doubtless, squatters, who refuse to recognize and respect valid titles, and waste in futile litigation the money that might make the lands they occupy indisputably their own. I blame no party exclusively, while I entreat the state and federal governments and courts to do their utmost to settle the titles to land in this state beyond controversy, at the earliest possible day. . . .

What of the contention that the high cost of litigation to secure confirmation of claims was responsible for many of the old California families losing their land?

In examining this indictment of the Act of 1851, it should be noted that many of the claims were not the claims of old California families to land long in their possession. Just before American occupation the granting of land by Mexican officials in California had been greatly accelerated. Of the 813 claims which came before the Commission, 494 were granted in the forties; of these 68 were dated 1845, and 87 were dated 1846. Many of these late grants to friends, business associates, and relatives of Governors Micheltorena and Pico were made in anticipation of the transfer of territory to American control and were not intended as colonization grants or as rewards for the development of land. Some, like Las Mariposas, had no improvements, nor were any put on them for some time after American occupation. Such grants were probably acquired for resale to land-hungry settlers. Justice N.H. Swayne, of the United States Supreme Court, later stated that testimony from reliable witnesses showed that a large number of grants had been made by Governor Pico on the day and night preceding his flight to Mexico in August 1846 and had been antedated.

Many of these later grants were acquired by Americans or other recent immigrants within a few months or a year or two after they were made and long before the scorned Land Commission had begun to function. Others were given directly to recent arrivals. Between a quarter and a third of all the claims had passed into the hands of Americans and other recent immigrants by the time the Act of 1851 was adopted.

Mexicans or native Californians, like the Creoles in Louisiana in the early part of the nineteenth century, had less regard for land ownership than did Americans, less foresight, little realization of the increase in land values that might occur. They lived extravagantly, were hard hit by taxes and drought, borrowed on their claims, showed little of the concern for their obligations that mortgage-ridden Americans felt, and were thus brought to bankruptcy or foreclosure of their estates. . . .

Historians judging the Act of 1851 showed little understanding of earlier handling of private land claims in other territories acquired from Spain, France, and England: their accounts have been unbalanced and subjective as their treatment of the squatters in California has been harsh and preju-diced. It has taken more than a Frank Norris to counteract Josiah Royce's savage blast at the squatters. Yet these squatters in the initial stages of their controversy thought they were fighting for exactly the same rights that the government conceded them elsewhere. Had early trial of the claims been pressed, had government prosecution of dubi-ous claims been more vigorously pushed by an adequately manned staff of competent attorneys, had the public land system with its surveys been early initiated, had free grants been given settlers as was done in Oregon, and had squatters been conceded the value of improvements they put on land later confirmed to others, most of the diffi-culties in California over rural property might have been avoided. Unfortunately, California was a mere pawn in the political conflict between North and South, and, when it desperately needed the sympathetic attention of statesmen, its claims on them were denied and it was permitted to drift, its problems unsolved until it was too late to avoid the consequences of that neglect. Not the Land Act of 1851 but congressional and administrative neg-lect and too much regard for inchoate rights of land claimants as against the pre-emptive rights of those making improvements on land were re-sponsible for the difficulties into which California fell over titles.

Outlaws and Bandidos in the Sagebrush Country

The 2,000 mile border between Mexico and the United States was not clearly marked in many places and the Rio Grande sometimes changed its riverbed. Outlaws from both sides of the border used the other country for refuge and profit. Cattle, sheep, and horses were stolen and traded back and forth. This illegal commerce gave each country a bad name in the eyes of the other. Mexican Ameri-cans suffered the bad effects of a reputation they did not deserve most of the time.

This brief reading from *A Vaquero of the Brush Country* by J. Frank Dobie is interesting because of the fair judgment it passes on a way of life in the West. The existing conditions led most westerners to pretty much make up their own law in many areas. Going back to Spanish times, unbranded cattle were fair game; thus many ranchers started herds with stray cattle that they promptly branded as their own. Much of the same applied to water sources as well. In many respects it seems that laws developed locally to recognize or finalize de facto situations.

Outlaws and Bandidos

As has been made clear, the *Brasada*—the brush country—marked the meeting of the East and the West. Desperadoes from eastern states as well as from Texas counties to the east sought the border brush and its security. Raiding Mexicans from below the Rio Grande slipped over the unguarded river, rendezvoused with American bad men, stole, murdered if necessary, and rode back into Mexico before they could be discovered, though plenty of them were trailed far beyond the borders of Texas and there ceased making tracks forever. In short, the Brasada was a strategic point for stealing and smuggling.

The white men who operated with the Mexicans were worse thieves and more hardened criminals than the bandidos; in some ways they were worse than the Comanches had been. They could steal a bunch of horses as far east as the San Antonio River, ride hard all night and a part of one day, and then, having crossed the Nueces River, lie up in some wild thicket of the Brasada. There Mexican confederates with a bunch of "wet" horses—horses stolen in Mexico and smuggled across the river—would meet them; the two outfits would exchange stolen stock; then each would turn back with horses to trade. Such operators could afford to offer horses at attractive prices. Many a Texas cowman bought Mexican horses for which his own remuda stolen a week or ten days before had been swapped. . . .

One rancher described the operation: "Of course the ranch people of the border country were con-

tinually losing horses. Sometimes we knew when they were stolen; sometimes it was weeks after they disappeared from the range before we found that they were gone. It took me a good while to put two and two together. . . .

Gregorio Cortez: A Mexican-American Farmer, Fugitive, and Hero

The life of Gregorio Cortez highlights several aspects of Mexican-American life in the Southwest after 1848. The mixture of Anglo and Mexican cultures was a force in his life that often helped him. However, the wrong interpretation of a couple of words from Spanish to English led to a gun fight in which Gregorio killed Sheriff Morris. He became a fugitive and was later caught, imprisoned, and finally released years later. The unfortunate life of Cortez tells us much about the way in which Mexican Americans and Anglos viewed each other well into the present century.

As was common among Mexican Americans, the life of Cortez gave rise to ballads about him, called *corridos*. Corridos spread his fame far and wide wherever Mexican Americans gathered together to talk or sing.

Gregorio Cortez

1
Como decimos, así es,
en mil novecientos uno,
el día veintidós de junio
fue capturado Cortés.

2
En junio día veintidós
por telégrafo supieron
que a Cortés lo aprehendieron
entre el Sauz y Palafox.

3
Se aprehendió en Campo de Oveja,
de don Abraham de la Garza,
él perdió toda esperanza,
ya en la frontera de Texas.

As we say, so it is;
In nineteen hundred and one,
On the twenty-second of June
Cortez was captured.

In June, on the twenty-second,
By telegraph it was known
That Cortez had been apprehended
Between El Sauz and Palafox.

He was captured in Sheep Camp,
Of Don Abraham de la Garza,
He lost all hope
When he was already on the Texas border.

4

Que viva nuestra nación,
aunque sufriendo revés,
Viva, Gregorio Cortés,
que ha honrado su pabellón.

5

Murieron tres aprehensores,
por falta en determinar,
y así han podido pagar
los justos por pecadores.

6

Todito el Río Grande estaba,
resguardando el litoral,
parece que se esperaba,
conflicto internacional.

7

La madre patria es hogar,
que hijo e hija ama,
pues México tiene fama,
disciplina militar.

8

Cortés a Morris mató,
la pistola que sirvió,
por otra luego cambió
a un amigo que encontró.

9

Su coche a tiro tomó,
toda esta advertencia tuvo,
tres millas y media anduvo
y allí se apeó y amarró.

10

De América su nación,
ha sufrido este revés,
pues nuestro hermano Cortés
ha honrado su pabellón.

11

Se oyen de Cortés querellas
lamentándose al Creador,
el pabellón tricolor.
idéntico a las estrellas.

12

Gregorio Cortés venía
de incógnito y lo entregaron,
y así lo determinaron,
porque así les convenía.

13

La grande alarma que hoy pasa
en San Antonio, Laredo,

Long live our country
Although suffering setback,
Long live Gregorio Cortez,
Who has honored his flag.

Three captors died
For lack of discernment,
And thus there have paid
The just for the sinners.

All the Rio Grande
Was guarding the shore;
It seemed that they were expecting
An international conflict.

The mother country is a home
That loves both daughter and son,
For Mexico has fame,
Military discipline.

Cortez killed Morris;
The pistol that was used
He exchanged for another
With a friend that he met.

His coach and team [?] he took,
He was careful to do all this;
He rode three miles and a half
And then got down and tied up.

Of America her nation
Has suffered this setback,
For our brother Cortez
Has honored his flag.

From Cortez are heard complaints,
Lamenting to the Creator,
The tricolor flag,
Identical to the stars.

Gregorio Cortez was coming
In disguise and he was betrayed;
Thus it was arranged,
Because it was to their interest.

The great alarm that now happens,
In San Antonio, Laredo,

por el gran furor y miedo,
querían acabar la raza.

14

Llegó a casa de Robledo,
allí con él conversó,
nada de esto les contó,
porque no tuvieran miedo.

15

Glover aquí lo asaltó,
descalzo salió de aquí,
volvió por calzado ahí,
y a Glover muerto encontró.

16

A Cortés llegan con fallos,
siendo íntegro mexicano.
Diciendo:—¿Cortés y hermano
son ladrones de a caballo?

17

¡Dios de mí tenga clemencia
adiós, esposa, ay de míl
por cincuenta añas salí
sentenciado, a penitencia.

18

Así difundió su amor,
nuestro Redentor Jesús.
Gracias mil, don Pablo Cruz,
Editor "DEL REGIDOR."

19

Pablo Cruz se distinguió
como íntegro mexicano,
este prominente hermano
que su ayuda me impartió.

20

Su indulgente Redacción
y su unión confraternal,
con su luz intelectuel,
él abrió una suscripción.

21

Participo esta noticia,
a gente culta y honrada . . .
los de lista enumerada,
la suerte le sea propicia.

22

¡Y aquí acaba de una vez,
la desgracia lamentando! . . .
Aquí se acaba cantando
el Corrido de Cortés.

From the great fury and fear
They wanted to exterminate our people.

He got to Robledo's house,
There he conversed with him;
He told them nothing of this,
So they wouldn't be afraid.

Glover surprised him here,
Barefoot he went out of here;
He returned for his shoes
And found Glover dead.

To Cortez they come with judgments,
Being an upright Mexican,
Saying, "Cortez and brother
Are thieves on horseback?

May God on me have mercy,
Farewell, wife, woe is me!
For fifty years I departed,
Sentenced to the penitentiary.

Thus did he diffuse His love,
Jesus, our Redeemer;
A thousand thanks, Don Pablo Cruz,
Editor of El Regidor.

Pablo Cruz distinguished himself
As an upright Mexican,
This prominent brother
Who gave me his help.

His indulgent Staff
And his confraternal union,
With his intellectual light,
He began a subscription.

I make this news known
To cultured and honest people;
Those on the numbered list—
May fortune be propitious to them.

And here ends at once,
The misfortune lamenting! . . .
This is the end of the singing
Of the ballad of Cortez.

Mexican Origins of the Cowboy Outfit

Many Anglo-American settlers arrived in the West with little knowledge of the strange, new terrain or of the best methods of adapting to it. Mexicans taught them much about the Western life-style: cattle and sheep raising, farming, construction, and irrigation.

One of the most important Mexican contributions was the horse lore they passed on to the newcomers. The horse was very important in the West, even after the railroads came.

This selection from *The Old-Time Cowhand* by Ramon F. Adams describes some of the practical, everyday things about horses that drew upon Spanish and Mexican culture. In addition to horse handling, elements such as music (guitar and songs), recreation (rodeos), and customs associated with the American cowboy stem from the Mexican *vaquero* (cowboy).

The Old-Time Cowhand

CHAPS

I reckon the most conspicuous part of the cowboy's riggin' was his chaps, or leggin's, as they were mostly called. The shorthorn looked upon 'em as the most affected part of the costume of a vain man, but it was a product of conditions that was adapted to the service it had to render. Handed down by the Mexicans, chaps were jes' two wide and full-length trouser legs made of heavy leather and connected by a narrow string called the "chapstring." This held the legs of the chaps together in front at the waist. It wasn't so strong that it wouldn't break when the wearer got hung up in the ridin' gear.

There's several styles in chaps, all developed from the armitas, a sort of loose-riding apron. This word's from the Spanish *amar*, meanin' to arm, to plate with anything that adds strength. Them were well cut aprons, usually made of home-tanned or Injun buckskin and tied 'round the waist and knees with thongs. They protected the legs and clothes and were cooler in summer than chaps. Their use practically passed with old-time range customs, although they're still used to some extent in southern California.

The first chaps in Texas to be developed from the snug-fittin' *chaperas* of the Mexican *vaquero* were the "shotgun chaps." These were pulled over the boots, and usually carried a leather fringe down the sides. The way the outside seams were sewn together they looked like the twin barrels of a shotgun, with a choke at the muzzle. In the more northern ranges they used "hair pants" a lot. Them were chaps made from skins, such as goat, bear, deer, and other animals with the hair left on and worn hair side out. They were a protection against cold, but in snow, sleet, or rain storms they proved mighty uncomfortable, for they got wet, soggy, and heavy, sometimes smelling stronger'n a wolf's den. They wasn't so pop'lar on the range as in the movies. . . .

ROPES

The rope's a simple thing, but it's the most important tool of the cowboy. Without it there'd have been no cattle business. In the early days it was the only way to ketch and hold hosses and cattle; the only way to throw an animal for brandin' and doctorin'. Even now, with fences, corrals, and chutes, it's still a necessary implement. Ever' workin' cowhand's got a rope coiled below his saddle horn, and it ain't there for pretty. No matter what job was to be done, he'd look it over to see if it could be done with a rope and saddle hoss. Ropin's an art, the most difficult of all cowboy attainments, and an expert started learnin' while he was fryin' size, and kept practicin' till he'd sacked his saddle.

The word "lariat" is a contraction of the Spanish *la reata,* which literally means a "tie back." The term was originally used for a rope in picketin' hosses. Some Eastern folks like to say "lariat" and "lasso" because it sounds Western, but the cowhand called his rope jes' plain "rope." "Reata," or "riata" is 'nother Spanish word meanin' rope," and is sometimes used, but usually it refers to a braided rawhide rope. Lariat may be used as a verb, as to fasten, or ketch with a lariat, but reata's never used as a verb, only as a noun. Some sections of the cattle country never used the word "lariat." California, for instance, don't like the word, but prefers "reata," or "lass rope."

The term "lasso" usually meant a hide rope, generally a long one with a runnin' noose. Mexicans introduced this name to the cattle range, although the word's not of Spanish origin, but comes from the Portuguese laco, which has a meanin' equivalent to "snare." Early in cattle-raisin' history cowboys began callin' a rope jes' plain rope. Out on the Pacific Coast, where they still use a lot of rawhide, they still say "lasso," but not in other sections except in fiction. In the Southwest where they mostly use a thirty-five-foot-length manila for ordinary ropin', a ropes' a rope—without any fancy label. And when they swing a loop and ketch a critter they "rope" it. They don't "lasso" or "lariat" it in spite of movie talk. . . .

THE REMUDA

The Spanish word *remuda* is from the verb *remundar*, meanin' "to exchange"; *remuda de caballos* means "relay of hosses." The cowman uses the word to mean the extry hosses of each cowboy herded together and not at the time under saddle. The word's pronounced "remootha" in the Southwest, but most Texas cowmen merely speak of "the hosses." The remuda's to the Southwest what the "cavvy" is to the Northwest, though the Northwestern cowhand usually calls them hosses the "saddle band." "Cavvy" is a shortened corruption of the Spanish *caballado,* meanin' a "band of hosses." It, too, refers to the broken "hosses" maintained by a ranch. . . .

The Decline of the Californios

The decline of the Mexican upper classes after 1848 in California may be a model of what happened in other states. Professor Leonard Pitt, who

wrote the following selection, calls these Spanish land holders "Californios." He explains how Anglo Americans and Californios developed different opinions about historical change after 1848.

In various parts of the Southwest, Spanish-speaking Mexicans helped the expansion of the United States in hopes of a better life. With few exceptions, this group acted independently in each region of the Southwest. Yet in time, most lost power and prestige. They were often put into the same class as mestizo Mexicans or Indians. Thus Mexican Americans lost what leadership they could have had and most Anglo Americans saw this as proof of their own superiority.

Schizoid Heritage

When Benjamin Hayes reflected that the Lugo family of southern California had possessed $150,-000 in 1852 but had practically no wealth by 1865, he concluded that "the finger of Providence seems to mark the decay of the old Californian families." Why God's wrath? "We must not judge," Hayes answered. "But the Indians have suffered great crimes and injustices from the later Mexican governors and people." In explaining the fall of the Californians, Hayes thus supplied the "unrequired toil" theory which Abraham Lincoln suggested in his second inaugural as an explanation of the Civil War. Since by Hayes's own reckoning the Yankees, too, should have felt the Lord's wrath for abusing Indians, the theory sounds smug and lacking in substance. Yet the question of the fall was a good one and perplexed both contemporary and later students of the California scene.

In Hayes's time the Yankee still felt sufficiently free of guilt to regard the Californians' defeat as self-inflicted. The oldest and perhaps most highly respected Yankee pioneer in the state, Alfred Robinson, in a late postscript of his famous *Life in California,* described the downfall as inevitable and regrettable, but as altogether the product of the Californios passivity. His argument supposes a belief in the idea of progress:

The early Californians, having lived a life of indolence without any aspiration beyond the immediate requirement of the day, naturally fell behind their more energetic successors, and became impoverished and gradually dispossessed of their fortunes as they idly stood by, lookers-on upon the bustle and enterprise of the new world before them, with its go-ahead-ative-ness and push-on keep-moving celebrity.

These words by Robinson, and also those of Hayes, are faintly colored by remorse, but not by guilt or romance; these came later.

The Californians also spoke of a mysterious Providence guiding their lives, but they added a human factor—the malevolence of gringos and Mexicans. Themselves they rarely blamed, except for tactical errors such as a failure to break completely with Mexico when it lay within their grasp to do so in the 1840s, which would have enabled them to appear before their Yankee conquerors as their own masters and to demand genuine Yankee guarantees of ownership of their ranchos. That the conqueror "seeks his own good fortune, not ours," Mariano Vallejo considered "very natural in individuals, but I denounce it on the part of a government (the United States) that promised to respect our rights and to treat us as its own sons." The Californios perceived themselves not merely as the victims of annexation or assimilation, but of deliberate betrayal and bone-crushing repression. By dint of strenuous effort, a few of them had managed to retain enough of their birthright to hand it on to their heirs; but few had held property as confidently as the conqueror had promised. Of the forty-five Californios representing the twenty-five families whom Thomas Oliver Larkin had enumerated in 1846 as the "principal men" of the old regime, the vast majority went to their graves embittered. Indeed, the gentry had experienced what might be called California's only true social revolution: they were a ruling class militarily conquered, bereft of national sovereignty and a constitutional framework, and alienated from

their land, homes, civil rights, and honor. They had retained little else besides their religion and a thin residue of honorary political influence. . . .

The native son Salvador Vallejo admitted that lower-class males had "gained to a certain extent" in the new era, but at the expense of upper-class women, who had lost all. Mariano Vallejo thought that the Americanization of California redounded generally to the benefit of agriculture and commerce "but to the moral detriment of the (original) inhabitants . . . demoralized by daily contact with so many immoral persons . . . and a large part of the blame and responsibility may be rightfully attributed to the national and state government. I ask you what has the state government done for the Californians since the victory over Mexico? But, what good will it do us to complain? The evil is done and there is now (1875) no remedy for it." His more mystically inclined brother, Salvador, added: "I abstain from repining (about our losses), for it is useless for mankind to protest against the decree of a wise Providence, whose deep mysteries we mortals are not allowed to fathom or interpret."

Given the irreversible political and diplomatic complications of 1845, few Californians regretted having become Yankees. Had he caviled over his new citizenship, a Salvador Vallejo would not later have joined the Union Army. But all wondered what they had accomplished in the transformation. Don Salvador thought that the old domestic amenities far surpassed anything he had since seen. Californios had bred their children well, he believed, having taught their sons the arts of ranching and their daughters housekeeping. Even the women who were cloistered by an army of Indian servants made good housewives in their own right. This resulted in "cleanliness, good living and economy." Moreover, none of the women formerly wasted money on cosmetics, high-heeled shoes, cotton bosoms, whale-bone corsets ("veritable instruments of torture"). All these novelties compared unfavorably with the "simple yet becoming" feminine garments of the "happy day"—and they were happy days, when people of all ages and both sexes roamed free of cost and free of worry "through the hills and plains, through meadows and ravines, with no critics' eyes to fear, no scandal-mongers to dread, no loquacious servants to bribe." Jose Eusebio Galindo developed the Arcadian image one step further and said that olden California had been a "true paradise."

Not to romanticize but to debunk Yankee myths and lies became the task of the moment. Mariano Vallejo and others had bristled at reading Robinson's Life; they could not fathom how a man could love his Californio wife and in-laws as fully as Robinson apparently did and yet write so condescendingly. Mariano started writing a multivolume history—"a true history of the country"—to tell the Americans that the early Californians "were not indigents or a band of beasts," but an "illustrious" race of people. Admittedly the scholarly project he had taken on surpassed the energies of one man, but duty drove Vallejo to work at it, lest "we . . . disappear, ignored of the whole world." In his usual luckless way Mariano lost 900 manuscript pages when fire ravaged his home in 1867, but in his equally persevering way he began again from scratch in 1873. . . .

In death, the Californios began to assume heroic importance. Grieving at the funeral invitations that came steadily in the 1870's and 1880's, old-time Yankee friends, themselves a dying breed, served as pallbearers to their dead compadres. The press showed belated sympathy, at least to the extent of giving the Californios favorable obituaries:

(He) . . . was one of the best known and most highly respected of our Mexican citizens, and at one time was one of the wealthiest men in this portion of the State. . . . (He saw) the few Mexican huts give way to the march of civilization and improvement, until it became to him a fairy dream. He was an honest, free hearted man. He leaves a long line of friends to mourn his taking away.

The notice of Juan Bernal's death in Santa Clara, September 23, 1878, could substitute for the obituary of a hundred rancheros. When Salvador Vallejo was laid to rest in February, 1876, Sonomo's flags hung at half-mast for the former Union Army officer. He lived his last days with his brother after going bankrupt in the panic of 1873, passing his time reading, painting, fishing, playing the guitar for his nieces, and drowning his bitterness in whiskey. His obituary included the observation that he was "a man of very strong prejudices, and never . . . reconciled to the American occupation." San Francisco's Spanish language weekly came to Salvador's defense by countering that he was, in fact, reconciled and had left the "wrong doers to God's mercy." The death of Salvador's brother Mariano in 1900 made banner headlines throughout the state.

Even with the aid of hindsight and detailed empirical research, the "final cause" of the Californio's pitiful collapse escapes the scholar. It remains a difficult exercise in historical causation to unravel the complex factors and extract the immediate from the remote causes, the human from the impersonal, the economic from the cultural or social; each contributed in its way.

5

THE MEXICAN AMERICAN
IN RECENT TIMES

Although Mexican Americans have been an integral part of life in the southwestern United States for well over a century, they have been a rather silent, almost invisible minority. Concentrated, as they were, in only five states, they were comparatively unknown to most Americans.

Forebears of many Mexican Americans lived in the Southwest long before it became part of the United States, but the overwhelming majority are either Mexican immigrants or second or third generation descendants of immigrants. Generally, their silence and invisibility can be attributed to the same factors that shaped the lives of many other minorities in America—poverty, discrimination, inadequate educational opportunities, and perhaps most importantly, a formidable language barrier.

Although they helped build the American Southwest and have been vitally important to its economic growth and development, Mexican Americans have, for the most part, been methodically excluded from the mainstream of life in that area. Generally, they were relegated to menial, low-paying jobs and inadequate housing. The educational establishment failed them miserably, for few educators ever considered their needs in terms of cultural difference or of the language barrier. The Anglo majority kept a firm grip on political institutions, excluding Mexican Americans whenever possible—even to the extent of preventing them from voting.

It would be difficult, if not impossible, to pinpoint the exact time when Mexican Americans began to say, "We've had enough." Although some efforts at improving conditions in the lives of Mexican Americans date back to the last century, the greatest thrust for equality and justice is only a little over 20 years old. In practically every area of the Southwest, Mexican-American leaders have emerged to fight for the rights of their people. The struggle has taken many forms. Some leaders have limited their fight to organizing Mexican-American workers to improve wages and working conditions. Some have struggled to impress on their people the importance of pride in their cultural heritage, and others have turned to politics.

Mexican Americans have posed the question whether Anglo Americans are correct in insisting that their language and culture are prerequisite to equality in America, just as blacks have forced the issue as to race. For generations since independence, millions have shed their "foreign name" (non-Anglo) or changed its spellings, selected their residence, intermarried, changed religion, or at a mundane level, dyed their hair in an effort to get lost in the great American crowd. How pathetically have millions tried to hide their shame to gain the advantages of cultural homogeneity. Clearly, nativism by which culturally different elements were suspect, rejected, or suppressed produced some benefits. However, the benefits are difficult to assess when compared to the human costs. How can we calculate the losses in vitality and creativity that extend from an inferiority complex, alienation, or hostility among Mexican Americans which prejuice against them has produced? Some Mexican Americans feel the losses are incalculable. The Mexican Americans who have assimilated in great numbers are hard to count. So are the countless who have "made it" and have preferred not to identify as Mexican Americans. We are concerned here with the fact that more and more Mexican Americans are assertive about their culture and demand acceptance as Americans on their grounds.

At one extreme we find Mexican Americans striving for assimilation, while at another we find some propounding separatism like that advanced by some blacks or French Canadians. Most Mexican Americans are not active politically, but others are working to build a separate *La Raza* Unida party. In areas such as education, we find Mexican Americans claiming that it is an asset to be bilingual, not a disadvantage. Every day the diversity among Mexican Americans becomes more evident and more relevant.

Many other "white" ethnic groups are responding to the call for a culturally pluralistic America. Germans, Swedes, Italians, Jews, and many others are becoming more assertive about their formerly submerged ethnicity. It is clear that the melting pot has not eliminated our differences, nor will it in the future. Mexican Americans pose an interesting case study in these respects. They also pose a riddle that will not be answered once and for all since as long as we share a border, Mexican Americans will come to our land legally (dry) or illegally (wet) and replay the old story over again.

Where America will go with respect to what it is to be American may be revealed by where Mexican Americans go. Their importance stems not only from their qualities or historical role, but from their numbers. Census data for 1970 reveals that the Indian population is soaring at about four times the rate of increase found among other Americans. Indians have doubled their number in twenty years, and they are living longer as well. From about 343,000 in 1950 Indians numbered about 792,000 in 1970. Mexican Americans have increased at a higher rate—in states like California more than doubling their number in ten years. In 1960 there were about 1,400,000 Mexican Americans in California; by 1970 the number reached just over 3,000,000 in this one state alone. Comparable developments have occurred in other states and there has been a great increase of Mexican Americans across the nation. Using California alone as a case study we can see some important implications for the future; doubtlessly, for many reasons Mexican Americans will figure more prominently in our national scene.

Selections in this unit were chosen to offer the reader a picture of today's Mexican American—his sense of pride in his rich cultural heritage, his advances toward the mainstream of American economic life, his cultural achievements, and the political role he is beginning to play in shaping his own destiny.

IMMIGRATION

Immigration is one of the most significant parts of the story of Mexican Americans. Many Mexican Americans are descended from forebears who lived in the American Southwest long before it became part of the United States. Many are descended from Mexicans who immigrated many decades ago, and and others were either born in Mexico or of parents who were born there.

In the early days of the United States and well into this century, immigration to the U.S. was relatively unrestricted for all but Orientals. For Mexicans and other Latin Americans, the policy of reasonably easy entry continued until the 1950's. For people of many other countries, however, immigration to the U.S. became far more difficult after 1924. In that year, Congress passed a law establishing a quota system. Under this system, the number of people allowed to immigrate from a particular country was based on the percentage of the U.S. population who were either born or descended from people born in that country.

Since the largest percentage of Americans were of Northern European ancestry, the system tended to preserve the Anglo-Saxon Protestant majority in the United States.

Laws passed by Congress in 1952 and 1965 limited immigration from Latin America, but the number of immigrants from Mexico, which is estimated at about 50,000 a year, still usually exceeds that of other nations.

National Origins of Mexican Americans in 1960 and 1970

Much information about Mexican Americans is missing because for many years, they were not counted as a separate group. Even in recent census studies, confusion about them has led to data which is often grossly misleading or not comparable to that of previous censuses. The 1970 Census was a great disappointment to many who hoped to get, at last, accurate, complete, and reliable data on Mexican Americans and other Americans of Latin descent.

Mexican Americans are nearly equally divided

into two groups: (1) those born in Mexico or those born in the United States whose parents were born in Mexico (Mexican Stock), and (2) Mexican Americans whose parents were born in the U.S. (Native or Native Parents). The 1960 Census described Mexican Americans as Mexican stock or as natives, shedding light on a special situation that affects Mexican Americans. The effects of Mexican culture are strong in at least half of the Mexican-American population. As the two graphs show, the percentage of Mexican Americans born in the U.S. was much greater in 1970 than it was in 1960.

Estimated Mexican Americans in the United States, 1960

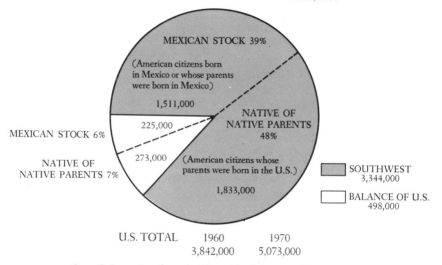

MEXICAN STOCK 39%

(American citizens born in Mexico or whose parents were born in Mexico)

1,511,000

225,000

MEXICAN STOCK 6%

NATIVE OF NATIVE PARENTS 7%

273,000

NATIVE OF NATIVE PARENTS 48%

(American citizens whose parents were born in the U.S.)

1,833,000

SOUTHWEST 3,344,000

BALANCE OF U.S. 498,000

U.S. TOTAL	1960	1970
	3,842,000	5,073,000

Spanish Origin Population by Place of Birth for United States, 1970

Estimated Mexican Americans in the U.S. in 1970
5,073,000

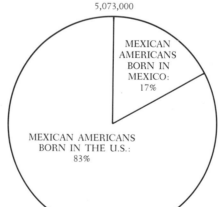

MEXICAN AMERICANS BORN IN MEXICO: 17%

MEXICAN AMERICANS BORN IN THE U.S.: 83%

Note: The data from the 1970 Census is not wholly comparable to the 1960 data. Each Census must be studied separately until further studies of the 1970 Census become available.

Where Mexican Immigrants Go in the U.S.

Mexican immigration has flowed steadily into the American Southwest, except during the years of the Great Depression (about 1930–1940). As they immigrated, Mexicans were, by law, required to indicate their intended state of residence.

Where immigrants wanted to live generally stemmed from information they had about an area. Such factors as job opportunities, the Mexican-American population of others from an area, and family ties usually influenced decisions about where to settle. After arriving in this country, immigrants often move about from state to state, usually seeking jobs, but sometimes in search of Mexican-American communities they would consider more compatible.

Much of Mexican-American life in barrios centers around clubs whose membership is determined by the Mexican state or region from which the immigrant came. Many important things stem from these social groups—job contracts, economic help, marriage ties, or simply the companionship of those from the same area back in Mexico.

As discrimination against Mexican Americans wanes, the need for such clubs lessens, but they have served a very important role in the lives of many Mexican Americans of the first and second generation.

The graph that follows shows how immigration patterns of Mexicans into various states has changed over the past 60 years.

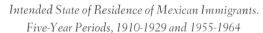

Intended State of Residence of Mexican Immigrants.
Five-Year Periods, 1910-1929 and 1955-1964

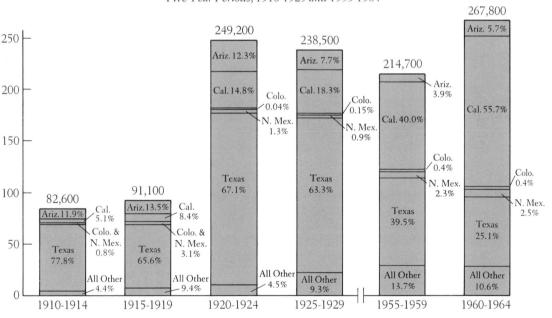

97

Distribution of Mexican Americans
(1910 to 1970)

The charts below demonstrate the concentration of Mexican Americans in the Southwest. Between 1960 and 1970 a significant number moved into other parts of the country. Illinois, Wisconsin, Michigan, and other eastern states each have hundreds of thousands of Mexican Americans while in the Northwest, Oregon and Washington now take them into account in various social, educational, and political respects. As Mexican Americans spread out across the United States they have attained national prominence and consideration rather than being purely a regional minority group.

Most Mexican Americans leave the Southwest to work in farm work, but many stay in the communities and start a barrio. This serves as a port of entry for others that come and enter other lines of work. Middle-class or professional Mexican Americans are harder to keep track of because they are not identifiable and are more socially acceptable. Although the center of social and political activity remains in Texas, Colorado, and California, other unlikely states such as Kansas, Michigan, and Wyoming now have surprisingly vigorous Mexican American social activity. Communication between the barrios across the nation improves steadily, and the increased speed of communication tends to accelerate social changes in the nation as a whole.

Geographic Distribution of Persons of Mexican Stock,
by Region and State, 1910–1960

	1910	1920	1930	1940	1950	1960
Arizona	13.4	12.6	8.2	7.3	6.1	6.0
California	13.4	17.4	29.3	32.9	35.8	40.1
Colorado	0.9	2.0	2.1	2.0	1.5	1.2
New Mexico	5.7	4.7	3.1	2.8	2.3	2.0
Texas	61.0	54.6	45.5	.45.0	42.8	37.9
Southwest	94.3	94.3	88.2	90.0	88.6	87.2
Other	5.7	8.7	11.8	10.0	11.4	12.8
U.S. Total	100.0	100.0	100.0	100.0	100.0	100.0

Spanish Origin Population for the United States, Five Southwestern States, and
Remainder: November 1969

	(Numbers in thousands)					
	UNITED STATES		FIVE SOUTHWESTERN STATES		REMAINDER OF U.S.	
ORIGINS:	Number	Percent	Number	Percent	Number	Percent
Total Spanish-speaking	9,230	100.0	5,507	100.0	3,723	100.0
Mexican American	5,073	55.0	4,360	79.2	713	19.1

ECONOMY

Like most minorities, Mexican Americans have found it very difficult to move into the mainstream of American economic life. While a small percentage has moved into professions, technical work, and clerical and sales jobs, the majority has been forced into such low-paying menial jobs as laborers and farm and domestic work.

While recent statistics indicate that Mexican Americans have begun to move up the economic ladder, the overwhelming majority still find many obstacles that block their way to more desirable, higher-paying jobs. In the decade ending in 1970, the percentage of Mexican Americans in professions and white-collar jobs increased rather dramatically. In 1960, for example, less than eight percent of the total Mexican-American work force were in white-collar jobs. By 1970, however, the figure had increased to 18.5 percent for men and to 37.7 percent for women. While these figures may, at first, seem impressive, the fact remains that the percentage of Mexican Americans in low-paying, menial jobs still is far higher than the national average.

Readings in this section will shed light on the occupations of Mexican Americans and their struggle to move upward on the economic ladder.

Mexican Americans and Rural Community Development

In this reading, Ernesto Galarza describes the difficulties Mexican Americans find in coping with the giant economic forces in U.S. agriculture. In the opinion of Galarza and many others both inside and outside the Mexican-American community, government agencies and programs favor the employer and offer almost no protection to the workers.

Of all the problems Mexican Americans face in dealing with farm owners, one practice of employers singularly stands out for its viciousness and is described by the author as a "black market in human toil." Instead of hiring Mexican Americans who are American citizens or who have legally entered the U.S., the farm owners often hire Mexicans who they know have entered illegally. With fear of exposure and deportation hanging over them, these Mexicans will work for much lower wages.

Galarza believes that present policies of government make it almost impossible for workers to protect their interests. He believes that the solution lies both in government policies on behalf of the workers and strong Mexican-American community organizations which can help the workers shape their own destinies.

Rural Community Development

The industrialization of agriculture, as of manufacturing, has been the end-product of a massive, complex and interacting change in a multiple of scientific, social and economic relationships. I have time to underscore only those factors which have directly produced the present condition of the rural working class of Mexican Americans.

Briefly they are as follows:

1. The employment of Mexican citizens who have entered this country illegally has become a regular feature of the agricultural labor market. This illegal supply of labor rests on the willingness of corporate farms to hire, of intermediaries to transport, of Congress to tolerate and of the Depart-

ment of Justice to accommodate to this vicious black market in human toil.

2. The contracting and hiring of Mexican citizens as *braceros* became an elaborate process of collective bargaining between three parties—the United States Government, the Government of Mexico and the associated corporate farmers of the Southwest. The other parties to the arrangement—the Mexican braceros themselves and the domestic Mexican-American laborers—have been missing—excluded—from the bargaining process.

3. The crossing or commuter system has become a growing and decisive element in the border economy. Its effects can now be felt hundreds of miles north of the border.

4. Mechanization has made great strides in agriculture. The experts of the Department of Labor can tell you that in some areas mechanical cotton pickers are now harvesting 90 percent of the crop. Machines have displaced the stoop labor of the tomato fields. With shakers and air cushions two men can do in one minute what a crew used to do in one hour in the harvesting of nuts. Machines are picking grapes. Electric, not human, eyes are sorting lemons.

5. The research that has made possible the chemical, physical, and genetic progress that underlies mechanization is subsidized research. The University of California campus at Davis has been for decades the publicly-supported Academy of Science of agri-business.

6. A second form of subsidy has been the public financing of the farm placement services. I have special knowledge of the farm placement service of California. During the past quarter century this service has at no time been what by law it is supposed to be—an agency to pursue and guarantee the job security of domestic farm workers. It has, and continues to be, an extension into bureaucracy of the power and influence of agri-business.

7. A third form of subsidy is, and has been, a powerful element in the conformation of agri-business. I refer to the gigantic irrigation projects by which corporate farming takes water at bar-

gain rates capitalizing this unearned dividend into rapidly rising land values that place it out of the reach of the small grower. The corporate farms can tap this no-cost benediction by laying a siphon into the nearest concrete ditch or sinking a $75,000 well. Their promised land is not over Jordan; it is just over the Central Valley Canal. Verily, the Federal government has laid a water-table for them in the presence of their critics.

8. Housing for farm laborers and their families has reached a point of absolute scarcity in some areas. For twenty years the barracks of the *bracero* made possible the elimination of the on-farm shanties, as they made possible the craven retreat of the Federal government after World War II from its wartime farm labor camp development.

9. The combined effect of the foregoing factors has destroyed or held in check the organization of Mexican Americans into unions. I pass it on to you, Mr. Chairman, as the declaration of a high official of farm placement—the policy has been to deal with associated agri-businessmen collectively and to deal with farm laborers individually.

10. The semi-urban farm labor pools have shrunk and their former residents have migrated in increasing numbers to the cities. You will find more Mexican-American ex-farm workers in the central city, poverty barrios of San Antonio, Phoenix, Los Angeles and San Jose than you will find in the fields. I will leave these neo-migrants there, for I am sure that other witnesses will bring to your attention how urban redevelopment is demolishing even these temporary reservations of the Mexican poor.

The brilliance of the technical performance of government and agri-business I am not questioning. I am only giving it as my opinion that the historical cycle of the last quarter century is more of the same thing. What was accomplished between 1850 and 1880 by the United States cavalry, legal chicanery, tax frauds and treaty violations is being carried forward by vertical integration, subsidies, mechanization, and rural renewal.

I therefore want to resurrect a recommendation

I made twenty years ago—the creation by agreement between Mexico and the United States of a Joint international border development authority to bring the border areas of both countries into balance by raising, at their point of contact, Mexican levels of income to American standards, not, as is happening now, by lowering American to present Mexican levels. By presidential or congressional directive, the funding of this authority should be made the keystone of United States financial commitment to Mexico. On this authority I recommend there be appropriate representation, through their own economic agencies, of the persons of Mexican ancestry, on both sides of the border, whose jobs and lives are affected.

The Cantaloupe Strike in Imperial County in 1928

Mexican Americans increasingly became the foundation of agriculture in the Southwest after 1910 when thousands crossed the border. Many products used nationwide and abroad have been grown in the Southwest where Mexican Americans were the main labor source. In view of the economic importance of agriculture, powerful financial and political forces have tried to control the supply of agricultural labor, its wages, and working conditions.

Mexican Americans have always struggled for justice in American society, although this record has been largely ignored. The following reading by Charles Wollenberg, published in the *Pacific Historical Review* in 1969 on the strike of workers in the cantaloupe fields in 1928, serves to illustrate how Mexican Americans have tried to protect their rights and advance their interests against great obstacles. Wherever Mexican Americans have followed the crops—in California, Arizona, New Mexico, Texas, Colorado, Illinois, and Michigan—they have been a great asset to America. As a minority group working in agriculture, they have not always been fairly treated.

An Early Farm Workers Strike

By 1928, then, Mexican workers had become an integral part of the Imperial Valley's economic and social system. They provided the growers with a source of cheap labor, and organizations representing growers acted energetically to protect this labor source. . . .

While Imperial County growers were exerting pressure to protect their labor force, the county's Mexican workers were organizing a union. The original idea of the union seems to have come from Carlos Ariza, Mexican vice consul at Calexico. In his official position, Ariza received many complaints from workers about defaulting contractors and poor working conditions. In early 1928 he decided that a union might protect the workers' interests, and discussed his idea with members of the valley's Mexican community. In the middle of April, these discussions led to the formation of the Union of United Workers of the Imperial Valley. On April 22 Ariza, now a private attorney, filed incorporation papers for the new organization. Offices were established in Brawley and El Centro, dues were set at one dollar per month, and an executive committee was chosen. By the time of the strike, the union claimed a membership of 2,754 persons, all of Mexican descent.

It appears that Vice Consul Ariza was the only "outside agitator" who played a role in the organization of the Union of United Workers. The union's leadership seems to have come from two *mutualistas,* or mutual aid societies that had long existed in the Imperial Valley. The Sociedad Mutualista Benito Juárez of El Centro (established 1919) and the *Sociedad Mutualista Hidalgo* of Brawley (established 1921) had memberships composed largely of Mexican agricultural workers. The two *mutualistas* provided small payments to their members in case of illness, injury, or unemployment. In return, members paid dues of two dollars per month. The two organizations were also the centers of the valley's Mexican social life, sponsoring dances and patriotic celebrations on

Mexican holidays. The mutualistas served as natural cores around which the Mexican labor union formed.

The Union of United Workers took its first important action on May 3, 1928, when the organization's executive committee sent letters containing specific requests for improvements in wages and working conditions to the valley's growers and to the Chambers of Commerce of Brawley and El Centro. . . .

The union's letters were either rejected or ignored. Dr. Louis Bloch, statistician for the state Bureau of Industrial Relations, found that most growers had little objection to the fifteen-cent wage, but considered most of the other requests to be "exorbitant." Bloch also found that growers were determined not to recognize or negotiate with a labor union. The Brawley *News* reported that growers felt that granting the union's "reasonable requests" simply would open the door for "unreasonable demands." "With a union there is no limit."

It does not seem that the union leadership intended to call a strike if its requests were not met. The letters to the growers were polite and did not contain any threats of work-stoppage. On May 8, the day after the initial incidents occurred at the Sears Brothers Ranch, the Brawley *News* published a letter signed by Union President Ramón Mireles which denied that the union was urging workers to stay out of the fields. Mireles claimed that his organization wished "to work in conformity with the laws" and "would gladly see agitators that try to commit unlawful acts punished." But at the same time that this conciliatory statement was being published in English-language papers, a leaflet in Spanish was being distributed which contained a different message. This document boasted of the union's strength and belittled growers' threats that strike-breakers would be brought in from outside of the valley. Thus the union disassociated itself from the strike in English, while buttressing the spirits of the strikers in Spanish. . . .

The Spanish-language leaflet bolstered striker morale, but did not specifically call upon workers to remain off the job. There is no evidence that the union issued any more published statements after May 8. On May 10, Imperial County Sheriff Charles L. Gillett closed the organization's offices and banned further meetings for the duration of the emergency. On the fifteenth, the union changed its name to the Mexican Mutual Aid Society of the Imperial Valley, perhaps in an effort to improve the organization's "image" and disassociate it from what by then was a clearly unsuccessful strike. . . .

On Tuesday, May 8, the County Board of Supervisors ordered Sheriff Gillett to "arrest agitators." Gillett also was given authority to add forty deputies to his staff, which he did, in part, by swearing in field bosses from some of the largest ranches. The sheriff also told Mexican workers in the Imperial Valley that, if they were not satisfied with conditions in the United States, they could go back to Mexico. Both Gillett and Heald [the district attorney] warned that troublemakers would be referred to the United States Immigration Service for possible deportation.

Sheriff Gillett believed that "Mexicans are excitable and if idle will gather into groups to their own detriment as well as hindering work in the fields." Given these premises, the sheriff's tactics were obvious: he would see to it that Mexicans in the Imperial Valley neither "remained idle" nor "gathered into groups." On Tuesday, May 8, Gillett arrested about thirty Mexicans for "loitering about the streets of El Centro." Learning that the union was planning a membership meeting in Brawley that evening, he announced that he would be "chairman of that meeting." One half hour after the sheriff arrived at the gathering, "there were few Mexicans left in the vicinity." On May 13, a Mexican newspaper distributor in Brawley was arrested for allegedly writing on his billboard, "Forty-eight Mexicans in jail—What for?—Nothing."

. . . By May 11, at least fifty persons of Mexican descent had been arrested. The offices of the Union of United Workers had been closed for the duration of the emergency, and so were five pool halls frequented by a Mexican clientele. All "congregations of foreigners" in the Imperial Valley were prohibited. The sheriff claimed to have a "secret service" operating in the valley's Mexican neighborhoods in order to identify agitators and troublemakers. Louis Bloch concluded that "the Sheriff's decisiveness in rounding up and incarcerating actual and potential disturbers of the peace undoubtedly had the effect of stopping a movement which might have resulted in an effective general strike and in heavy losses to the growers." . . .

By the beginning of 1929, an informed observer such as Dr. Bloch could be cautiously optimistic about the future of Mexican farm workers in the Imperial Valley. The state government had taken action to alleviate some of the workers' difficulties. Federal restriction of Mexican immigration certainly would have improved the bargaining position of the valley's resident Mexicans. And workers had shown a willingness to form labor unions and strike for better wages and working conditions.

But Bloch could not foresee the events which, for the next thirty-seven years, would weaken the ability of Mexican field workers to improve their economic and social positions in California. The depression of the 1930's created a disastrous drop in wage rates and caused the introduction of hundreds of thousands of Anglo workers into the field-labor market. Violent strikes organized by outside radical groups occurred in the valley during the thirties but were not successful. World War II helped create the bracero program, which gave California growers a government guarantee of cheap migrant labor from Mexico. Not until Congress ended the importation of braceros in 1965 did anything approximating the agricultural labor situation of the 1920's return to rural California. Perhaps, then, it is no accident that in September of 1965 Mexican workers in Delano again walked out of California fields. . . .

Braceros: *Hands Across the Border*

This selection helps the non-Mexican American see the question of contract labor from a perspective that cannot be charged with bias. As time passes and the economics of the U.S. and Mexico become more integrated, contract labor could return, or free labor flow could come about across the border. In some respects, contract labor could be a stepping stone to an American common market.

Mexican braceros have played an important role in the economy of the United States because of their service to agriculture. They have also affected life in Mexico during at least two decades (1940–1960). Braceros manifest the interdependence of the U.S. and Mexico. The word *bracero* refers to one who works with his hands (*brazos*—arms).

This selection by N. Ray and Gladys Gilmore originally appeared in the *Pacific Historical Review*. It offers a sketch of the bracero program and some of the basic economic and political forces that gave rise to it. The effects of the vast traffic in low cost labor are difficult to evaluate. One's interest can affect one's judgment. In any case, the selection helps us understand the basic forces that affect our life.

The Coming of the Braceros

When Charles E. Warren told the Commonwealth Club of California in May, 1918, "We all know we need labor. . . . What we need is forty thousand to fifty thousand good young Chinamen," he was challenging two generations of anti-Orientalism. It was a challenge born of wartime needs and one which had already resulted in the development of an informal bracero program in which the Mexican national replaced the traditional Chinese coolie. The apparently bottomless reservoir of agricultural labor south of the border seemed a fortuitous circumstance that it would be folly to ignore. In consequence, the coming of the bracero (defined here as a temporary agricultural laborer from Mexico, usually unskilled or semi-skilled) has become for many growers an annual miracle now regarded as a necessity.

California farmers have never constituted a homogeneous group because of a great range in farm size and variety of crops, each crop with its often highly specialized requirements. The state is large; the growing season is long, ranging from 240 to 365 days; the geography varies from below-sea-level deserts to rain forests; over 200 crops are produced—more than any other state. All this has created a complex and unique agricultural picture.

[A] significant trend has been shifting crop patterns: a tremendous expansion in field crops since 1930, with cotton now the state's leading crop and sugar beets, hay, barley, fruits, melons, and vegetables showing varying increases. Citrus, on the other hand, registered serious declines. The growing substitution of capital for labor has been marked in crops like cotton which employ mechanical harvesting equipment but still depend upon hand labor for cultivating and thinning. Irrigation has increased enormously in the last two decades.

The peaking and overlapping of various crop demands has led to a dependence upon a variety of labor sources. Only 35 percent of the state's farm labor is family labor which means that almost two-thirds must be supplied by other means. Most of the permanent as well as the casual laborers are local workers who do agricultural labor near home for at least a part of the year. Migratory labor, largely intrastate, generally constitutes the remainder of the temporary force although there has been a tendency since the early fifties for this group to settle down and become part of the local feeder supply. As a result, out-of-state labor is once again being recruited by farm labor organizations. Another source of casual farm labor is the "day-haul": recruiting the inhabitants of skid row through the local Farm Labor Service or directly by touring the other side of the tracks in cars or

busses. In addition, wetbacks, before the drive against them became effective in 1954, were always present in significant, though necessarily unknown, numbers in California's fields. Growers have long tapped all of these labor sources through labor contractors. Finally, California has historically relied upon foreign labor, usually contract labor, as a supplement or a replacement for domestic farm workers.

The passage of a law in 1885 making it illegal to import contract labor placed Californians who needed labor in a difficult position. . . .

Before World War I railroads imported Mexicans for temporary maintenance work. They allowed farmers to borrow from their labor camps in order to stimulate the production of crops which would find shipment by rail. In 1917, the Literacy Test Act . . . contained more carefully defined contract labor proscriptions which might have eliminated Mexico as a source of labor supply had it not been for provisions exempting temporary agricultural and skilled labor. . . . It was probably the pressure of sugar beet growers, supported by the railroads, which led to the exemptions and the order of the secretary.

These steps produced an informal bracero program. The growers signed agreements with the United States government specifying the conditions of import and return. Employers made arrangements for the transportation, housing, and feeding of the Mexicans, all such costs being deducted from the bracero's wages.

Out-of-state migrants fed the farm labor force during the depression, and for several years after the outbreak of World War II in 1939, they met most of the needs when farm workers took jobs in industry.

By 1942 sugar beet growers once again began to demand an end to the growing agricultural labor shortage, this time supported by the small farmer, the Grange, and the liberals, whose spokesman, Senator Sheridan Downey, asked for the importation of 100,000 braceros. The federal government responded with a program arranged through informal executive agreements with Mexico. . . .

Finally, in 1951, came both P.L. 78, an act to amend the Agricultural Act of 1949, and P.L. 319, containing the text of the Migrant Labor Agreement between Mexico and the United States. The former outlined the bracero program while the latter spelled out detailed arrangements and contained the standard work contract. Although the two acts have been amended, they remained the basis of the current bracero program, the most carefully worked out agreement for the importation of contract workers ever engaged in by the United States.

By far the most controversial section of the act is Section 503 which requires the Secretary of Labor to certify: that 1) "domestic workers who are able, willing, and qualified" are not available "at the time and place needed to perform the work" for which braceros are being contracted; that 2) the employment of braceros "will not *adversely affect* the wages and working conditions of domestic agricultural workers similarly employed," and that 3) "*reasonable* efforts have been made to attract domestic workers . . . at wages and standard hours of work comparable to those offered to foreign workers" [emphasis ours]. What constitutes adverse effect and how this is to be measured, what is a reasonable effort, whether the requisite kind of domestic workers is available, and whether the wages and hours offered to the foreign workers should be used as the yardstick in trying to attract domestic workers—have been the subject of continuing arguments between the supporters of the program and its opponents.

The long list of specific conditions under which this labor contracting system operates is carefully detailed in the Migrant Labor Agreement. Essentially the worker pays for his food (not to exceed $1.75 a day), medical insurance, Mexican Social Security payments, and any purchases. The employer is responsible for transportation to and from reception centers and the daily job, contracting fees, tools and equipment, housing (according to prescribed standards), occupational risk insurance, wages, adequate food at the specified cost to the worker, and almost all of the paperwork.

In practice the system works something like this: About ten days before he expects to need labor, the prospective employer files an order for workers at the local Farm Placement Office. He probably has already reviewed his labor requirements with these same local officials. His request is sent through area offices to the state department of employment which has received preseason labor need estimates from all of its farm placement branches. These estimates are revised weekly and monthly and sent on to the Bureau of Employment Security (BES) of the USES in the Department of Labor where the secretary himself must finally certify the labor need. At any stage the request may be revised or disallowed. The Secretary of Labor notifies the Mexican government of expected recruitment needs and Mexican officials round up the braceros into camps, screen them, and send them on to reception centers across the border where prospective employers (usually representatives of growers' associations) pick them up. The grower is in charge of them from then until the end of the contract period.

The State Senate's Fact-Finding Committee on Labor and Welfare concluded that, although California growers pay very nearly the highest farm wages in the nation, domestic workers generally get lower wages in those areas and crops where bracero labor dominates. Certainly the impossibility of a labor shortage prevents the agricultural labor organizer from operating from a bargaining position.

That the operation of the program tends to depress wages, destroy the domestic worker's bargaining power, and drive away local labor, that the domestic agricultural worker has no safeguards and benefits comparable to the bracero—all these criticisms have been repeatedly made by public officials and private individuals and organizations. . . .

Who then benefits from the program? Clearly someone benefits or thinks he benefits. Over the years it was the growers who procured Mexican labor. Their recorded testimony at innumerable hearings overwhelmingly opposed restrictions which might affect their labor supply. They demanded and secured the wartime bracero program. In the late forties the inadequacies of the informal arrangements necessitated either an end to the program or more specific legislation and more carefully circumscribed international agreements. The growers were willing and able to fight to secure these in 1951 and to continue them down to the present despite difficulties and opposition.

The farmer who uses braceros argues that he must have a guaranteed supply of labor when he needs it. Domestic labor varies in skills and dependability, whereas the bracero, although frequently unskilled, is willing to learn. He is dependable and he is there. "Foreign labor is more expensive and ten times the trouble . . . but more efficient and dependable." The State Senate Fact-Finding Committee summed it up this way: "The chief advantage found in the employment of the Mexican National . . . is not his particular skills or the amount of work he can or will do. The main appeal of the bracero is his dependability—the fact that he is there when he is needed and can be counted upon."

Without any question, there is some economic benefit to Mexico which received an estimated $83,000,000 in wages in 1959, about 17 percent of the total wage bill paid by the United States farmer. Bracero earnings were the fourth largest source of dollar income in the State of Chihuahua in 1956. . . .

The individual worker makes money or he would not return. The disadvantages to Mexico need to be studied in great detail: draining off good workers, creating artificial labor shortages, the sociological problems connected with breaking up homes for a part of the year, and many other serious problems which are not immediately apparent.

In this country the bracero program has had the powerful support of the Farm Bureau Federation and numerous farm labor recruitment organizations, and the somewhat mild support of the Grange. Opposition has come from the unions, the AWOC of the AFL-CIO and the National Farmers Union particularly, and a variety of civic groups such as the Social Action Department of the National Catholic Welfare Conference, the National Consumers League, the National Advisory Committee on Farm Labor, and the National Council of Churches of Christ in America.

The future of the bracero program is in question. The number of braceros recruited has [decreased] since 1957 for a variety of reasons: stricter assessment of the need for foreign labor, more rigorous enforcement, stricter regulations, improved recruitment and use of the domestic labor supply, higher wages and better working conditions to attract domestic workers, and mechanization of agricultural tasks. The last three seem to be the major elements of any future agricultural planning designed to dispense with the bracero program. . . . The unionization of agricultural workers is under way, however chaotically. . . . [Some] suggest the use of student labor in the fields. Growers are resorting to "green card" holders—that is, permanent immigrants certified by prospective employers and admissible under special provisions of the McCarran Walter Immigration Act of 1952.

The consensus is that the days of the bracero program are numbered and the real question is simply the date. While many growers are preparing for this event, almost all government sources as well as growers insist that the program was, and still is, essential [until an adequate substitute can be found].

Wetbacks and Braceros

During the Second World War, the U.S. needed more manpower than it had. Mexico and the United States, as allies, decided to meet this need by a treaty which sent Mexican workers (braceros) to labor in the United States as farm workers. However, after the war, the bracero program continued and grew. All the while, thousands of Mexicans entered the United States illegally. Wetbacks, as they were called, caused great problems for both braceros and Mexican Americans, for wetbacks were willing to work for lower wages.

Ernesto Galarza, the author of this selection from *Merchants of Labor,* is an authority on the subject of Mexican labor in the U.S. The selection concentrates upon wetbacks. This insight will help shed light on all Mexican-American life in the United States, for in the eyes of the Anglo Americans, wetbacks, braceros, and Mexican Americans often look alike.

In some respects, the use of illegal Mexican labor displays shortcomings in the societies of each country. The practice may not be admirable to some, but it does represent some harsh realities we must deal with.

Mexican Government Protects Interests of Braceros

Between 1943 and 1947 the Mexican farm labor program was maintained by a series of informal amendments which reflected mainly the changes requested by the Mexican Government to safeguard the interests of the braceros. In 1944 President Avila Camacho expressed his satisfaction with the results of the program which, in his view, assured the workers under contract full protection of their rights and interests. Ezequiel Padilla, the Mexican Foreign Secretary, praised the agreements warmly. "They provide," he said, "an opportunity to earn high wages, a noble adventure for our youth and above all, proof of our cooperation in the victory of our cause."

Victory having been won, the Department of State notified Mexico on November 15, 1946, of its desire to end the current agreement. Mexican war workers were no longer thought necessary and termination was proposed within 90 days. Notwithstanding the views of the Department, some employers continued to plead an acute need for braceros and it was on their behalf that recruitment was extended through 1949. . . .

The smooth course of the noble adventure was severely disturbed while the 1948 agreement was in effect. In October of that year the border was shaken by a controversy between the two governments which for a time threatened to leave scars on the Good Neighbor policy, of which the migrant labor agreements were an outstanding exhibit.

The agreement of February 21, 1948, had replaced that of March 10, 1947, and was in effect when recruiting was proceeding for the fall harvest of cotton in Texas. The Texas growers, as was their custom, had met and determined that the prevailing wage for the first picking was to be $2.50 per hundred pounds. Mr. Don Larin, acting for the U.S. Department of Labor, accepted that figure as the effective wage, since at that time the Department was making no surveys of its own to determine prevailing wages.

Unexpectedly, the Mexican representatives insisted that the wage rate be fixed at $3.00. The Texas growers, whose right to set the prevailing wage had never been challenged even by their own government, were outraged. Mr. Larin gave point and direction to their resentment. He appeared in El Paso to cooperate with the Immigration and Naturalization Service in opening the border to thousands of waiting Mexicans, destitute men eager to pick cotton at any wage.

Word was passed to the milling *braceros* within sight of the Rio Grande that picking was available —at $2.50. This information was embellished as it moved through the twists and loops of the grapevine telegraph with hints that all applicants should hurry because it was understood that the Mexican Government intended to close the border. The braceros began to move up the line. They waded the shallow river in sight of the Border Patrol, which received them with formality, herded them into temporary enclosures and immediately paroled them to the cotton growers, who trucked the men at once to the fields.

Between October 13 and October 18 some 6,000 Mexicans entered the United States in a massive break. They glutted the Texas labor market and, according to press reports, wages dropped to $1.50.

The flagrant violation of the agreement with which Mexico charged the United States could have led to the suspension of contracting altogether. Some 25,000 braceros who were legally in the United States at the time of the border incident could have been recalled without any means for replacing them. The Mexican Government received expressions of regret from Washington along with an admission that the entry of those Mexican Nationals was indeed illegal and "the painful incident was considered closed." . . .

A passing phase of the national migrant labor program was the assignment of braceros to railway construction and maintenance during the war years.

Late in 1941 the Southern Pacific Company filed a request for braceros which was turned down by the War Manpower Commission. The request was made again in the spring of 1942 by a number of carriers who contended that they could not meet manpower shortages by drawing on the national labor market. After consultation with the railway Brotherhoods the War Manpower Commission gave its approval and delegated authority to the Railroad Retirement Board to supervise the non-agricultural phase of the Mexican program.

Understandings between the two governments, the companies and the Brotherhood of Maintenance of Way Employees were reached in April and by June 15, 1943, there were 6,000 Mexicans at work on the Southern Pacific, Sante Fe and Western Pacific lines. The ceiling fixed in April for contracting was raised by stages during the latter part of 1943 and new petitions for contract labor were granted. By April 1944 approximately 40,000 Mexicans were working on twenty-four railroads. The total number of men contracted during the year for track maintenance was above 80,000. . . .

In the West, meanwhile, the system was growing in favor with commercial farmers. In California the braceros were received with eagerness and often with jollity. Festivities were organized for them in Imperial County, Yolo and Butte with welcoming bands, parades, dining and speeches. Mexican national holidays were appropriately observed with free barbecues at the expense of growers and townsmen.

This good will was stimulated by the close resemblance that employers had begun to discover between their ideal of a farm laborer and the bracero. A special committee made this recommendation to the governor of California in 1947: "Mexican workers . . . should constitute a flexible group which can be readily moved from operation to operation and from place to place where local help falls short of the numbers needed to save the crops. These workers should be in a sense 'shock troops' used only in real emergency as insurance against loss of valuable production." Since by definition a real emergency exists perpetually in California's harvests the advantages of a bracero labor pool were plain. Flexibility and transferability added up to the best kind of crop insurance. The bracero was, in another respect, the answer to commercial farming's prayers. As Mr. G.W. Guiberson, representing the Agricultural Labor Bureau of San Joaquin, phrased it: "We are asking for labor only at certain times of the year—at the peak of our harvest—and the class of labor we want is the kind we can send home when we get through with them." The braceros had eminently proved to be the kind of workers who could be sent home when they were got through with. . . .

The illegals gravitated toward those types of employers who hired most of the labor, that is to say the corporations and the large individual operators. In 1948 the Border Patrol raided the DiGiorgio Farms at Arvin near Bakersfield, on one occasion pulling 29 illegals from the ranch. Two raids in 1949 resulted in the apprehension of 315 wetbacks at DiGiorgio, where they mingled freely with contracted braceros. These raids were euphemistically described as "surveys" by a ranch official, Mr. Webdell. No one seemed to be astonished over the situation. A congressional committee which investigated conditions on the model corporation farm in November 1949 was told that "Illegal aliens, have from time to time been found on DiGiorgio Farms, just as they have been found on almost every farm in Texas, New Mexico, Arizona, and southern California." DiGiorgio was in a numerous and reputable company.

Although corporation farms provided most of the cash custom for illegals, none used such labor exclusively nor was it by any means monopolized by them. Mr. Keith Mets, president of the Imperial Valley Farmers Association, himself only a middling commercial farmer and an experienced user of contraband labor, was not exaggerating when he said in 1951: "Every farmer from Brownsville to San Diego uses these people."

Cesar Chavez: Plight of Farm Workers Breeds a Great Leader

In recent years, Cesar Chavez has become internationally known as a leader of Mexican-American farm workers. In his fight to improve the working and living conditions of workers, he has emerged as one of the most controversial figures of our times. To many of his opponents, he is a devil, but many people throughout the world consider him practically a saint.

Chavez is the son of Mexican-American farm workers. He started working in the fields of the Southwest when he was very young, and he has shared back-breaking toil, economic deprivation, and other hardships with hundreds of thousands of his countrymen of Mexican ancestry. Rather than submit to bitterness, indifference, and defeat, he chose to try to change what he did not like. Around the world, Chavez has a reputation as a skillful organizer. The issues he deals with are products of American society, and so, too, are the many methods which he uses on behalf of farm workers.

The following selection from *Delano: The Story of the California Grape Strike* by John Gregory

Dunne will help the reader understand how Chavez's early background underlies the course he chose to lead in life.

Delano: A Cross-Section of Much of the American Southwest

Cesar Estrada Chavez was a barrio baby. He was born in Yuma, Arizona, into a family of five children whose father scratched out a precarious existence on a small farm near the Colorado River. His father went broke when Cesar was ten years old, and the family began trailing the crops from Arizona to California and back. Home was a succession of labor camps or the back of a ramshackle automobile. The time was the Depression and there were more workers than there was work. Labor contractors papered the Dust Bowl with the promise of employment, and regiments of Okies swept into California like tumbleweed, only to discover that they were too many and too late. School was something to be fitted in whenever the opportunity presented itself. To this day, Chavez cannot remember how many schools he went to; the number escalates from thirty-one to sixty-seven, although this last is probably the total number he and his brothers and sisters together attended. It was an education that was to leave a lasting mark.

"Those early days when we first came to California were rough," Chavez recalled in a series of interviews for the Farm Worker Press, a subsidiary of the NFWA set up to publicize the plight of the *campesinos* (farm workers). "We were really green, and whenever a labor contractor told us something, we fell for it hook, line, and sinker. We didn't know the ropes yet and got hooked every time. I remember the first year we ended up in the fall picking wine grapes for a contractor near Fresno. They were bad grapes, there were very few bunches on the vines, and we were the only family working in the field. But we were too green to wonder why we were the only ones, you see. After the first week of work, my father asked the contractor for his pay. 'I can't pay you because I haven't been paid by the winery,' the contractor told my father. But we were broke, absolutely broke, with nothing at all to eat, so the contractor finally gave us twenty dollars and said we'd get a big check later when the winery paid him. We worked for seven weeks like that, and each payday the contractor said he couldn't pay us because the winery hadn't paid him yet. At the end of the seventh week, we went to the contractor's house and it was empty. He owed us for seven weeks' pay and we haven't seen him to this day.

"We were desperate. We ran into another labor contractor in Fresno. 'There's lots of money in the cotton near Mendota,' he told us. It was late November by now and it was cold and raining almost every day. Because of the rain, there was almost no work at all. Well, we finally learned the ropes. We learned where the crops were and when they needed workers and we learned little tricks like living under bridges and things like that. Once we learned the ropes, we began helping other green families like we had been, so they wouldn't have it as rough as we did. About 1939, we were living in San Jose. One of the old CIO unions began organizing workers in the dried-fruit industry, so my father and uncle became members. Sometimes the men would meet at our house and I remember seeing their picket signs and hearing them talk. They had a strike and my father and Uncle picketed at night. It made a deep impression on me. But of course they lost the strike, and that was the end of the union. But from that time on, my father joined every new agricultural union that came along— often he was the first one to join—and when I was nineteen, I joined the National Agricultural Workers Union, but it didn't have any more success than any of the other farm workers' unions."

In time, Chavez left home and began to follow the crops on his own. One of his stops was in Delano, where he met and married his wife, Helen. It was at this time that he had his first brush with the Delano establishment. He and Helen were sitting in a movie one night when an usherette asked them to move. Chavez refused and the usherette called the manager, who in turn called the police. Under duress, Chavez was taken from his seat and escorted to the police station, where he was charged with violating the theater's seating policy—Mexicans on one side of the aisle, Anglos on the other.

Chavez's odyssey finally took him back to San Jose, where he went to work in the apricot orchards. At this juncture, in 1952, fate stepped into his life in the person of Fred Ross of the Community Service Organization. Of all the people who have attached themselves to Chavez, Ross is by far the most impressive. I talked to him about his early days with Chavez one afternoon in the coffee shop of the Stardust Motel. "Cesar was living in an area called Sal Si Puedes, which means 'Get Out If You Can,' " Ross said. "It was a tough slum with a high proportion of San Quentin alumni. I was trying to organize CSO chapters, and Helen Chavez's name had been given to me by a Mexican-American public-health nurse. Cesar wasn't at home the first several times I called, but on the fourth time he had about thirty people in the house and I could see that they were going to give this gringo a hard time. I could almost hear them thinking, 'What's he know about our problems?' At first they were very hostile when I started to tell them about the CSO. But then they began recognizing certain names and certain incidents like 'Bloody Christmas.' " (This was an incident in which seven Mexicans were beaten up one Christmas Eve by drunken police officers at the Lincoln Heights police station in Los Angeles. The CSO took on their case and after a continual protest got the police department to investigate. As a result, six police officers were sent to jail for from one to ten years.)

"Well, they'd all heard about 'Bloody Christmas,' " Ross continued, "and that got them interested. Now, instead of refusing my cigarettes when I passed them around, they began to accept them. No one there was more enthusiastic than Cesar. I was keeping a diary in those days, and that night when I got home I wrote in it, 'I think I've found the guy I'm looking for.' You could tell it even then."

Chavez became chairman of the CSO's voter-registration drive and in a period of two months he registered over 4,000 people. "It was the first time there had ever been a voter-registration drive among the Mexican-Americans," Ross said, "and the local Republicans were plenty worked up. They announced they were going to have challengers at the voting places because the CSO was registering braceros and dead people. So we had our own challengers at the polls to challenge the Anglos. Pretty soon the literacy-test line was longer than the voting line."

After the election, Chavez was laid off his job, but he got hold of an office and went to work helping Mexicans obtain their citizenship. It was the first time such an organized program had been set up, and in the next eight years it helped some 30,000 Mexicans get their papers. At the beginning, Chavez was out of a job, living on unemployment, but Ross finally got Saul Alinsky to hire him as a paid staffer for the CSO at a salary of $325 a month. "It was pretty tough for me at first," Chavez recalled in another interview, taped for *Ramparts Magazine*. "I was changing and I had to take a lot of ridicule from the kids my age, the rough characters I worked with in the fields. They would say, 'Hey, big shot, now that you're a politico, why are you working here for sixty-five cents an hour?' "

Chavez ranged over the Valley, setting up new chapters in Madera, Bakersfield, and Hanford. "That was during the McCarthy era and there was a great deal of opposition," Ross told me. "In every town, people were calling us Reds and pointing the finger at Alinsky, who they were convinced was a Communist." To gain new members more rapidly, Chavez set up a service program to deal with the most basic bread-and-butter problems. He got Mexicans out of jail, inquired about their welfare payments, helped them get driver's licenses, settled their immigration status with the proper authorities. "One of his big things was trying to get people who were in trouble with the law not to plead guilty because they had no money to hire an attorney," Ross said. "He scrounged around and got them lawyers, and when they were acquitted, a lot of them were tied up to him for good in gratitude."

During this period, Chavez's ideas were beginning to jell. "I learned to keep away from the established and so-called leaders, and to guard against philosophizing," he says. "Working with low-income people is a lot different from working with professionals, who like to sit around talking about how to play politics. When you're trying to recruit a farm worker, you have to paint a little picture, and then you have to color the picture in. We found out that the harder a guy is to convince, the better leader or member he becomes. When you exert yourself to convince him, you have his confidence and he has good motivation. A lot of them who say okay right away wind up hanging around the office, taking up the worker's time.

"And I learned quickly that there is no real appreciation. Whatever you do, and no matter what reasons you may give to others, you do it because you want to see it done, or maybe because you want power. And there shouldn't be any appreciation, understandably. I know good organizers who were destroyed, washed out, because they expected people to appreciate what they'd done. Anyone who comes in with the idea that farm workers are free of sin and that the growers are all ———— either has never dealt with the situation or is an idealist of the first order. Things don't work that way."

La Huelga

By 1971, many California grape growers had signed labor contracts with the United Farm Workers of America (UFWA). Soon after, Chavez moved to obtain labor contracts with growers of lettuce in the Salinas Valley of California and strawberry growers in other places. Clearly, the issue over grapes serves to illustrate other similar issues between farm workers and their employers.

The strike of grape pickers started in 1965 when certain employers refused to bargain over wages with the union representing the grape workers. Many have condemned the strike and subsequent consumer boycott for different reasons. This selection is essentially the views of a major grower who employs thousands of migrant workers every year. At various times, other opponents have claimed the strike was illegal and immoral, and they began to use a variety of tactics to break it, including the use of local law enforcement officers and harassment of the striking workers.

The issues raised in the strike spotlight what many consider a grave injustice that stemmed from the Federal Labor Relations Act of 1935. Through that act, most industrial workers gained the right to conduct secret elections to select a union to represent them. Farm workers, however, were excluded. The federal law, however, was only one of the obstacles that those who attempted to organize farm workers faced. Many farm workers are migrants who "follow the crops." They work in one area until harvest season is over, and then move to another area where other crops are ready for harvest. Understandably, it is difficult to organize people who are constantly on the move. Opposition of growers was, of course, another formidable obstacle to organizers. Most farm workers live a day-to-day existence, and the threat of being fired by their employers prevented many from getting actively involved in a union movement.

In his attempts to organize the workers in California vineyards, Chavez met a solid wall of resistance from growers, but he was encouraged by the support of other labor unions and of people all over the United States who refused to buy California grapes. In the end, his persistence paid off, and some growers voluntarily recognized the UFWA and negotiated contracts with their workers.

A Grower Explains His Opposition to the Grape Strike

I knew little about the care and cultivation of grapes when I arrived in Delano in the summer of 1966, save for the fact that table grapes presented a greater opportunity for union organizers than any other seasonal crops. Unlike lettuce or asparagus,

grapes require attention for some ten months a year. They must be sprayed, trimmed, and girdled. Each process takes a certain degree of skill. As a result the labor force is relatively stable. There are few migrants, except during the harvest, and since the residents can put in nearly a full year's work, their income levels are accordingly higher. As the richest of the poor, they are less apathetic than migrants whose overriding considerations are the next job, the next meal, and hence more susceptible to an organizing effort.

A day or so after I checked into the Stardust Motel, I drove down to the DiGiorgio Corporation's ranch in Arvin, some thirty miles south of Delano, to see how grapes are grown and how a huge corporation ranch is run. The Arvin ranch has 9,000 acres, slightly less than half planted in grapes, the rest in plums, potatoes, asparagus, cotton, peanuts, wheat, barley, and black-eyed beans. Unlike DiGiorgio's 4,400 acre Sierra Vista ranch in Delano, it was not then being struck. I was met by Joseph A. DiGiorgio, a vice president of the DiGiorgio Corporation and head of its farming operation. (Farming accounts for less than ten percent of DiGiorgio's annual sales of $230 million; the bulk of its income derives from food processing and grocery wholesaling.) Joseph DiGiorgio is a short, tanned, muscular man in late middle age, with the classic profile of a Renaissance people. He wore a straw planter's hat with a madras band, a neatly pressed blue buttoned-down sport shirt and work shoes so brightly polished that they would have done credit to a member of a military drill team. He suggested that the best way to see the ranch operate was to drive around with him for the rest of the day, and so I got into his car. There was a two-way radio in the car, and periodically through the morning and afternoon he would call back instructions to his office and receive reports from field foremen.

DiGiorgio explained that the grape season is progressive, proceeding from Coachella and Borrego over to the high desert in Arizona, then back to Arvin, up to Delano, and on up the Valley. In the best of years, the seasons do not overlap and there is no price break, but when they do, as they did in 1965, so many grapes hit the market at the same time that the price plummets. Thus, though 1965 was a vintage year in quality and quantity, many grape ranchers took a serious beating. We passed through vineyards of Cardinals, Thompsons, Ribiers, Red Malagas, Emperors, Amerias, Calmerias, and Muscats, and at each we stopped to sample the grapes. Some were quite tart and not yet ready for picking. I was told that it takes five years to bring a vine into full production and that the productive life of a quality vine ranges from twenty-five to thirty years. Then the vines are pulled out and the land reworked for several years with other crops, such as cotton or potatoes. Throughout the year, there is constant cultural work to be done. Girdling is one example. A strip, or girdle, of bark is cut out of the vine, disrupting its natural intake and outflow and thus forcing the moisture already in the vine up into the berries, swelling their size. Girdling is done strictly on a piece-work basis, the workers making two or three cents a vine.

We drove down a dirt lane and stopped by a picking stand. There was a sunshade over the stand, and a radio playing Mexican music. DiGiorgio showed me the tally sheet for one crew of field workers. The day before, the crew had picked 117 lugs of grapes, an average of 2.17 boxes an hour, giving the workers an hourly wage of $1.73. "It's hard work," he said. It was an understatement. The workers hunch under the vines like ducks. There is no air, making the intense heat all but unbearable. Gnats and bugs swarm out from under the leaves. Some workers wear face masks; others, handkerchiefs knotted around their heads to catch the sweat. I asked if there were not some way to automate the picking process. He shook his head and brought me under a vine to explain why. "If it were just a matter of picking, it might be feasible," he said. "You could do it for raisins or for wine grapes, but there are too many quality checks for table grapes." He clipped a bunch of grapes and handed it to me. "A picker has got to check color, the size of the berry, the size of the bunch, and trim

bad berries before a bunch can be packed," he went on. "How are you going to mechanize these functions?" He examined the bunch and threw it away. "That one would never pass muster."

On the way back to lunch, we passed a plum orchard where a bulldozer was neatly uprooting trees and laying them in symmetrical rows. The trees had been planted in 1947, I was told, but they were no longer economically productive because of poor root stock. I asked if I could see one of the labor camps before lunch. Arvin employs Mexicans, Filipinos, Puerto Ricans, Negroes, and Anglos, and, as they are at every large ranch, the workers are segregated by nationality. At the height of the harvest, the work force runs to a peak of between 1,200 and 1,400 men, dropping to between 400 and 500 during slack periods. "Our basic concept here is to have enough crop diversification so that we'll be harvesting ten months a year," DiGiorgio said. "That gives greater employment."

He chose to show me a Mexican camp. The mess hall reminded me of the army. In the kitchen, cooks were preparing a lunch of steak, corn, and tortillas. (A machine stamps out over three thousand tortillas a day in the Mexican camp.) "This is just a normal meal," he said. "Nothing special." Outside, I saw a cluster of older living quarters with pipe chimneys but I was steered into a newer building which still smelled of wet paint. The building was air-conditioned and accommodated forty-eight men. In the bathroom there were four toilets, six showers, and eight sinks. Four men live in a room. They sleep on cots and have their own wardrobes and shelves. Room and board costs $2.25 a day, which is deducted from their pay. There was nothing shabby about the building, but it was as cold and as impersonal as a barracks.

After lunch DiGiorgio showed me Arvin's family housing, which, depending on the size of the unit, rents for five dollars, seven-fifty, or ten dollars a month. There was a playground with a baseball field and a tennis court. "We fix up the tennis court every couple of years," he said, "but they never use it except to play basketball on." We then drove to the packing house. It is an enormous building, roughly the size of two football fields. Trailer trucks were backed up along the side of the shed. On the second floor, there were rooms where the truckers could sleep while their trailers were being loaded. We watched the packing from a balcony outside the shed office. The packers were women and most were the wives and daughters of field help. They packed each box of plums and grapes by size and quality of the fruit, picking it off a conveyor belt, examining it, and then placing it in the appropriate box. It seemed a tedious, exacting job.

Before I left Arvin, Joseph DiGiorgio drove me out to see what the land looked like when his uncle, the founder of the company, bought it nearly fifty years ago. We were at the edge of the ranch property line. There was nothing but sand, sagebrush, and cactus. With some pride, DiGiorgio told me he had helped level the land himself.

"Nobody stops to think of the farmer's problems," DiGiorgio said. "We have a tremendous capital investment in packing, boxmaking, storing mechanical equipment, in trucks and cooling systems.

"Rain can spoil an entire crop, and when a crop overlaps, as it did last year in grapes, the price breaks because of overproduction. Our profit margin is at the mercy of the elements. We've got to know when to plant, what to plant, when to irrigate, when to rotate, when to pick. Five years from now, is the public going to go for a certain type grape we plant today?" The question was rhetorical, and as we shook hands he answered himself. "It's a gamble, that's all it is."

Mexican Americans Change Occupations

The following charts demonstrate how Mexican immigrants change occupations when they come to the United States, and how more and more Mexican Americans are gradually moving into new vocations. The first chart compares the occupations of the Mexican-born labor force in the U.S. in 1960 with occupations in Mexico.

As compared to workers in Mexico, Mexican Americans find some jobs easier to get in the U.S. Thus, Mexican immigrants work less frequently at some jobs than they did in Mexico. With their language problem, however, immigrants still find much less freedom to choose jobs than do native-born Mexican Americans.

The second chart shows occupational distribution of Mexican Americans in 1970. Since the first chart deals with the Mexican-born labor force and the second one with the Mexican-American labor force in general, a valid comparison between the two cannot be made. From the 1970 chart, however, it does seem obvious that more and more Mexican Americans are moving into professions, technical work, sales, and other white-collar jobs. While the largest percentage of Mexican Americans still are in farm and service work and other blue-collar jobs, the 1970 statistics, nevertheless, reflect a rather remarkable upward movement. Note on the second chart the percentage of Mexican Americans who are now in white-collar jobs.

Mexican Americans have suffered much discrimination in hiring practices in practically every field of employment. Like other minorities, they have often been excluded from consideration for jobs, even when they were extraordinarily well qualified.

The shortage of labor during World War II helped bring down barriers in many areas where Mexican Americans had previously been excluded. After the war, ground was lost in some areas, but other opportunities opened up with specialized training for returning Mexican-American servicemen and as the result of good work records.

Unions, especially the skilled-craft and white-collar organizations, have been a formidable handicap in the past. Only in the recent years have unions made vigorous efforts to recruit Mexican Americans into fields of employment which were previously closed to them. Although Mexican-American workers are still not represented in unions in proportion to the percentage of the population they constitute, nevertheless, considerable progress has been achieved in getting them accepted into many unions.

While progress is being made toward bringing Mexican Americans into the mainstream of American economic life, the fact that most Mexican Americans are still in menial, low-paying jobs should not be overlooked.

Occupational Distribution of Mexican-Born Persons of Spanish Surname in the United States Compared with Occupational Distribution of the Mexican Labor Force, 1960[1]

Occupational Group	Mexican-Born in U.S.	Labor Force in Mexico
Professional, technical and kindred	2.5%	3.6%
Clerical, sales and kindred	5.6%	9.0%
Craftsmen, foremen, operatives and laborers except farm and mine	45.4%	18.9%
Service workers including household	9.5%	7.0%
Farm laborers and foremen	31.1%	53.5%
All groups included	93.1%	92.0%

[1] The U.S. figures are from the 1960 Census and refer to employed white persons of Spanish surname born in Mexico. The Mexican data pertain to the total labor force.

*Occupational Distribution of Mexican Americans, 1970 ***

Total employed	1,513,000	Female	513,000
Male	1,000,000	Percent	100.0
Percent	100.0	White-collar workers	37.7
White-collar workers	18.5	Blue-collar workers	53.6
Blue-collar workers	64.4	Service workers	7.8
Service workers	8.4	Farm workers	1.2
Farm workers	8.7	* 1970 Census, Population Characteristics	

EDUCATION

Education, rather than economics and politics, may be the key to what the future holds for Mexican Americans. Most Mexican-born Americans arrived in the United States with two formidable barriers to economic advancement—limited education and a language handicap.

With the knowledge that these limitations were detrimental to economic and social progress, more and more Mexican Americans began to look toward education to help solve their problems.

Unfortunately, however, the American school system all too often failed them miserably. Educational methods were carefully planned to meet the needs of the Anglo-American majority. Rarely did educators take into consideration the language problem and cultural differences of Mexican-American youngsters and gear educational programs to meet their needs. Such glaring deficiencies led educators, finally, to begin to reappraise the system.

Educators can testify to the lower achievement of Mexican-American pupils and offer many suggestions as to why they cannot measure up to other children. Usually, the fault has been assigned to the pupil, his family, or background. Very few professional educators have imagined (or were willing to admit) that their teaching was deficient. The fact that there are very few Mexican-American educators helps explain the absence of a professional group which would undertake the study of basic causes of this underachievement.

The time comes when school life becomes a great force in shaping the character of the child. When attitudes and values in school vary much from those at home, then a stressful situation arises for the child. Generally, since educators have not taken such factors into consideration, schools have been a destructive force to Mexican-American values at home. Schools often place the Mexican-American child in a position of having to reject values of his family in order to gain acceptance in the dominant school society. In addition, vast numbers of Mexican-American children must learn the content taught at the same time that they struggle to learn the language in which it is being taught.

Only recently have educators started to ask meaningful questions about what is wrong with schools and why they are failing to meet the needs of *all* the children. A new and irreversible period in education has started, best typified, perhaps, by the Bilingual Educational Opportunities Act passed by Congress in 1967, and by new approaches and techniques which have emerged from the basic philosophy that inspired that act.

Education for Mexican Americans:
An Anglo View in 1928

In formulating plans for educating Mexican Americans today, more and more educators are seeking approaches which will nurture the unique culture of the Mexican American—the customs, traditions, and language that are a rich and diverse heritage from forebears who were a true blend of the Old and New Worlds.

As the following reading from *California Controversies: Major Issues in the History of the State* by Leonard Pitt shows, such was not always the case. Most of the time, both the goals of education and the system to achieve them were set by Anglos. Generally, the goal was to Americanize Mexican Americans and prepare them for certain roles.

Some well-intentioned people failed Mexican-American children by not fully considering the difficulties imposed on them through cultural differences and language problems. Others, however, preferred minimal schooling for Mexican Americans, realizing, of course, that a large, uneducated group provided a cheap, exploitable labor supply and posed no threat to the political status quo.

This selection offers an insight into some ideas for teaching Mexican Americans that were common in past years. While such ideas may have come from people of good intentions, they were, nevertheless, often very destructive for two principal reasons. First, they cast the Mexican-American child in an inferior role and made him doubt both his abilities and his worth as a human being. Secondly, such an approach often alienated the child from his home, family, community, and rich cultural background, and made him feel estranged from his group.

An Americanization Program for the Ontario Schools, 1928

In the five preceding chapters it has been shown that:

1. Mexican children constitute one-fourth of the elementary pupil population of San Bernardino County, and nearly one-fourth of the pupil population of the elementary schools of the Chaffey Union High School District.

2. The Mexican population in San Bernardino County is on the increase, for three-eighths of the babies of San Bernardino County are Mexican.

3. The children of the thirty races other than American and Mexican composing the pupil population of San Bernardino County constitute no serious problem in educational administration.

4. The Mexican children are actually making only 42% as satisfactory progress through the schools as are the children of other races.

5. The Mexican pupils have only 58% as good ability to do the work of the schools as have the American pupils; yet they have 90% as good ability as have American pupils to do manual work, they show equal capacity in penmanship.

6. The Mexican adult peons are illiterate and ignorant; 42% of the men and 48% of the women have had no schooling; less than one-fifth of the adults can write English; less than one-fourth of the adults can read English; while less than one-fourth of the adults can speak English.

7. The economic status of the Mexican adults is low; there is a high infant death rate among Mexicans; the homes are unsanitary, crowded, and possess little or no furniture, books, or magazines; unemployment exists to a marked degree; while the average income of the Mexican parents is not sufficient to provide a satisfactory educational background for the children. . . .

The program here suggested will largely solve the Americanization problems by accomplishing the following:

1. The problems involved in Americanization will be recognized.

2. Separate courses of study will be developed for the education of Mexicans.

3. Equipment and buildings will be secured that will make possible carrying out the program.

4. Consistent effort will be made to enroll all Mexican adolescents and adults in classes that will be conducted to meet their actual needs and assure their educational and economic advancement. . . .

The comparatively few [Mexican] adults should be enrolled in classes where English is taught when needed. Then there should be provided naturalization classes where American geography, the principles of American government, and American ideals are taught. The ultimate objective of these classes is full citizenship in the United States. Such classes have been maintained in the Chaffey Union High School for many years; the class work culminates each year in the awarding of citizenship certificates to those who are ready for their final papers at the annual commencement exercises of the Chaffey Union High School.

The educators who are concerned with an Americanization program must set up clearly defined objectives as to what ought to be taught the Mexican peons. The latter will be required to use the English language. To meet this need language lessons should be developed by teachers and by boards of education to be adaptable to children, to adolescents, and to adults. Word or vocabulary lists should be worked out and developed into lesson units. Constant use of these words should be required in class work to accustom the Mexicans to their use. Simple arithmetic lessons leading to a mastery of the four fundamental processes should be developed. This should be done for the mere protection of the adults in their small business relations. Penmanship lessons should be developed, and the Mexican pupils and adults given an opportunity to learn our written language, for they appear to be adept in a certain manual dexterity that leads to proficiency in penmanship. Lessons in hygiene and health should be developed, together with lessons on pre-natal care and that of infants, that the high mortality amongst Mexican babies may be arrested. As the Mexicans are lovers of music and art, lessons should be developed so that they may become trained along these lines wherein they show great proficiency. As the average Mexican adult has had no training in the "home-owning virtues," it will be necessary to develop lessons regarding thrift, saving, and the value of keeping the money in the banks. As the Mexicans show considerable aptitude for handwork of any kind, courses should be developed that will aid them in becoming skilled workers with their hands. Girls should be trained to become domestic servants, and to do various kinds of handwork for which they can be paid adequately after they leave school. . . .

PROBLEMS

The greatest problem confronting southern California today is that of dealing with the Mexican element that is forming year by year a larger proportion of the population. According to present tendencies the time is not far distant when every other child in the elementary schools will be Mexican. The Mexican families live in segregated districts of city and rural districts and import their native standards of living. How shall this element be taken care of? Can the Mexican be raised to the American standards of life? Can American schooling figure in the upbringing of a race? What lessons should be taught and how much should be taught? What skills should be developed? Can the English language replace the Spanish as a medium of current use? Can the high infant death rate be overcome? Can sanitary methods be adopted to replace the less desirable methods that now prevail? Can Mexican adults be led to seek and secure naturalization? And finally, can the Mexican peon be assimilated into the American population as have the races of Europe? These are the problems involved everywhere, and an effective Americanization program must take them into account. The considerations involved are:

1. Mexican children can acquire both information and skill.
2. Mexican adults can learn the English language, can acquire useful information about our government, and can learn methods of sanitation.
3. Mexican parents should be taught as well as their children; teach both and prevent rifts in the home.
4. The regular course of study is developed to meet the needs of normal American children and does not meet the needs of Mexican children.
5. Mexican adults will not go to afternoon or evening schools very far from their homes; the school must be taken to them.
6. A new course of study must be created to meet the needs of the Mexican elementary pupils.
7. Separate courses must be set up for Mexican adolescents.
8. Courses must be developed for Mexican adults that will be based upon the actual needs and experiences of those adults.
9. An Americanization program will be justified from an economic standpoint.

10. Every inhabitant or dweller within the territory of the United States has an effect upon the success or failure of the American people; any racial group that numbers from one-fifth to one-fourth of our population has a tremendous effect upon the destiny of our country.

11. Raising the standards educationally, economically, and spiritually should be the aim of any system of education.

From these considerations it seems perfectly clear that there must be set up an Americanization program to take care of the foreign element of any community; it will be the purpose of this chapter to present an educational program for a typical union high school.

How Mexican-American Children Have Learned To Believe They Are Inferior

This reading points to common occurrences which twist and stunt Mexican-American children's intellectual development long before they know what is being done to them.

Schools teach children in ways determined by local authorities who, in turn, reflect community feelings. Sometimes schools show favoritism, thus teaching all students that some are considered more important than others.

Many teachers and schools do not understand the life-long effects upon Mexican-American children when they are treated in a less favorable manner. Most Mexican-American children have such experience outside their homes early in life and this affects them greatly. Sometimes schools show prejudice even when they are trying to help Mexican-American children. Better understanding will help eliminate experiences like those we read about here from an essay by the author who quotes from a doctoral dissertation written by Theodore Parsons at Stanford University in 1965. Parsons did extensive research on the subject in Mexican-American communities in California.

A Doctoral Dissertation on Prejudices Against Mexican Americans

The following material is taken from a doctoral dissertation which Parsons entitled, "Ethnic Cleavage in a California School" (Stanford, October 1966). The material in this work reflects conditions in a central California town which are typical in several respects of others in the state and the Southwest. He made the following observations:

1. A teacher, asked why she had called on "Johnny" to lead five Mexicans in orderly file out of a school room, explained: "His father owns one of the big farms in the area and . . . one day he will have to know how to handle the Mexicans."

2. Another teacher, following the general practice of calling on the Anglos to help Mexican pupils recite in class, said in praise of the system: "It draws them out and gives them a feeling of importance."

3. The president of the Chamber of Commerce declared in praise of the school principal: "He runs a good school. We never have any trouble in our school. Every kid knows his place . . . We believe that every kid has to learn to respect authority and his betters."

4. The school principal expounded the "grouping" and departmentalized reading programs instituted under his administration: "We thought that the white children would get more out of school if they would work faster and not be slowed down by the Mexicans. We thought that maybe we could give them some special attention.

"Everybody is happy about the grouping programs. The Mexican parents have never said anything but the kids in school are doing better. I guess the Mexicans are more comfortable in their own group."

5. By admitted subterfuge, the Chamber of Commerce committee sees to it that the artichoke festival "queen" is always an Anglo with the Mexican candidate in second place as her attendant. An influential citizen told Parsons: "We could never have a Mexican queen represent us at the county fair."

6. Two of the three churches do not accept Mexicans. At the Catholic Church, when both groups are assembled for special occasions, the Mexicans sit in the back or stand if seating is inadequate.

7. At school graduation, the Mexicans march in last and sit at the back of the platform. A male teacher explained that this is traditional and makes for a better-looking stage. Also, he explained that the Americans, who have all the parts in the program, can get more easily to the front. He added:

"Once we did let a Mexican girl give a little talk of some kind and all she did was to mumble around. She had quite an accent, too. Afterwards we had several complaints from other parents so we haven't done anything like that since. That was about 12 years ago."

Scientific tests conducted by Parsons disclosed that even the Mexican children came to share the view constantly held up to them that the Anglos are "smarter" and their good opinion of special value.

"In general, the Anglo informants characterized the Mexicans as immoral, violent, and given to fighting, dirty, unintelligent, improvident, irresponsible, and lazy," wrote Parsons.

"Mexican informants often described Anglos as being unsympathetic, aggressive, interested only in themselves, cold, and demanding."

Not one of the several hundred people contacted during the field investigation had ever visited a home outside of his own ethnic group.

An Educational Crisis: Lower Performances by Mexican-American Students

The Mexican American Education Commission, which was created by the Los Angeles Board of Education in 1969, has gathered information that shows a serious educational crisis. The lower performances in school by Mexican-American children contributes to dropout rates as high as 50 percent in high school years. Thus, close to one half of Mexican-American children who enter elementary school do not graduate from high school. Most of those who do graduate have done poorly when compared to Anglo-American students.

Reading ability and native intelligence are common measures for educational success and potential for a creative life. The chart and graph show how Mexican-American students in the Los Angeles school system ranked when compared to Anglo students and to the national average. The chart is an analysis of published scores of individual schools where children were tested in the fall of 1968. Note that Black and Mexican-American children in the sixth grade were two years behind the national average in reading ability. Note also their IQ scores in comparison to Anglos in Los Angeles and to the national average.

The high school section of the chart shows that Blacks and Mexican Americans have fallen even farther behind by the time they reach the tenth grade.

The graph shows how Blacks and Mexican-American children in the sixth grade ranked in comparison to Anglos in reading ability in 1971. Each dot on the graph represents one school whose pupils were tested in reading ability. The highest possible score was 85. The score is not shown, but only the percentile which the score represents. The percentile shows how an average reading score of all the pupils in one school compares with the average of all other schools. For example, a reading score of 65 (out of a possible 85) would place a school on the 55th percentile, meaning that the school's score was as good as or better than 55 percent of all other schools.

Note that as the percentage of minorities (mostly Blacks and Mexican Americans) goes up in a school, the school's standing in reading ability goes down. For example, the school that ranked highest had less than ten percent minority students. And most schools that had 90 to 100 percent minority children ranked lowest in the entire school sytem.

Some believe that the poor showings are the result of faulty tests which are unfair to Blacks and Mexican Americans, and there is substantial evidence to support such a claim. Psychologists today are almost unanimous in their conclusion that people of all nationalities and ethnic groups are about equal in intelligence. After years of extensive testing, they found no noticeable differences between various ethnic groups.

Many standard IQ tests have been widely criticized by psychologists who contend that they are geared to the middle-class child whose enriched background and language abilities enable him to score higher and, thus, appear more intelligent. Who could doubt that an extremely intelligent Mexican-American child with a language problem would score lower than a less intelligent Anglo-American child who has no problem with the language on the test?

Obviously, there are also other factors which might affect test scores—poverty, poor health, bad nutrition, and little parental encouragement.

Elementary (6B Grade)

Number of Schools	% Minority	Kind	I.Q.	Reading Level
154	94%	Anglo	104	6.0
80	97%	Black	87	4.1
47	94%	Mexican	87	4.1
150	42%	Mixed	96	5.0
	National Average		100	6.1

High School (10B Grade)

Number of Schools	% Minority	Kind	I.Q.	Reading Level
15	04%	Anglo	105	57%
12	97%	Black & Mexican	88	18%
20	38%	Mixed	96	38%
		National Norm	100	50%

I.Q. (100 is average)

	Q1	Median	Q3
Majority Schools	93	105	114
Minority Schools	73	81	91

Reading Ability
(100 percentile is the national average)

	Q1	Median	Q3
Majority Schools	36	57	79
Minority Schools	12	28	48

Note: Q1 means lowest ¼ of scores
Q3 means highest ¼ of scores
Median represents middle ½ of scores recorded.

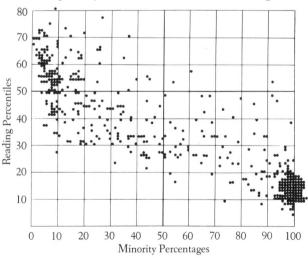

Los Angeles City Schools Sixth Grade Fall 1971 – Reading Scores

The Psychology of Mexican-American Students

Philip Montez, part of whose address before the California State Senate is quoted below, claims most Mexican Americans are caught in a special psychological situation which few educators understand. He says that teaching goals and methods do not meet the needs of most Mexican-American students, so they do poorly in school. Educators usually place the blame on the students and their families, but Montez believes the schools share the responsibility for the poor results in teaching because they do not fully understand the Mexican-American child.

Some believe that Mexican-American children share equal potential in grade one, but fall behind because schools, in effect, discourage them from learning. Many Mexican Americans come to believe they cannot succeed in English-speaking schools, so they stop trying and in time drop out of school.

The questions raised by educators, such as Mr. Montez, cause much discussion. New books, tests, and teaching methods are emerging as educators discuss ideas we find in this selection.

The Problem of Motivation for the Mexican-American Student

For some time we in school psychology have been concerned with what happens to a bilingual-bicultural child when he is placed in a monolingual situation—such as our schools. Our Mexican-American children do not live in a vacuum for the first five years of life. The period prior to entering school is one of constant bombardment with dual language and cultural forces. This varies with each child. Consequently, when the child enters school he may be 10 percent "Mexican" and 90 percent "Anglo." Another child may be 90 percent "Mexican" and 10 percent "Anglo." Each one is different.

In a recent study in the El Rancho School District, under the able direction of Dr. Henry Johnson, we found that the Mexican-American child is just as motivated in kindergarten and first grade as his Anglo counterpart. But in about the third or fourth grade a change begins to take place in the child's motivation patterns. He begins losing educational "ground," so that by the time he reaches the eighth or ninth grade he is anywhere from 1 to 2 years educationally retarded. Under this system of "rejection," is it no wonder that he can't succeed educationally? This rejection is very subtle and seldom intentional and no one seems to know what the problem of education is relative to the Mexican-American child. They are asked questions such as: "Why aren't Mexican-American children interested in education?" "Why won't the parents help us motivate their children?"

This educational rejection makes the child feel that he is different. Consider the child who enters kindergarten overjoyed and enthusiastic because he is in school. He finds that his communication is somewhat different because of an accent. He may even be corrected in his pronunciation by some well-meaning teacher who is trying to help. He is not given any reasons why his speech is different, only that it must be corrected. He begins to feel that all he has been prior to entering school must now be corrected and revamped. The self-image becomes more and more negative and by late elementary school we find him going one of two directions. He becomes a psychological "drop-out," which is now being called a "sit-in," or he develops a personality with a great deal of hostility and he becomes known as a trouble-maker and a discipline problem. This has happened because a great part of this human personality has never been recognized. He knows this and feels it. The system has created rejection and all human beings suffer under rejection. Some don't even survive.

As we look around the Mexican-American community, is it any wonder that the rates of anti-social behavior are so high? We lead in narcotics addiction; we lead in juvenile delinquency; we lead in illegitimate births, low income, and many other social ills that confront a rejected group.

Yet, we are told that we do not want to help ourselves. This is not true. Our children can be taught to be productive in this great American system. But they need help in the area of acceptance—to be accepted as they are, be they 10 percent "Mexican" and 90 percent "Anglo"—or 95 percent "Mexican" and 5 percent "Anglo."

Now to the specifics: I'm sure legislation can do much in this area. Legislation could encourage teachers to utilize Spanish in those areas where it is needed. By this we do not mean merely teaching it as an academic discipline, but as a means of communication. A natural process with children and parents, language should start in the early grades. I have never understood why, with all the natural potential we have in this area, we are now having trouble finding teachers to teach Spanish.

What is wrong with all our children graduating from high school being bilingual? This would make a great contribution to our American system, with the millions of persons in 21 nations just south of us speaking Spanish. We will be needing this to a greater extent as the political complex of Latin-America continues to change and our own position becomes undermined by other factions.

A Theory of Bicultural Education

Recently, many educators have called for a new approach to education for Mexican Americans. Typical of these, Marcos de León argues for the preservation of Hispanic and Mexican culture in schools for both Mexican-American children and others who would benefit from it. His views are based on the assumption that most Mexican Americans will not be completely assimilated.

He feels that a Mexican American should be able to choose whether he will assimilate. He points out that self-respect and creativity are more likely to occur where an individual is proud of his ancestry, rather than when he is ashamed of it. It is interesting to note that de León envisioned new educational approaches to help Mexican Americans as an opportunity to enrich all students.

Edward Moreno, Robert Rangel, and other Mexi-can-American educators believe Anglo-American children are losing as much as Mexican-American children by the systematic destruction of bilingual ability and an appreciation for cultural diversity. Their work leads to the conclusion that Mexican-American children represent a rich creative source and have much to teach others.

The following reading, in which Mr. de León states his views, was originally published in the *California Journal of Secondary Education.*

Wanted: A New Educational Philosophy for the Mexican American

Today the Mexican-American is faced with three areas which demand of him continual adjustment: (1) the community to which he has been relegated and in which he has surrounded himself with those ancestral cultural elements rendering optimum security; (2) the total community which in spite of himself will not accept him as a bona fide citizen; and (3) the school, which ignores the fact that his life is molded by living in two worlds: a cultural dichotomy not touched by the curriculum. . . .

Efforts to identify himself with the representative culture have been attempted in various degrees, depending on the social level of the person and the community in which he resides. Yet, in spite of it all, he still remains a foreigner, a stranger, and for all intents and purposes a "Mexican" with the common stereotyped connotations brought on by some one hundred years of cultural conflict.

Moreover, the partial disintegration of the parent culture and the fact he has been taught through social pressure to be ashamed of and even to disown his ethnic ancestry, has made the Mexican American a victim of confusion, frustration, and insecurity.

A very practical teaching of mental hygiene is that one cannot run away from himself, or what he is, or from that in which he believes. To do so is to invite disaster. Somewhere along the way, the Mexican American must make a stand and recognize the fact that if there is to be progress against those barriers which prevent and obstruct a more functional citizenship, he must above all retrieve his dignity and worth as a person with a specific ethnic antecedent, having a positive contribution to make to civilization. No man can find a true expression for living who is ashamed of himself or his people.

Whatever progress in education and community consciousness has been achieved by Mexican Americans can be attributed to (1) becoming realistically aware of their nonacceptance by American society; (2) finding a personal dignity and worth in their ethnical and cultural background; and (3) sacrificing immediate ethnic integration and assimilation by excelling in education and the professions, thereby making a greater contribution to American democracy.

Educational practice and community organization should be directed toward creating conditions which contribute to the security and well-being of all its members. Where two basic cultures such as the English and Spanish have come to throw circles of influence over one another, the method whereby this takes place and its relation to the growth of youngsters should be a matter of concern for administrators and teachers. . . .

Throughout the Southwest, elements of the cultures peculiar to the United States and Mexico have thrown constant and continuous circles of influence over one another for over a century. In every village and city this rubbing of elbows of the two cultures, involving food, art, music, religion, architecture, clothing, language, ideas, and attitudes, is actually occurring, albeit undirected, but serving the only purpose that culture was meant to fulfill: adjustment and security of its members. . . .

If we are to utilize the community and its needs to strengthen the school's program, elements of food, art, clothing, music, language, and history, peculiar to the Mexican area, should certainly be included in the curriculum of those schools serving large numbers of Mexican Americans. In the average school program, however, one finds almost ex-clusively those cultural elements peculiar to the American scene composing the curriculum. This not only violates the best recommended procedures and methods for setting up the curriculum for a bicultural community, but prevents the school from assuming its role as an educational institution for the total community and leaves very little leeway for anything but a frustrating and sometimes sterile learning situation. . . .

In the past, the process of acculturation apparently was left unguided and without direction. The idea that the United States is the "melting pot" of the world does not necessarily hold true. The frustration and insecurity brought on by a "melting" process, carried on at random and conditioned by cultural conflicts, are too great to permit this "catch as catch can" philosophy to reign over and control the life of the Mexican American any longer. The school cannot continue to function as an isolated unit, or continue to carry on practices based on tradition for the bicultural community, under the present "all or none" concept as an educational philosophy.

⤷ Bilingual Educational Opportunities Act of 1967

As in certain provinces of Canada, where both French and English are spoken, some areas of the United States are becoming more and more bilingual. Until comparatively recent times, the bilingual areas of the country were concentrated in the Southwest. In the past few decades, however, the Spanish-speaking population of New York and Florida has grown tremendously with new arrivals from Puerto Rico and Cuba, respectively.

Recognizing the national interest in preserving bilingual abilities, Congress passed the Bilingual Educational Act of 1967—the document which follows. Many members of the U.S. House of Representatives and Senate from both parties joined together to sponsor the bill. The original financial support proposed was scaled down, but an appropriation of several million dollars was committed for distribution to states to meet bilingual educational needs.

While there are still some areas which probably have not taken advantage of the money appropriated, nevertheless, a giant step has been made, and a new period in bilingual education has begun.

Some Provisions of H.R. 8000

EXTENSION OF REMARKS OF

HON. EDWARD R. ROYBAL OF CALIFORNIA

IN THE HOUSE OF REPRESENTATIVES

Mr. ROYBAL. Mr. Speaker, because of the fast-growing evidence of widespread national support for a program of bilingual education to offer America's millions of non-English-speaking elementary and secondary school children a better chance to realize their full educational aspirations, I ask unanimous consent to insert in the Congressional Record the text of my bill, H.R. 8000, the Bilingual Educational Opportunity Act:

H.R. 8000

A bill to amend the Elementary and Secondary Education Act of 1965 in order to provide assistance to local educational agencies in establishing bilingual educational opportunity programs, and to provide certain other assistance to promote such programs.

Be it enacted by the Senate and House of Representatives of the United States of America in Congress assembled, that the Congress hereby finds that one of the most acute educational problems in the United States is that which involves the more than two million bilingual and bicultural children of non-English speaking ethnic or nationality background that little headway has been made in finding adequate and constructive solutions to this unique and perplexing educational situation; and that the urgent need is for comprehensive and cooperative action now on the local, State, and Federal levels to develop forward-looking approaches to meet the serious learning difficulties faced by this substantial segment of the Nation's school-age population. . . . .

DECLARATION OF POLICY

Sec. 702. In recognition of the special educational needs of the large numbers of students in the United States to whom English is a second language. Congress hereby declares it to be the policy of the United States to provide financial assistance to local educational agencies to develop and carry out new and imaginative elementary and secondary school programs designed to meet these special educational needs.

AUTHORIZATION AND ALLOTMENTS

Sec. 703. (a) For the purpose of making grants under this title, there is authorized to be appropriated the sum of $5,000,000 for the fiscal year ending June 30, 1969, and $15,000,000 for the fiscal year ending June 30, 1970, and the succeeding fiscal year.

(b) From the sums appropriated pursuant to subsection (a) for each fiscal year the Commissioner shall allot an amount to each State based upon the number of non-English-speaking elementary and secondary school students in such State and the per capita income in such manner as he determines will best carry out the purposes of this title. For the purposes of this title non-English-speaking elementary and secondary school students means elementary and secondary school students born in, or one or both of whose parents were born in, a non-English-speaking area such as Mexico, Puerto Rico, Cuba, or French Canada, and in States for which such information is available, other students with Spanish surnames, and where the Commissioner establishes additional objective criteria which he deems appropriate for carrying out the purposes of this title, other students determined on the basis of such additional criteria.

(c) A State's allotment for a fiscal year pursuant to subsection (b) shall be available, prior to such date in such year as is established by the Commissioner, for grants to local educational agencies in such State pursuant to this title. Allotments not reserved prior to such date may be reallotted to other States and made available for grants pursuant to this title prior to the end of such fiscal year in such manner as the Commissioner determines will best carry out the purposes of this title.

Sec. 704. Grants under this title may be used in accordance with applications approved under section 705, for—

(a) planning for and taking other steps leading to the development of programs designed to meet the special educational needs of students who speak English as a second language, including—

(1) special bilingual and bicultural educational research and demonstration projects; and

(2) pilot projects designed to test the effectiveness of plans and programs so developed; and

(b) the establishment, maintenance, and operation of programs, including minor remodeling of classroom or other space used for such programs and acquisition of necessary equipment, designed to meet the special educational needs of students who speak English as a second language through activities such as—

(1) intensive preschool, Headstart-type programs specifically designed to orient and prepare non-English-speaking children for smoother transition to and more rapid advancement in the elementary education environment:

(2) the utilization of the ability to speak a language other than English as a bridge to the learning of English;

(3) regular, ongoing comprehensive bilingual educational programs;

(4) the teaching of English as the first or primary language;

(5) the teaching of the language spoken in the home as a second language;

(6) programs designed to impart to non-English-speaking students a knowledge of and pride in their ancestral culture and language;

(7) programs to attract and retain as teachers promising individuals of non-English-speaking ethnic or nationality background;

(8) efforts to establish closer cooperation between the school and the home; and

(9) other activities which meet the purposes of this title.

Educational Attainments

Three of the Tables that follow (1, 2, and 4) clearly show the effect of education on the incomes of Mexican Americans. Note the correlation between higher educational achievements and higher annual incomes. Study Table 3 in which there is a comparison between the educational achievements of Americans of Mexican origin and those of other Hispanic Americans.

Table 1 *Educational Attainments and Median Income of Mexican Americans, 1960*

	Median School Years Attained	Median Income
All	8.1	$2,804
Urban	8.4	3,197
Rural, non-farm	6.9	1,871
Rural, farm	4.6	1,531

(Figures are for Spanish surnamed males, including Mexican Americans.

Table 2 *Educational Attainments and Median Income of Mexican Americans, 1970*

	Median School Years Attained	Median Income
All Spanish Surnamed, 25 years and older	9.3	(See Table 4
All Spanish Surnamed, 25 to 34 years	11.7	on next
Mexican Americans, 25 to 34 years	10.8	page.)
Mexican Americans, 35 years and over	7.3	

Table 3 *Educational Attainment for Persons 25 Years Old and Over by Origin and Age, November, 1969*

(Numbers in Thousands) Age and Origin	Total	Elementary		High School		College, 1 or More Years	Median School Years Completed
		0 to 7 Years	8 Years	1 to 3 Years	4 Years		
SPANISH ORIGIN							
Total, 25 years old and over	3,815	1,345	495	675	850	452	9.3
25 to 34 years old	1,239	238	124	291	399	187	11.7
Mexican	565	131	68	138	182	46	10.8
Puerto Rican	214	68	19	69	45	13	9.9
Cuban	109	12	14	13	36	34	12.4
Central or South American ...	125	11	15	21	44	35	12.4
Other Spanish	226	16	8	50	92	59	12.4
35 years old and over	2,576	1,107	371	384	451	265	8.5
Mexican	1,343	737	182	187	161	76	7.3
Puerto Rican	335	179	54	39	45	19	7.5
Cuban	211	47	46	22	52	45	10.8
Central or South American ...	147	37	18	23	37	32	11.4
Other Spanish	540	107	71	113	156	93	11.4
OTHER ORIGIN AND NOT REPORTED							
Total, 25 years old and over	102,466	13,350	13,749	18,010	35,135	22,228	12.2
25 to 34 years old	22,643	826	1,027	3,860	9,989	6,946	12.6
35 years old and over	79,823	12,524	12,722	14,150	25,146	15,282	12.0

Table 4 *Median Family Income by Origin and Age of Head, November, 1969*

Origin of Head	Total	Age of Head		
		18 to 24 Years	25 to 44 Years	45 to 64 Years
Total	$7,894	$5,498	$8,478	$7,819
Spanish	5,641	4,614	6,122	5,209
Mexican	5,488	4,276	6,261	4,860
Puerto Rican	4,969	(B)	5,097	5,000
Cuban	5,957	(B)	6,042	(B)
Central or South American	5,595	(B)	5,607	(B)
Other Spanish	6,889	(B)	7,412	6,964
Other and not reported	8,011	5,553	8,606	7,920

B Base less than 75,000.

POLITICS

Mexican Americans generally have not been very successful in American politics, so they have had little to do with shaping political decisions that affect them. Despite their numerical strength in some areas, laws and voting practices have made it hard for Mexican Americans to exert influence. Because they have not voted in large numbers, political parties have not tried to please them. Indifference or prejudice towards them has made most Mexican Americans avoid politics. Their lack of political involvement has continued the vicious cycle of political leaders ignoring the needs of minorities who stay aloof from politics.

Since World War II, however, the generation of GIs among Mexican Americans has entered politics more often. In recent years, younger Mexican Americans are even more involved in politics, changing old cultural patterns in the barrios and awakening others to their needs. More and more Mexican Americans are beginning to understand that their future depends upon political activity.

Attesting to the recognition of this imperative need for political involvement was the very active role that many Mexican Americans played in the 1972 Presidential election. Mexican Americans served as delegates at the national conventions of both the Democrats and the Republicans, and were later active in the campaigns.

The election of President Nixon in 1968 commenced a period of national Republican attention to Mexican Americans. Republicans began an attempt to woo them away from their old ties with the Democratic Party, at the same time bold young Mexican Americans were forming their own party, *La Raza Unida*. This section offers a broad view of politics as they affect Mexican Americans as a group.

An Overview of Politics in the Southwest

The following selection from *The Southwest: Old and New* by W. Eugene Hollon sketches a broad picture of political life in the Southwest. For the most part, Anglos have dominated state and local politics. They have often discouraged Mexican Americans from participating in politics by various methods. It may seem easy for others to say Mexican Americans deserve what they get politically. But such an attitude may unfairly hold the oppressed guilty for the acts of the transgressor. In many cases, bribes, economic pressure, character assassination, or outright violence have been used to suffocate a Mexican-American political move-

ment. Mexican Americans are not a violent people and have not returned the treatment in kind. Generally, even courts and law enforcement have been at the service of the dominant group. Concern for one's job and safety of family explain why so many Mexican Americans have settled for less than they wanted from politics. Thus, on the whole, Mexican Americans have not been a political force.

Understanding the role of the Mexican Americans depends upon understanding political realities in the particular areas where they have lived. Political bodies, such as school boards, city councils, state legislatures, and the courts, have established the conditions of life. In many cases, special groups have influenced political institutions greatly. Mexican Americans have not been influential in these circles of political power, despite their numbers. These historic traditions are now changing rapidly, as more Mexican Americans realize that their destinies depend on political involvement.

Politics in the Southwest

Until 1940, as we have already noted, the entire Southwest was more rural than urban, more oriented toward agriculture than industry. Almost two decades later the region still led the nation in livestock production and remained among the top producers of cotton, wheat, peanuts, and other crops. But industry now surpassed agriculture in economic importance and more people lived in cities than in rural communities. These changes brought shifts in political thinking also. The pattern evolved similarly in the four states, yet local traditions, racial groups, diversity of natural resources, geography, and climate were factors that contributed to sectional differences. . . .

TEXAS

On the national political scene Texas presents a slightly different picture from the rest of the nation. The two most powerful men in Congress during the decade of the fifties were both Texans: Lyndon Johnson and Sam Rayburn. Though neither is considered an outright liberal, both are far more progressive than the last half-dozen Texas governors. . . .

Texas's legislature has generally been as conservative as its governors. A political writer once described it as an organization controlled by the three B's—Bourbon, Beefsteaks, and Blondes—and one of its members in the 1959 session summarized the situation as follows: "In Austin, the climate is very corporate, cloudy, and full of oil."

Both statements contain as much truth as metaphor. Well-financed lobbyists consistently exercise more influence over legislation than the people do, blocking more bills than they advocate. This will remain possible as long as rural Texas and conservative urban elements combine to resist political transformations in a rapidly changing state. But as cities continue to attract an even greater majority of voters, a more balanced political picture seems inevitable. Texas has not completed the 180-degree turn from conservatism to liberalism, but it has grown weary of demagogues and clowns; it has outgrown the Solid South; it is outgrowing Bourbon democracy; and many Texans no longer believe that mere "bigness" is everything. . . .

NEW MEXICO

This section of the Southwest is often described as a land where comic-opera politics flourish, party labels mean little or nothing, and issues are subordinated to personalities. And the early years of New Mexico's statehood saw the development of "the most gorgeously corrupt political systems imaginable."

Republicans dominated New Mexico politics during territorial days. Thus, at the time of its admission to statehood in 1912 they determined the membership of the constitutional convention. Among other failings, the convention neglected to provide primary-election laws, and for a full generation all candidates obtained nominations through the convention system. This meant that the man with the most money possessed an overwhelming advantage, for party organizations were scarcely more than bargain counters where votes were sold to the highest bidder. . . .

Because New Mexico politics are always close to the individual, almost everyone is interested in them. Before the great population boom in the early forties, most candidates for state offices knew the majority of voters personally. A democratic society hardly existed, for a large portion of the population consisted of illiterate sheepherders, vaqueros, and peons. Unable to read or write and uninterested in affairs beyond the home range, they voted according to the orders of the "Big Boss."

This was known as the patron system, and it endured until the beginning of World War II. Many patrons owned original Spanish land grants larger than the state of Rhode Island and employed hundreds of workers over whom they exercised feudal powers. Individuals voted as they were told, considering it a part of their job. The Big Boss in turn expected political "plums" for his hacienda and henchmen when he delivered the vote. . . .

Before World War II most of the large land grants were divided and the system withered away in its social and economic aspect. But the patron in the guise of the politico remains after a half-century of statehood. The average voter tends to give his allegiance to the individual leader rather than the party. The leader, if he is successful, rewards his supporters by means of patronage. Most of the jobs are petty, but they are tempting to a group that has been, as a whole, underprivileged. "It is a thin mess of pottage to accept in place of favorable laws or wages, health, welfare, taxation, etc., but it is the pottage that they have demanded and both major parties have found that they could get more votes by delivering jobs to shrewdly selected leaders than by a direct appeal based on issues." . . .

Broadly speaking, New Mexico's population consists of three distinct groups: the Indians who live on the reservations and who have only recently begun to play an effective role in politics, the natives of Spanish descent, and the citizens of Anglo-American descent. . . .

Despite the unpredictableness of New Mexican political behavior, the situation as a whole is much healthier than a generation ago. A sizable proportion of the new residents since World War II are well-educated people, and they are difficult to deceive. They enjoy comedy by professional comedians, not by politicians. More important, the legislature is reapportioned according to population regularly—and cities such as Albuquerque and Santa Fe are adequately represented. "Second-floor governors" are no longer in vogue, and the practice of counting the sheep and dead men is declining. Inevitably the state will have to elect its congressmen from districts rather than at-large. This will almost certainly mean that Republican Albuquerque will control one of the two seats, for a third of New Mexico's population lives in this metropolitan area. It will also mean a stronger two-party system.

ARIZONA

Arizona has a long-standing Democratic tradition of conservatism similar to that of Southern cotton-planters and Texas-ranchers—bolstered by the mining interest. In the days when free silver ranked as a national issue, the territory's economic welfare depended on federal price supports. When the Democrats staked their future on "free and unlimited coinage of silver" in the nineties, they won the grateful support of the silver barons. No other issue mattered in Arizona as long as silver was king.

Since World War II this traditional conservatism has been strongly spiced with Midwestern Republicanism. Party labels mean comparatively little, and party registration figures are easily misconstrued. In 1940 the Democrats outnumbered Republicans eight to one; by 1958 the figure was two-and-a-half to one. This change does not reflect a swing from left to right, but rather the fact that being an avowed Republican is no longer a political liability. It has long been a practice of Arizona conservatives to register as Democrats in order to have an effective voice in state and local affairs. A large proportion of these are called "pinto" Democrats, by those who consider themselves "real" Democrats, for the "pintos" are indistinguishable from conservative Republicans. Since the war thousands of bona fide Republicans have arrived in the state, about one third of whom do not need to earn a living. These newcomers have been less hesitant to register according to their true affiliation. And under the enthusiastic leadership of Republican Party workers additional thousands of so-called Democrats have been persuaded to do likewise. Many realistic "pintos," however, particularly those in the urban centers of Phoenix and Tucson, are reluctant to surrender a strategic advantage; by retaining their Democratic registration they succeed in obtaining desired results as members, candidates, and manipulators of the dominant party. . . .

Between 1912 and 1950 Arizona elected only two Republican governors, Thomas E. Campbell (1917–21) and John C. Phillips (1929–31) and one United States senator, Ralph H. Cameron (1921–7). In 1950 Republican Howard Pyle won the governorship and repeated his victory in 1952. When Ernest W. McFarland vacated his United States Senate seat in 1952, Republican Barry Goldwater replaced him in Washington. Eisenhower and Nixon carried the state that year by a large majority, and they did even better in 1956. Two years later things went badly for the Republicans throughout most of the nation—but not in Arizona. Goldwater defeated McFarland for the Senate in a contest that attracted national attention. . . .

Before the senatorial campaign of 1958 few contests created much excitement; candidates did not conduct vigorous campaigns, and a relatively small percentage of the total population bothered to vote. Seldom has a defeated candidate made charges of fraud. There has been little evidence of racial bigotry, and no blind following of political bosses.

Yet the political climate in Arizona is not completely healthy. With the election of a new governor everybody loses his job, even members of the state highway patrol. Legislators are generally undistinguished, and conservatives dominate the House so thoroughly that sometimes they can elect the speaker by acclamation. This body, like the Senate, spends most of its time during a typical sixty-day session in squabbles with the governor. The upper chamber is so small that fifteen members constitute a majority and whoever controls them frequently can control state legislation.

The question naturally arises as to who or what actually runs Arizona. I asked numerous residents during a week's visit to Phoenix and Tucson in April, 1959, and the answers were in general agreement. "Nobody runs the state," explained Orme Lewis, a prominent Phoenix attorney. "But there is a powerful veto power in the Senate representing mining, utilities, cattle, big farmers, big ranchers. They don't initiate much, but they can and do check expensive bills. It used to be that copper ran things by itself, but not so much any more." . . .

Discrimination in Jury Selection and Voting

In a society with democratic institutions, the selection of juries and voting rights provide the foundations for liberty and equality. In some locations, Mexican Americans have filed court actions against the methods by which grand juries and ordinary juries are selected. Such actions allege that Mexican Americans are systematically excluded from juries, thus denying their judgment by peers. This reading describes conditions in Texas during the 1960's and explains how such conditions have restricted the liberty and equality of many Mexican Americans. The reading is the testimony which James de Anda gave before a cabinet committee hearing in El Paso, Texas, in 1967.

The conditions reported here have not been universal, but similar conditions have been common in most of the Southwest. Many Mexican Americans have moved from one place to another, and this mobility has made it more difficult to satisfy local laws that govern civic participation. In view of the different obstacles, most Mexican Americans have not played a major role in civic life. This has made it difficult for them to protect their own interests.

James de Anda's plan for federally supported legal assistance to the poor has been started. In some states, groups such as the California Rural Legal Assistance (CRLA) now help Mexican Americans in court. The U.S. Commission on Civil Rights has started to investigate and expose injustices that affect the civil rights of groups like the Mexican Americans. Many governmental agencies are changing in order to extend equality to everyone.

Testimony of James de Anda

The fact that I have been asked to speak on the problem concedes the existence of it. Therefore, I will not dwell on the admitted fact and references to specific instances of discrimination are made only to show more clearly the need for prompt and meaningful administrative action.

When we speak of remedies for the denial of constitutional rights as they pertain to schools, voting and jury service, we are in the domain of the lawyer. So we must look not only at the Mexican American, the injured party, but to the private practitioner as well.

First, what of the party on whom the harm is inflicted? What kind of complainant does he make? Does he have a "damn the torpedoes, full speed ahead" approach? Unfortunately, no. There appears to be a uniformly fatalistic tolerance to the intolerable on the part of those whose rights are denied. Fear of reprisals, fear of failure, and ignorance of those rights are calculated to make a reluctant litigant. These factors are magnified in smaller communities where economic necessity requires a subservience to those who control the purse strings. In these areas, oftentimes the persons who make unlawful school board policies are the employers of the parents of children who are being discriminated. Suing your boss, when a job is not easy to come by, is a very unhappy event calling for almost unnatural courage. The usual situation requires that a stimulus be provided to precipitate action by the injured parties to protect these cherished rights.

Can the individual lawyer provide this needed impetus? And will he? To date, the answer, with rare exception is "no." The traditional role of the lawyer, the canons, and mores of the legal community, oppose the instigation or fomentation of lawsuits. Apart from this philosophical barrier, there are practical considerations which make it difficult to find an advocate. Shakespeare observed rather strongly that "There is no breath so foul as that of the unfee'd lawyer." In defense of the profession, it can be honestly stated that the quotation is an exaggeration, but the fact remains that the lack of funds for legal expenses is a detriment. Furthermore, identification with civil rights causes of this nature is calculated neither to enhance a lawyer's social status in his community nor his acceptance by the established economic interest. Again, these factors weigh most heavily in rural areas and in smaller urban centers.

How can this void be filled? How can these problems be exposed and corrections be made? One possible remedy would be for the administration to recommend legislation to provide for attorneys' fees in school, jury and voting cases as is now provided under the equal employment provisions of the statutes. But this would not relieve the community pressures, economic reprisals and social stigma involved. The solution lies in executive action through investigators whose responsibility would be to ferret out violations, to consult and negotiate with school officials and to recommend court proceedings to the Attorney General in appropriate cases. This approach has been successfully used in practically all areas of government concern and regulation. The Equal Employment Commission is very active and openly solicits complaints and follows through on those complaints. The Labor Department is most active in enforcing minimum wage provisions. The accomplishments of these agencies, in a relatively short time, illustrates the good that can flow through an aggressive agency, competently staffed.

Attention is now focused on the specific areas which are the subject of our concern.

JURY DISCRIMINATION

Other than the field of criminal law, where the defendant claims violation of his constitutional rights, little has been done to insure cross-section participation of the community on jury panels. Criminal lawyers are never hesitant to raise defenses based on violations of constitutional rights; and the protective court decisions touching on jury discrimination have been almost exclusively in this area where cases have been reversed because of illegalities in the jury selection process. These same illegalities occur in civil cases. An example of this was exposed in Corpus Christi, Texas, where I live. A study was made of civil juries and it was found that although forty-five percent (45%) of the people of Nueces County were of Mexican extraction, that only about five percent (5%) of the jury panels were Mexican Americans. This was attributed to disqualifications of jurors due to language handicap, absenteeism and a general group reluctance to serve on juries. However, a study made by a group of lawyers disclosed that residents of certain precincts, comprised almost exclusively of Mexican Americans and Negroes, were never called for jury service. The evidence was damning and overwhelming. The local bar association reviewed the facts presented by the study and consultations were had with the officials involved in jury selection. Unofficially the reason given for the situation was that "these jurors would never appear for jury service anyway and the county would lose money, that these people were not qualified for jury service." The official reason given was that the jury wheel was too small and that the name cards did not properly mix. Solution—get a larger jury wheel. This was done and amazingly enough the following year the number of Mexican-American names appearing on jury rolls increased to as much as forty percent (40%) of the total persons selected. The composition of the juries changed and so did the results of jury trials. A jury system is fair only if the jury selection is fair and only if the jury truly reflects a cross-section of the people. . . .

Token representation on jury panels is not enough because under our system of pre-emptory challenges, the attorneys for each side have the right to strike a certain number of jurors without stated cause or reason. I do not criticize my adversaries for taking advantage of the situation. These are advocates whose duty is to do anything legal to win their case. I can and should criticize officials who permit this situation to exist. One other exam-

ple might serve to illustrate the importance which all attorneys attach to the make-up of the jury. Court records in my county revealed that for a long period of time the prosecutors in criminal cases without exception struck from the jury list all Mexican-American names in cases where a Mexican American was the defendant. One prosecutor had the habit of numbering his strikes in the order in which he made them. Invariably, the first names he struck were the Mexican-American names. . . .

My purpose in relating this story is to point the need for more than token representation on juries of a particular ethnic group. Jury selection in federal courts has also been discriminatory and in many areas it has been accepted practice to use service club lists and personal knowledge to make up a jury list. In many areas federal juries have a reputation of being "blue ribbon juries." Voter registration lists have not been used but should be to get a true cross-section representation. The excuse that there will be inconvenience due to disqualified jurors may have some validity, but it does not override the necessity of an impartial jury of one's peers to pass judgment on a case. . . .

VOTING DISCRIMINATION

It is a statistical reality that the Mexican-American group falls far behind other ethnic groups in its participation at the polls. This applies both to persons registered to vote and to those who vote after being registered. In Texas the reasons for this state of affairs have been a poll tax now abolished; an unreasonable and unfair deadline for registering to vote (January 31 of each year); rigid and unrealistic interpretation by our state officials of our registration laws; and setting general elections on a weekday.

We must acknowledge with some embarrassment that our voter participation is less than just about any country in the world which holds free elections. In Vietnam we have been told that approximately seventy-five percent of the electorate went to the polls in the recent elections. Texas could seldom top or equal this figure. The precincts of the wealthy, of the controlling interests, of the well-to-do, invariably vote much more heavily than do the precincts of the minorities. Indifference plays a part, but like the jury wheel situation I discussed earlier, it is not the answer. I do not know how much effort has been made to change our general election day from a Tuesday to a Saturday but I do not hesitate to make this recommendation, or as an alternative, to declare election day a national holiday. Although our election laws provide that the polls shall be opened from 7 A.M. until 7 P.M., for all practical purposes, the poor working man can come only late in the afternoon and early evening. Job requirements, not infrequently artificial, may deprive a person of his right to vote.

The legality of unnecessary and unreasonable voter registration procedures should be challenged at every turn by the Attorney General. Only a few days ago, the Attorney General of the State of Texas, issued an opinion (in direct contradiction to a previous opinion issued by another attorney general) that persons who send in their registration applications by mail, must send those applications in individual envelopes, and that voting registrars could not accept applications mailed in bulk, nor presented in bulk by civic organizations or others. The stated reason for this interpretation was that "it would prevent fraud." Our Attorney General has never stated why mailing applications separately rather than together makes for a more honest registration. In view of the fact that it is the duty of the registrar in each county to mail the registration certificate only to the applicant at the applicant's residence, I have been unable to find anything beneficial in the interpretation. It does make it most difficult for civic organizations and volunteer public spirited citizens to hold registration drives and register voters. It would appear to me that such an interpretation should be challenged in the courts but to date, nothing has been done. In Texas, voting instructions can be given only in the English language. Such a rule has no valid purpose in areas where representatives of all interests are bilingual.

Conclusions: Despite the real or fancied impediments to immediate, effective administrative action, the Executive Branch and its agencies must recognize that we can no longer afford to wait, to make studies, to gather statistics and then shake our heads in anguish. The problems that I have discussed demand immediate solutions. I hope that my suggestions will help, even in a small way, in bringing about change. . . .

Mexican Americans and the U.S. Forestry Service Compete for Land

Many thousands of Mexican Americans in New Mexico and Colorado depend upon the use of U.S. forest lands to graze their cattle, as their ancestors have done since the 16th Century when they settled this region. In recent years, the Forest Service has cut back lands available for grazing and increased the lands open for recreation. This change has hurt the ability of Mexican Americans to earn a living in their traditional manner. Some, like Reies Tijerina, have formed groups to demand the return of lands they believe were unjustly seized by the Forest Service and other Americans.

Mexican Americans believe that their rights to graze cattle on public lands were protected by the Treaty of Guadalupe Hildalgo in 1848. The park service is concerned with present land use, rather than rights gained in treaties. While the legal arguments continue, many Mexican Americans grow poorer. They claim that the honor of the U.S. government is at stake, as well as their rights and welfare. Somehow, two opposing claims must be reconciled.

The first reading, which covers the controversy and provides an historical overview of events that led to the clash, is the testimony of Tomas C. Atencio before a cabinet committee hearing on Mexican-American affairs in El Paso in 1967.

The second article, a news story from the *Los Angeles Times,* is an account of direct action against the Forest Service by Reies Tijerina, a

Mexican-American leader, and members of his group.

The Conflict Over Grazing Rights

The following statement reflects the conflicts and problems prevalent in the relationship of a traditional folk, agrarian society and an impersonal United States Government Bureau.

HISTORICAL OVERVIEW

In 1598 Don Juan de Oñate, the first New Mexican colonizer, arrived at San Juan de Los Caballeros in northern New Mexico with about one hundred and thirty Spanish soldiers. Some had their families as well as some Indian servants. A small contingency of soldiers with families arrived two years later. Battle casualties, mutinies, and mass desertions, however, reduced the original number considerably and only a few settled on the land. Until the Pueblo Revolt in 1680 that placed settlers in exile, only a few other soldiers arrived. This marked the beginning of European colonization in what is now part of the United States of America.

After the reconquest in 1692, led by Don Diego deVargas, second colonizer, the Kingdom of New Mexico began to grow. Military men and other influential leaders acquired large portions of land through the Spanish crown. Small groups of colonists were given portions of land to establish communities in the outlying areas of New Mexico.

Generally, the settlers were isolated from Mexican and Spanish influence. In the quest for survival, the colonists developed a new way of life. Spanish and Indian patterns of living began to blend as the one group established close contact with the other.

One salient pattern of living that became a very important factor in the life of the Spanish settler was his relationship to the land. The land was used for stock raising. He exploited it and carved a meager livelihood. This way of life helped the settler survive and was subsequently perpetuated. The

consequences of this attitude still prevails today. Many small subsistence farmers still depend on the land for survival—if not only for meaning in life.

While the Spanish settler and his dependents struggled for mere survival in the southwest, the Anglo-Saxon immigrant built what is now known as the United States of America. The former preserved his values and orientations to life and raised cattle and sheep for subsistence. The latter built large industries, cities, transportation systems, and the like. While New Mexico was changing hands from the Spanish to the Mexican Government in 1821, the United States continued to grow and by 1846, in effect, conquered the kingdom of New Mexico. The same population changed hands again. This time they were captives of the United States Government, having been betrayed by their own leaders. They were now subject to impositions of a new and powerful nation whose cultural orientation and social and legal systems were diametrically opposed to theirs. . . .

POINTS OF CONFLICT

Land tenure and land use are perhaps the most prominent areas in which conflict between the government bureaus and the native population of northern New Mexico exist. The traditional subsistence stock farmer continues to perceive that the land surrounding his community that was there for his ancestors, is there for him to enjoy. Forest Service officials have informed him to the contrary and have imposed procedures consistent with its own priorities.

It is not uncommon for the native population to see the forest ranger in his olive drab uniform as an American occupational trooper guarding the spoils of the Mexican-American War. The injustices of the past are manifested in the attitudes of the northern New Mexican commoner. There is an enemy in those hills. It is that forest ranger. . . .

Meanwhile, the Forest Service, responding to urban pressures for recreation, has designs for the region that are incompatible with the culture and its values. Instead of developing programs compatible with the small subsistence farming community and cottage industry, the Department of Agriculture supports large programs that increase opportunities for the native businessman and outside investors. External capital gets on a conveyor belt that passes through the region and bleeds it of its potential. The reason, again, seems to be that the Federal Bureaus respond to the business-industrial complex pressures which forces containment of rural areas for recreation purposes. The following data on estimated obligations for fiscal year 1968 provide support to the conclusion drawn above that the Forest Service places higher priority on recreation than on range management.

For Colorado, for example, $242,868 are proposed for range and re-vegetation. As opposed to range management, recreation has an appropriation of $2,433,169. In New Mexico, $240,753 are proposed for range and re-vegetation, while $1,235,823 are committed to recreation. . . . While these broad, general programs instituted through the Forest Service come in conflict with a class or group of people, there are other instances in which the individual is personally hurt. Although the Forest Service may have good reasons for their policies, the individual is seldom informed in a rational or courteous manner. Accordingly, the native New Mexican perceives Forest Service action on reduction of grazing allotments as a deliberate act to hurt the small owner. . . .

CONCLUSION

The inevitable conclusion is drawn that either the Forest Service is deliberately trying to displace the northern New Mexico resident by reducing one of his sources of livelihood or because of the Department policies that respond to urban pressures is trying to contain the Forest area to provide a recreation mecca for urban dwellers.

Side effects of the containment policy are that it hurts the native resident who is attempting to survive in the land of his choice. On the other hand, it may be that the Forest Service policy is one

of assisting everybody, including the Mexican American of northern New Mexico, but the personnel employed, for personal reasons, exploit people like the illiterate sheep rancher. The fact that the American aggressive business-industrial system is in conflict with a minority group is exemplified by the conflicts outlined above. Resolution to this conflict must be found if the Mexican American as a group in northern New Mexico is to survive. The following suggestions are recommendations and part of an attempt to improve the situation in general. . . .

New Mexico Land-Grant Rebels Found Guilty

Las Cruces, N.M.—Reies Tijerina and four of his followers, who seized a national forest campground, saying it was necessary to attract attention to their Spanish land-grant claims, were convicted by a federal jury here Saturday.

Tijerina, founder-leader of the Federal Alliance of Land Grants, was found guilty on two counts of assault for manhandling and running off two U.S. Forest Service officers at the Echo Amphitheater campground in Carson Forest on Oct. 22, 1966.

He was found innocent on two counts of converting to his own use two U.S. Forest Service pickup trucks. The jury could not agree on a fifth count, charging conspiracy, in respect to any of the defendants, and U.S. Dist. Court Judge Howard Bratton declared a mistrial on that count.

Judge Bratton continued bond of $2,000 for each defendant and set Dec. 15 for sentencing. The trial began last Monday and the jury of seven women and five men deliberated 12 hours before reaching a verdict.

While Tijerina has a minor police record, this was his first conviction on a criminal charge. The maximum penalty on each count is three years in prison and a $5,000 fine.

The jury's verdict indicated it adhered closely to the court's instructions to assess the evidence without consideration of the defendants' motivation.

Sixty percent of the defense testimony was motivational, seeking to show the underprivileged condition of Spanish-American farmers in northern New Mexico and also their long-standing grievances against the U.S. Forest Service, which controls grazing permits on national lands in their area.

Two of the defendants—Alfonso Chavez and Jerry Noll—were found guilty on four counts—two of assault and two of converting U.S. vehicles to their use—and face maximum possible sentences each of 26 years imprisonment and fines of $10,000.

Tijerina's brother Cristobal and Ezekial Dominguez were each found guilty on a single count of assault. Maximum sentence for them would be three years in prison and a fine of $5,000 each.

All five are among 10 defendants accused in the wounding of two law officers and the kidnaping of two other men during the invasion of a rural courthouse in Tierra Amarilla last June 5. The preliminary hearing in that case is set for Jan. 29.

The Grapes of Wrath: Mexican-American Style Politics

There is probably no single event in the history of Mexican Americans in the United States that focused as much international spotlight on the group as the California grape strike. This selection from *Time*, July 4, 1969, presents a fair summary of the basic issues that affect workers, growers, unions, consumers, and political leaders at local, state, and national levels.

The skillful use of established law and non-violent methods stand out as principal elements in the strike. Cesar Chavez expressed a common sentiment among many grape strikers and other Mexican Americans when he said that if you gain your goals through peaceful methods, you gain two prizes: your objective and the preservation of your freedom.

The absence of direct political action is noteworthy. Although powerful political interests are involved, the grape strike has not produced a political party, a new elected figure, or an ideology. Chavez, himself, has not tried to enter politics or to become a national public figure. Few would remember him as a failure, however. The success of the strike and boycott may lie beyond the actual economic gains. Although massive political power has been directed against the strikers, the movement has survived. This survival suggests there are elements in the American political scene that bear closer study.

The Little Strike that Grew to La Causa

ITEM: At a dinner party in New York's Westchester County, the dessert includes grapes. The hostess notices that her fellow suburbanites fall to with gusto; the guests from Manhattan unanimously abstain.

ITEM: At St. Paul's, a fashionable New Hampshire prep school, grapes are the only part of the meal invariably left, untouched.

ITEM: In San Francisco, a Safeway official observes: "We have customers who come to the store for no other reason than to buy grapes. They'll load up their car with grapes and nothing else."

ITEM: In Oakland, a conscience-ridden housewife explains apologetically to her dinner companions: "I really wanted to have this dessert, and I just decided that one little bunch of grapes wouldn't make that much difference."

ITEM: In Honolulu, the Young Americans for Freedom organizes an "emergency grape lift" by jet from the mainland, inviting "all of those starved for the sight of a California grape to come to the airport."

Why all the excitement about this smooth, sweet and innocent fruit? The answer is that the table grape, *Vitis vinifera*, has become the symbol of the four-year-old strike of California's predominantly Mexican-American farm workers. For more than a year now, table grapes have been the object of a national boycott that has won the sympathy and support of many Americans—and the ire of many others. The strike is widely known as *la causa*, which has come to represent not only a protest against working conditions among California grape pickers but the wider aspirations of the nation's Mexican minority as well. La causa's magnetic champion and the country's most prominent Mexican-American leader is Cesar Estrada Chavez, 42, a onetime grape picker who combines a mystical mien with peasant earthiness. La causa is Chavez's whole life; for it, he has impoverished himself and endangered his health by fasting. In soft, slow speech, he urges his people—nearly 5,000,000 of them in the U.S.— to rescue themselves from society's cellar. As he sees it, the first step is to win the battle of the grapes. . . .

Governor Ronald Reagan calls the strike and boycott "immoral" and "attempted blackmail." Senator George Murphy, like Reagan an old Hollywood union-man-turned-conservative terms the movement "dishonest." The Nixon Administration has seemed ambivalent, putting forward legislation that would ostensibly give farmworkers organization rights but would also limit their use of strikes and boycotts. The Pentagon has substantially increased its grape orders for mess hall tables, a move that Chavez and his followers countered last week by preparing a lawsuit to prevent such purchases on the ground that grapes are the subject of a labor dispute. Some auto-bumper stickers read: NIXON EATS GRAPES. The growers' answering slogan: EAT CALIFORNIA GRAPES, THE FORBIDDEN FRUIT. . . .

The fact that it is a movement has magnified *la huelga* far beyond the economic and geographic confines. At stake are not only the interests of 384,-100 agriculture workers in California but potentially those of more than 4,000,000 in the U.S. Such workers have never won collective-bargaining rights, partially because they have not been highly motivated to organize and partially because their often itinerant lives have made them difficult to weld into a group that would have the clout of an industrial union. By trying to organize the grape pickers, Chavez hopes to inspire militancy among all farm laborers. Because most of the grape pickers are Mexican Americans, he also believes that he is fighting a battle on behalf of the entire Mexican-American community, which as a group constitutes the nation's second biggest deprived minority. . . .

BOYCOTT AND BREAKTHROUGH

Chavez has never been able to get large numbers of laborers to join the strike. Many of those who do follow him are fanatic in their loyalty, but a large segment of the shifting, transient work force continues to be indifferent to unionism. Wages have been rising even in the absence of contracts, and few farmworkers can afford to go unpaid for long. Although federal regulations theoretically prohibit the hiring of aliens, or "green-carders," as strikebreakers, the owners have nevertheless continued to use imported workers of Mexican citizenship.

Chavez decided to resort to the boycott to keep pressure on the table-grape growers. He applied it first in 1967 to the Giumarra Vineyards Corp., the largest U.S. table-grape producer. Giumarra started using the labels of other growers—in violation of Food and Drug Administration rules—to circumvent the boycott. In retaliation, the Chavez people began to appeal to stores and consumers not to buy any California table grapes at all. The boycott has been extended overseas to Britain and Scandinavia.

Chavez has now finally achieved a breakthrough: nationwide grape sales were off 12% in 1968, and prices for this year's first California grapes are down as much as 15%. Last month ten growers representing about 12% of the state's table-grape production announced that they would sit down with Chavez to write a contract. If negotiations with Chavez succeed, some other vineyards may also sign contracts, but a determined majority still barely acknowledge his existence and remain adamantly opposed to union recognition.

If the union does begin to win contracts with an increasing number of growers, a new difficulty could arise. How is the consumer to tell the difference between union and nonunion grapes? Boxes can be labeled easily, but not loose bunches of grapes in a market. The union claims that existing boycott machinery can be turned around to promote the produce of those who have signed; they could be marketed through the chain stores that have refused to handle the produce of struck growers. However, any such confusing procedure is bound to dilute the boycott's effectiveness.

Most of the growers bitterly dispute Chavez's contentions. His claim to represent the workers is false, they say: only 3% of California's grape pickers have joined his union. Chavez has not been able to strip the fields of workers and, they argue, even if he personally preaches nonviolence, his followers do not practice it. Packing sheds have been set afire, foremen threatened, tires slashed. Chavez also has outside help. Long-haired pickets came down from Berkeley in the early days of *la huelga,* and the union gets $14,500 a month in grants from the A.F.L.-C.I.O. and Walter Reuther's United Automobile Workers. By insisting that all workers join his union, moreover, Chavez wants what amounts to a closed shop (which is illegal under the Taft-Hartley Act but the act does not apply to agricultural workers). This means that, for now at least, Chavez's goal, however unpalatable, is a legal one. Chavez opposes placing farmworkers under the National Labor Relations Board precisely because that would make the closed shop he seeks unlawful.

The growers of Delano are difficult to cast as villains. Many are self-made men, Yugoslavs and Italians, who came to the valley between 1900 and 1940 with nothing and worked hard to amass enough capital to practice the grape-growing arts they learned in Europe. Most of the Delano spreads are family enterprises, and many of them have had rough going. Costs have risen sharply over the past decade, and grape prices have now begun to decline. The California growers also pay the second highest agricultural wages in the U.S. (after Hawaii, where unionized workers average $3 an hour).

While they generally belittle the extent of his support, however, the growers have gone to some lengths to counter Chavez's moves. The anti-U.F.W.O.C. campaign even included for a time a group called Mothers Against Chavez. The growers are using the J. Walter Thompson agency to place $400,000 worth of ads extolling the benefits of table grapes. The California public relations firm of Whitaker & Baxter has been retained to advise the growers about how to counter the boycott. Whitaker & Baxter helped to manage Richard Nixon's unsuccessful campaign for governor of California in 1962, and masterminded the American Medical Association's attempt to defeat Medicare.

PLURALISM VS. THE MELTING POT

That Chavez has dramatized the problems of Mexican Americans in the city as well as on the farm seems beyond dispute. Father Bernardo Kenny, a Sacramento priest with a sizable Mexican-American congregation, believes that even if Chavez never wins his strike he will have made a "tremendous contribution." Says Kenny: "He focused attention on the problem of the farm workers, and he made the Mexican Americans proud to be Mexican Americans. Chavez must be given credit, I think, for really starting the Mexican-American civil rights movement." Ironically, mechanization hastened by unionization may eventually diminish Chavez's farm-labor base—but it will not slow the momentum of *la causa.*

The new Mexican-American militancy has turned up a mixed *piñata* of leaders, some of them significantly more strident than Chavez. In Los Angeles, 20 year-old David Sanchez is "prime minister" of the well-disciplined Brown Berets, who help keep intramural peace in the *barrio* and are setting up a free medical clinic. Some of them also carry machetes and talk tough about the Anglo. Reies Lopez Tijerina, 45, is trying to establish a "Free City State of San Joaquin" for *Chicanos* on historic Spanish land grants in New Mexico; at the moment, while his appeal on an assault conviction is being adjudicated, he is in jail for burning a sign in the Carson National Forest. Denver's Rudolfo

("Corky") Gonzales, 40, an ex-prizefighter, has started a "Crusade for Justice" to make the city's 85,000 Mexican American *la causa*-conscious.

As with the blacks, the question for those who lead the *Chicanos* is whether progress means separatism or assimilation. Cal State Professor Rafael Guzman, who helped carry out a four-year Ford Foundation study of Mexican Americans, warns that the barrio is potentially as explosive as the black ghetto. He argues for a new pluralism in the U.S. that means something other than forcing minorities into the established Anglo-Saxon mold; each group should be free to develop its own culture while contributing to the whole.

Yet there is no real consensus in the *barrio*. The forces for assimilation are powerful. A young Tucson militant, Salomon Baldenegro contends: "Our values are just like any Manhattan executive's, but we have a ceiling on our social mobility." While federal programs for bilingual instruction in Mexican-American areas are still inadequate, that kind of approach—if made readily available to all who want it—leaves the choice between separatism and assimilation ultimately to the individual *Chicano* himself. He learns in his father's tongue, but he also learns in English well enough to find that language is no longer a barrier; he retains his own culture, but he also knows enough of the majority's rules and ways to compete successfully if he chooses to do so.

Cesar Chavez has made the *Chicano's* cause well enough known to make that goal possible. While *la huelga* is in some respects a limited battle, it is also symbolic of the Mexican-American's quest for a full role in U.S. society. What happens to Chavez's farm workers will be an omen, for good or ill, of the Mexican-American's future. For the short term Chavez's most tangible aspiration is to win the fight with the grape growers. If he can succeed in that difficult and uncertain battle, he will doubtless try to expand the movement beyond the vineyards into the entire Mexican-American community.

Catolicos Por La Raza: *A Challenge to a Cardinal*

Most Mexican Americans are Roman Catholic. Like Catholics of other origins and members of other sects, they vary greatly as to attendance and support of the church.

When the U.S. took over the Southwest after the Treaty of Guadalupe Hidalgo, American Catholicism, dominated by people of New England stock, took control of the church. For the new Mexican Americans, the American-dominated church was strange and different. Nevertheless, they accepted the changes without challenging the authority of church leaders or the style, practices, or policies of the church.

In recent years, however, younger Mexican Americans have begun to challenge church policies and to demand that the church become more involved in social and economic problems confronting the Mexican-American community. One such group, *Catolicos por la Raza* (Catholics of the People), picketed St. Basil's in Los Angeles on Christmas Day in 1969. The two readings that follow are accounts from the *Los Angeles Times* of the group's confrontation with the church and the reaction of James Francis Cardinal McIntyre, the former Archbishop of the Archdiocese of Los Angeles.

Chicano-Catholic Conflict: A Split Over Philosophy

One day in early December a small, newly formed group called Catolicos por la Raza, later involved in a Christmas Eve melee at St. Basil's Roman Catholic Church, demanded that the Los Angeles archdiocese become more relevant to Mexican-American needs.

The following day, James Francis Cardinal McIntyre appeared in East Los Angeles for the groundbreaking of a 100-bed $4 million hospital that will serve a portion of the Mexican-American community. The Los Angeles prelate had pushed the project, getting president-elect Nixon to speak a year ago at a dinner at which $3.5 million was raised for the hospital.

A priest, speaking at the ground-breaking ceremony, said that when Cardinal McIntyre first came to Los Angeles in the 1940's he visited every East Side parish to learn of the needs, that he built schools and had expanded the church's welfare work in the area.

"In coming to Los Angeles," added Cardinal McIntyre in his talk, "my first commission was to serve, and serve well, the Mexican people."

Now, while archdiocesan leaders appear confident that they continue to serve well the material and spiritual needs of the vast majority of the Mexican-American community, the Catolicos por la Raza has challenged the cardinal's conservative approach to economic and educational problems and social-political issues.

"The church teaches us to fight for the poor," said Ricardo Cruz, a co-chairman of CLR. "We need priests like Father Mark Day (a chaplain and aide to farm worker organizer Cesar Chavez), Father James Groppi (a militant civil rights leader in Milwaukee), and Bishop Antulio Parrilla."

SAYS MASS IN VACANT LOT

Bishop Parrilla celebrated Mass in a vacant lot near St. Basil's Church last Sunday in commiseration with the CLR's cause. The Puerto Rican bishop on tour of the United States is sponsored by an organization called Clergy and Laymen Concerned About Vietnam. Bishop Parrilla, currently without a diocese, teaches in Ponce, Puerto Rico.

A study of the archdiocese's defense of its health, education, and welfare work in Spanish-speaking communities and the demands of the CLR and sympathetic Anglo groups shows that the difference lies in the contrasting philosophies of what the role the church should be in the community.

The exception might be in education. There the question is posed by the activists: "Is the church doing all it can?"

Educational demands include parochial schools that do not charge tuition, church-subsidized expenses for educational needs through graduate school and bilingual classes in Catholic schools.

The archdiocese notes that it built 206 schools between 1948 and 1963, it has the Don Bosco training school in East Los Angeles, and it has promoted and supplied facilities for a bilingual adult education program established in San Fernando and East Los Angeles by the Los Angeles City Schools.

Tuition is waived in Catholic schools for families who cannot afford the costs, archdiocesan school officials say. The CLR's Cruz, on the other hand, said he knows of families that cannot really afford tuition but pay it anyhow.

The archdiocese recently announced it operated its schools in four counties in the last school year on a $9 million deficit, making up the amount not covered by tuition from other collections . . .

MOSTLY PHILOSOPHICAL

On other questions, the differences between the archdiocesan leaders and the church reformers are mostly philosophical.

"The true nature of our protest," Cruz said, "is that we want the Catholic Church to identify with the struggle of our people to obtain self-determination and to give us spiritual leadership."

CLR's set of demands urged the church leaders to support Cesar Chavez's United Farm Workers Organizing Committee and its grape boycott, to support efforts for educational improvement and to support the anti-war movement.

While Cardinal McIntyre and other Catholic bishops in California have issued statements supporting the right of farm workers to organize, the cardinal has not publicly supported the grape boycott and has not supported liberal-to-radical causes.

Msgr. William R. Johnson, director of the Catholic Welfare Bureau, said Tuesday he thinks the distinction in the current controversy is that "we function along the line of service and development as opposed to trying to change the power structure through building up massive public support for particular issues."

Oscar Acosta, another spokesman for the Mexican-American group, said that whenever a community group wants to take a clergyman with them to see a police board or other organization with a grievance "we have to go to a Protestant minister."

Allowing more community members to be involved in the church decision-making is still another demand.

The archdiocese, in turn, has described in the last two years instances of greater participation by Spanish-speaking Catholics in church affairs, plus the assignment of community organizers to East Los Angeles and the formation of a parish priests' group in East Los Angeles to keep the chancery informed of the area's needs.

As for the desire to make the church more democratic, archdiocesan spokesmen in the past have said that the church cannot be compared to political democracy.

"There is no question that we are sympathetic to the needs and desires of the community," said Msgr. Johnson. "We don't feel every institution including ours, is perfect; they are all subject to change and we are happy to work with them."

Four CLR representatives who met with Cardinal McIntyre at the chancery before Christmas, however, said they came away convinced that the archdiocese would not make any significant changes in direction.

In housing, the group said the church should establish a community-controlled lending agency to approve loans and grants for home building and repair and should create an agency to build low-cost housing.

The archdiocese's response often has been that the church is not in the housing business although it has been noted that the San Francisco archdiocese has recently participated in a low-cost housing project and some other dioceses have done likewise.

The extensive social, health, and community work of the archdiocese's Catholic Welfare Bureau, which is funded primarily by the United Way in Los Angeles County, has been criticized in the activist Chicano community as charitable, often paternalistic work.

"For example, the Catholic Charities," said an article in the monthly newspaper *La Raza,* "has millions of dollars earmarked for the poor. But often the money is spent for food baskets for the needy instead of for effective action to eradicate the cause of poverty."

Church spokesmen argue they contribute heavily to solving basic problems, citing their transferral in the last six years of more than $13 million from affluent parishes to poorer parishes in the four-county archdiocese to keep the inner-city parishes in the black.

DISBURSEMENTS LISTED

The Archbishops' Fund for Charity disbursed a record $313,833 during the past year to cover services not covered by United Way and Community Chest.

Cruz and Acosta said they were aware of many of the church's programs. But they said the church still should spend more money in Spanish-speaking areas and promote Mexican-American Catholics into the hierarchy—commensurate with the high percentage of such Catholics in the Southwest. The CLR and Anglo sympathizers also feel the church should identify with their socio-economic causes with the same vigor that it has opposed liberal abortion laws and urged state aid to Catholic schools.

The group's methods of drawing attention to its demands, however, prompted archdiocesan priest John Urban to characterize it last Sunday as "an articulate, professionally organized minority (plotting) revolution."

Msgr. Johnson put it more mildly: "There is some question about the methods they want to solve some of these problems. I think they desire the church to be a militant social action agent, which it has not been."

Cardinal Forgives Mexican-American Demonstrators

James Francis Cardinal McIntyre, in a letter Wednesday to the militant Catolicos por la Raza, said he could forgive the demonstrators involved in a Christmas confrontation, but would not have sought dismissal of charges against those arrested.

Charges of disrupting a religious meeting were dropped Tuesday in Municipal Court, pending further investigation, against one woman and three men arrested at St. Basil's Catholic Church during a Christmas Mass. The four were the only members of the group arrested that night.

Richard Cruz, a co-chairman of the Mexican-American group and a Loyola University School of Law student, had written Cardinal McIntyre Dec. 26, giving his account of the group's actions and asking the prelate to forgive them and seek dismissal of charges.

The cardinal wrote that he forgave the demonstrators "who are truly sorry for this regrettable occurrence" and would repeat the prayer he had made at the Christmas Mass, imploring God's forgiveness.

Cardinal McIntyre had told the St. Basil's congregation that the conduct of the demonstrators had been comparable to the "rabble" at Jesus' crucifixion, but that they should be forgiven, "for they know not what they do."

However, the cardinal wrote that "under no circumstances would we interfere with the performance of duty by the police and other officers of the government in prosecuting persons charged with crimes."

The cardinal also warned Cruz of setting in motion forces that cannot be controlled.

Promoting Prejudice Through Advertising

Professional politicians say that people vote against something more often than for something. The same might apply to candidates as well as issues. Where two otherwise equally qualified candidates come before the public, does the minority or majority candidate have an advantage? What people know about others depends greatly on the media. This selection points to the social and political impact which the media has in shaping the opinions one group of people has about another.

Advertising is one of the most common methods by which the public is taught prejudice about Mexican Americans. Daily, millions of people see magazine ads or T.V. commercials where products are sold by making fun of Mexicans. They have been commonly pictured as fat, lazy, dirty, comical, or as thieves. The use of Mexicans in such a way in advertising makes an impression on both old and young who may not know a Mexican in person. The commercial image of Mexican inferiority is all too often transferred to Mexican Americans.

Advertisers have, of course, denied that they intend to teach prejudice, and they point to the comical use of people of many other nationalities. In spite of the denials, however, the U.S. Civil Rights Commission has charged that prejudice is taught through advertising that pictures Mexicans in ways listed in the following selection.

Promoting Racism: A Partial Listing

	The Medium	The Message
Granny Goose	†*Fat Mexican toting guns, ammunition	Mexicans = overweight, carry deadly weapons
Frito-Lay	†*"Frito Bandito"	Mexicans = sneaky, thieves
Liggett & Meyers	*"Paco" never "feenishes" anything, not even revolution	Mexicans = too lazy to improve selves

A. J. Reynolds	*Mexican bandito	Mexicans = bandits
Camel Cigarettes	*"Typical, Mexican village all sleeping or bored	Mexicans = do nothings, irresponsible
General Motors	†*White, rustic man holding three Mexicans at gunpoint	Mexicans = should be and can be arrested by superior white man
Lark (Liggett & Meyers)	†Mexican house painter covered with paint	Mexicans = sloppy workers, undependable
Philco-Ford	†*Mexican sleeping next to TV set	Mexicans = always sleeping
Frigidaire	*Mexican banditos interested in freezer	Mexicans = thieves seeking Anglo artifacts
Arrid	*Mexican bandito sprays underarm, voice says, "If it works for him, it will work for you."	Mexicans = stink the most

† = newspaper or magazine ad
* = TV commercial

Mexican Americans Form a New Political Party

Many young Mexican Americans believe that a new political party must be established because other parties have failed to serve their needs. The issue raises much heat because vested interests feel threatened by such a development. The issue frequently divides older and younger Mexican Americans, as it does others, who differ on the value of existing parties.

The GI generation returned from World War II with a desire to join the system and gain acceptance as equals, if not full assimilation. The Chicano generation of today includes those who champion separatism. They may or may not be correct in their analysis of practical considerations, but the effort is provocative.

Mexican Americans differ over how they can gain a voice in our government institutions. In Las Vegas, New Mexico, Spanish Americans elected all Mexican-American members to the city council in 1970, after Anglo Americans had dominated it since 1948. In addition, the New Mexico Highlands University in that city gained its first Spanish-American president in 1971. All this was accomplished through greater civic involvement with little political party activity as such. Differences in conditions locally may be as important as ideology or institutional factors in explaining how the past has shaped the present. Proponents of *La Raza Unida* Party are charting a new course for the future, similar, in some respects, to that of the American Independent Party. By 1972, several local elections in Texas and California were decided by the margin of votes cast by voters of this new party.

The origins of La Raza Unida Party are in South Texas. It has spread to other states since it was formed in 1970. In Texas, its members gained control of the City Council and the Board of Education of Crystal City. These victories have affected other places where young Mexican Americans seek more political power.

Jose Angel Gutierrez is the leading figure in the formation of La Raza Unida Party. The following excerpts from a speech he recently made display some ideas he believes in and his opinions of how Chicanos or Mexican Americans fit into our political scene.

Mexicanos Need to
Control Their Own Destinies

As you know, there is a new political party in Southwest Texas. It's called *La Raza Unida* Party. The history of this party is rather interesting.

For years the Chicano farmworker has made up the majority of the population in the South Texas counties. But he goes trucking across this country on his summer vacation (laughter), and so he's never there to vote. Yet this is precisely the time the primaries are held—in May. And he is already vacationing in his resort area by the time the runoffs are held in June. So, you see, we are in fact not even able to vote.

We have had other problems which we have known about for a long time. For instance, the fact that the Mexicano can't cope with the culture of the monolingual creatures that abound in South Texas. You see, we're literate in Spanish, so we can't recognize the name of John Waltberger on the ballot, but we sure as ——— recognize Juan Garcia. (Laughter)

Supposedly in this kind of a democratic society the citizenry is encouraged to participate in the political process—but not so in South Texas.

Someone asked me recently whether I thought any type of system other than the American political system could work in South Texas. I thought about it for a minute and suggested that the question be reworded because we ought to try the American system first. (Applause)

They accuse me and Mexicanos in Cristal [Crystal City], in Cotulla and Carrizo Springs, of being unfair. One gringo lady put it very well. She was being interviewed around April 6, right after the school board elections and before the city council elections. The guy from *Newsweek* asked her to explain the strange phenomena that were occurring in these counties: a tremendous voter turnout and a tremendous amount of bloc voting. She said, "Well, this is just terrible! Horrible! A few days ago we elected a bunch of bum Mexicans to the city council." And the reporter said, "Well, they are 85 percent of this county." And she replied, "That's what I mean! They think they ought to run this place!". . .

The formation of this party came about because of the critical need for the people to experience justice. It's just like being hungry. You've got to get food in there immediately, otherwise you get nauseous, you get headaches and pains in your stomach.

We were Chicanos who were starved for any kind of meaningful participation in decision making, policy making and leadership positions. For a long time we have not been satisfied with the type of leadership that has been picked for us. . . .

These parties, or party, have traditionally picked our leadership. They have transformed this leadership into a kind of broker, a real estate guy who deals in the number of votes or precincts he can deliver or the geographical areas he can control. And he is a tape recorder—he puts out what the party says. . . .

You know, civil rights are not just for those under 21. They're for everybody—for grandma, for daddy and mama, and *los chamaquitos* [children] and *primos* [cousins] and sisters, and so on. We've all got to work together. That means that all of us have to pitch in. And this is why in Crystal City you no longer hear "Viva La Raza" and "Chicano Power" and "La Raza Unida" all over the place. We don't talk about it anymore because it's a reality. You see, there *la familia mexicana esta organizada* [the Mexican family is organized]. Aztlan has begun in the southwest part of Texas. . . .

You have three choices. First, you can be very active in this thing. For once we are not talking about being anti-Democratic or pro-Republican or pro-Democrat and anti-Republican. We are talking about being for La Raza, the majority of the people in South Texas. So there are a lot of things you can do and be very actively involved in.

If you don't choose that route, you can stay home and watch baseball and just come out and vote. But otherwise stay home. Don't get in the way.

The third thing you can do is lend your support, your general agreement. Often we are too critical of ourselves, and the gringo misunderstands that. He says, "You're disorganized, there's no unity among you." He can't understand an honest discussion when he hears one.

So, you've got these three roles that you can play. Or you can get very, very defensive and say, "This is wrong, this is un-American because you're bloc voting." But don't forget that the Democrats do it too. You can say that this is racism in reverse, but don't forget that we are the majority. And you can say that this is going to upset the whole situation in the state of Texas because we will never be able to elect a senator, because we're segregating ourselves and cutting ourselves apart and that this is not what we should be trying to do, that we should be trying to integrate, etc., etc. . . .

Build your constituency, build your community —that's how we will be electing three and possibly four congressmen in the very near future. There's going to be another congressman in Bexar County, and there's not room for all of them on the North side [Anglo section of San Antonio]. (Laughter and applause) So we have some very interesting developments coming up. . . .

The Lettuce Boycott: A National Political Issue

On July 13, 1972, Senator Edward M. Kennedy opened an address before the Democratic National Convention in Miami with these words: "Mr. Chairman, delegates, and fellow lettuce boycotters." Senator Kennedy's remark about lettuce boycotters referred to the fact that thousands upon thousands of Americans were trying to help Cesar Chavez and the United Fruit Workers in their negotiations with lettuce growers in the Salinas Valley of California and in parts of Arizona. These Americans were trying to help by refusing to buy iceberg lettuce.

In addition to the remark by Senator Kennedy, the lettuce boycott was mentioned time and time again by speakers from various delegations to the convention. The attention the boycott received is

a tribute to Mr. Chavez and thousands of Mexican-American farm workers, who, only a few years ago, were fighting a lonely and what sometimes seemed like a hopeless battle in their efforts to achieve decent wages and decent working conditions.

Although Woody Guthrie, Lois Hudson, Michael Harrington, Dorothy Day, and Deane Mary Mowrer have written poignantly of the conditions of Mexican-American migrants in California, the plight of these workers remained largely unknown until the workers themselves began to risk their meager livelihoods and strike against the growers.

In spite of threats, harassment, and deprivation that, at times, almost reached starvation for some, they courageously persisted, and soon they had sympathy and support from all over the nation. The Delano grape strike and the subsequent nationwide boycott focused international spotlight on the deplorable wages and living conditions of migrants.

Although many Americans, including such prominent ones as Senator Kennedy, have come to the support of Mexican-American farm workers, it is the workers themselves who must be given much of the credit for the gains they have made. It was their courage, their persistence, and their willingness to suffer hardships and deprivation that made such gains possible.

While the grape workers and other farm laborers have made gains, unfortunately, there are some Mexican-American farm workers who have not, and the lettuce boycott focuses attention on this fact. The average annual wage of the migrants who harvest lettuce is less than $2400.

The first selection about the lettuce boycott and the conditions that led up to it is from the *New York Post*. The letter from Cesar Chavez is from *The Catholic Worker*.

Delegates: No Lettuce

During the Democratic National Convention, nationwide television attention was often focused on a side issue which might be described as a recipe for Cesar (Chavez) Salad: no lettuce.

Organizers of the Chavez-led lettuce boycott are hoping that the free publicity given the campaign by delegation after delegation by convention stars such as Sen. Kennedy will revitalize it.

The boycotters are setting their sights on the same 200 growers of iceberg or crisp-head lettuce primarily in the "salad bowl" of the Salinas Valley in California and parts of Arizona, who refuse to bargain with the United Farm Workers of America.

Growers in the far west produce some 85 percent of the entire iceberg lettuce market. The boycott does not include the other longer-leaved and greener varieties of lettuce which are more nutritious than iceberg: Boston, romaine and bibb lettuce, escarole, endive and other green vegetables.

IMPOSSIBLE TO DIFFERENTIATE

Some six growers of iceberg lettuce have already signed union contracts, but boycott organizers are urging consumers to avoid buying any iceberg lettuce at all.

"A very small amount of union lettuce is coming into the city," said Jose Gomez, the boycott's New York State coordinator. "And, in most cases, it's impossible for the shopper to tell if the lettuce he's buying is union or nonunion."

The boycott first began two years ago, but a moratorium was declared in April, 1971, when the growers agreed to negotiate. Two months ago, the talks broke down and the boycott was resumed.

Organizers here says the campaign will soon enter a new phase, from mere concentration on winning consumer support to applying pressure on food chains to boycott scab lettuce.

Such tactics as picketing stores and other demonstrations may be used.

The price of lettuce has been going down recently but it's hard to tell whether this is a·result of the boycott or of weather and seasonal factors. Union spokesmen here declined to assess the impact of the boycott since it was resumed but spokesmen for the merchants said it was minimal.

UNAFFECTED

"I've gotten just one letter from the members on it," said Clarence Adamy of the National Food Merchants.

In addition, an Associated Press survey of supermarket chains across the country showed the boycott thus far was having little effect.

Adamy called the boycott "like all secondary boycotts, immoral, indecent and improper."

Wholesalers at the Bronx's Hunts Point Market agreed that boycott was ineffective.

Union organizers, however, urge patience.

"When we plan for a boycott we plan for a couple of years," said international boycott director Marshall Ganz. "The success of the boycott depends on reaching many, many Americans and convincing them not to eat lettuce."

WAYS VS. PRICES

UFWA spokesmen stress that unionization of the farm workers would benefit the consumer too since, in their contract demands, they insist that the growers not use certain poisonous pesticides and that they provide field toilet and hand-washing facilities for the workers, insuring more sanitary crops.

Furthermore, they claim, as of now only one penny of each 29 cents for a head of lettuce goes to the farm worker.

"Theoretically," Gomez said, "You could double the laborer's wage, which is not likely to happen, and still the price would only go up one penny. But we still don't advocate that the increase be passed along to the consumer.

A Letter from Cesar Chavez

As the lettuce boycott began, Cesar Chavez started a fast for the "spirit of justice" in connection with the plight of the farm workers who harvest lettuce. On May 11, 1972, he sent the following letter to farm workers and the supporters of the farm workers' cause.

147

Dear Brothers and Sisters:

Our people have been poor for more years than we can remember. We have made only a small amount of progress these past ten years of work and struggle. Our women and children still die too often and too young. There is too much hunger and disease among us. Not even 5% of America's migrant farm workers are protected by union contracts. Yet there is a great fear of our union—a fear that I do not fully understand, but that I know is present with most growers and especially among the lettuce growers in their current resistance to the rights of their workers. Growers through the Farm Bureau are seeking to bring the whole machinery of government against us. Why are they so afraid of a union for migrant farm workers?

In Arizona—one of two major lettuce producing states—the growers and the politicians have just passed a law that destroys the right of farm workers to have a union. Farm workers under this law cannot engage in consumer boycotts. Supporters of our union could be arrested for telling their friends not to buy lettuce. Farm workers are put in the humiliating position of having to go to a special Agricultural Labor Relations Board (appointed by Republican Governor Jack Williams) for a government-conducted election to determine their right to strike. The law provides for union representation elections but establishes so many steps and procedures that seasonal and migrant workers would never have a chance to vote. Growers can not only frustrate an election for 2–3 months, they can actually avoid elections by a minor change in hiring practices. Even if workers should vote for the union, an employer can seek a decertification election after only a 3 month waiting period. The bill is discriminatory. It is aimed only at farm workers who are mostly Black, Brown and Indian. No other labor force is asked to live with these repressive measures. This is what the Farm Bureau means when they advocate "free elections" and "responsible legislation."

Farm workers in Arizona tried to tell their legislators about the unfairness of this law. They collected letters and petitions and brought them to their representatives. They were met with cold indifference. They were patient but could not get appointments. In many cases, their letters were thrown into trash cans in front of their eyes. After the bill passed, it was brought to the Governor by the Highway Patrol. He signed it immediately. The next day the Governor was asked by a reporter to comment on the farm workers who wanted to meet with him. He responded: "As far as I'm concerned, these people do not exist."

What is it that causes sane men to act so hastily and so cruelly? It cannot be that we are so powerful. In the context of the great corporations, we are like a mosquito on an elephant's back.

This attack on our union in Arizona and in every major state is also an attack on the spirit of justice in America. Why shouldn't farm workers finally have a chance to hold their heads high in their own organization? Why shouldn't there be food on the tables of the families who work so hard to harvest that food?

My major concern is not this particular Arizona law and the fast is not out of anger against the growers. My concern is the spirit of fear that lies behind such laws in the hearts of growers and legislators across the country. Somehow these powerful men and women must be helped to realize that there is nothing to fear from treating their workers as fellow human beings. We do not seek to destroy the growers. We only wish an opportunity to organize our union and to work non-violently to bring a new day of hope and justice to the farm workers of our country. It is long overdue and surely it is not too much to ask. Justice for farm workers is our only goal; it is the goal of our non-violent lettuce boycott. Will you help us by making a commitment not to eat or buy lettuce? This is a small sacrifice that can bring a great change for migrant farm workers. I ask for your prayers and your continued help in our struggle.

Your brother,
Cesar E. Chavez

POCHO AND CHICANO CULTURE

Pocho is a term used by Mexicans to describe Mexican Americans. It implies that the *pocho* is neither Mexican nor American and is used in a negative manner. Mexican citizens have mixed feelings about Mexican Americans. Often, their attitudes seem to be a mixture of envy, admiration, and resentment. Except for kin, many Mexicans consider Mexican Americans sort of traitors to the motherland. Such feelings are probably pretty much like those of the relatives of Americans elsewhere. The proximity of Mexico and the special history of the two people accentuates such feelings and attitudes.

Mexican Americans started to build a new culture after 1848. Much of this story essentially remains untold, but, as more and more about the unique culture of Mexican Amerians comes to light, it focuses attention on the inescapable fact that most Mexican Americans are neither wholly Mexican nor American.

Readings in this section reveal the many ways in which Mexican Americans are finding a path between the Anglo and Mexican worlds. Much of what they are borrows from both worlds. Their speech, which often mixes both tongues and forms new words in the process, makes linguistic purists claim they speak neither language. So, too, with other elements in their culture. Obviously, there are some who deplore the mixture, but many, especially among younger Mexican Americans, contend that the mixture can produce a worthwhile and viable culture.

Today, Mexican Americans are shaping a new self-image, free from Mexican and Anglo-American concepts. Thus, *pocho* is rejected as a negative Mexican term, and *Mexican American* is losing popularity because of its Anglo-American sociological origins. *Chicano* appears to grow more popular all the time as a general term for all Mexican Americans. Like Negroes who have redefined blackness into something positive with such reflections as "Black is beautiful," so, too, young Mexican Americans have taken *Chicano,* an old Mexican slang term with a negative meaning, and transformed it into something admirable by simply saying that is what it means. *Chicano,* then, is replacing *Mexican American* as a term, and it reflects a state of mind, as well. This change in terms was clearly evident among Mexican Americans by 1970, and it gained acceptance by many other Americans, as well.

This section will examine major areas of social change in which Mexican Americans have taken a role. Changes in their life and self-image of the Mexican American affect the nation as a whole and point to trends for the future.

The Pachuco as a Mexican-American Type

Pachucos were perhaps the first Mexican American generation to break with the past. The so-called generation gap in America today bears many resemblances to the Pachuco movement of the 1940's.

Octavio Paz in *The Labyrinth of Solitude: Life and Thought in Mexico* has tried to interpret how the Mexican thinks and feels, as compared to other people. He also has interpreted how the young Mexican American felt about life in the United States during the period of the Second World War (1939–1945). His opinions about Mexican American youth arouse controversy, but they also help us to understand Mexican Americans a little better.

The "Pachuco," as a type of Mexican American youth, was a common term for several years. Both young men and young women formed new ways to talk, walk, and live. They also dressed differently in their effort to reject traditions and form something better for themselves. In the 1960's the hippie movement contained many similar elements to "pachuquismo," or the pachuco way of life. Adults and youths saw this question in opposing lights. Pachucos were not juvenile delinquents, but some delinquents gave a bad name to pachucos by using their style and manners. Pachucos were Mexican American youngsters who felt the impact of having to live in two worlds—the Anglo American and the Mexican American barrio.

The Pachuco

When I arrived in the United States I lived for a while in Los Angeles, a city inhabited by over a million persons of Mexican origin. At first sight, the visitor is surprised not only by the purity of the sky and the ugliness of the dispersed and ostentatious buildings, but also by the city's vaguely Mexican atmosphere, which cannot be captured in words or concepts. This Mexicanism—delight in decorations, carelessness and pomp, negligence, passion, and reserve—floats in the air. I say "floats" because it never mixes or unites with the other world, the North American world based on precision and efficiency. It floats, without offering any opposition; it hovers, blown here and there by wind, sometimes breaking up like a cloud, sometimes standing erect like a rising skyrocket. It creeps, it wrinkles, it expands and contracts; it sleeps or dreams; it is ragged, but beautiful. It floats, never quite vanishing.

Something of the same sort characterizes the Mexicans you see in the streets. They have lived in the city for many years, wearing the same clothes and speaking the same language as the other inhabitants, and they feel ashamed of their origin, yet no one would mistake them for authentic North Americans. I refuse to believe that physical features are as important as is commonly thought. What distinguishes them, I think, is their furtive, restless air: they act like persons who are wearing disguises, who are afraid of a stranger's look because it could strip them and leave them stark naked. When you talk with them, you observe that their sensibilities are like a pendulum, but a pendulum that has lost its reason and swings violently and erratically back and forth. This spiritual condition, or lack of a spirit, has given birth to a type known as the pachuco. The pachucos are youths, for the most part of Mexican origin, who form gangs in Southern cities; they can be identified by their language and behavior as well as by the clothing they affect. They are instinctive rebels, and North American racism has vented its wrath on them more than once. But the pachucos do not attempt to vindicate their race or the nationality of their forebears. Their attitude reveals an obstinate, almost fanatical will-to-be, but this will affirms nothing specific except their determination—it is an ambiguous one, as we will see—not to be like those around them. The pachuco does not want to become a Mexican again; at the same time he does not want to blend into the life of North America. His whole being is sheer negative impulse, a tangle of contradictions, an enigma. Even his very name is enigmatic: pachuco, a word of uncertain derivation, saying nothing and saying everything. It is a strange word with no definite meaning; or, to be more exact, it is charged like all popular creations with a diversity of meanings. Whether we like it or not, these persons are Mexicans, and one of the extremes at which the Mexican can arrive.

Since the pachuco cannot adapt himself to a civilization which, for its part, rejects him, he finds no answer to the hostility surrounding him except this angry affirmation of his personality. Other groups react differently. The Negroes, for example, oppressed by racial intolerance, try to "pass as whites" and thus enter society. They want to be like other people. The Mexicans have suffered a less violent rejection, but instead of attempting a problematical adjustment to society, the pachuco actually flaunts his differences. The purpose of his grotesque dandyism and anarchic behavior is not so much to point out the injustice and incapacity of a society that has failed to assimilate him as it is to demonstrate his personal will to remain different.

It is not important to examine the causes of this conflict, and even less so to ask whether or not it has a solution. There are minorities in many parts of the world who do not enjoy the same opportunities as the rest of the population. The important thing is this stubborn desire to be different, this anguished tension with which the lone Mexican —an orphan lacking both protectors and positive values—displays his differences. The pachuco has lost his whole inheritance: language, religion, customs, beliefs. He is left with only a body and a soul with which to confront the elements, defenseless against the stares of everyone. His disguise is a protection, but it also differentiates and isolates him.

The pachuco tries to enter North American society in secret and daring ways, but he impedes his own efforts. Having been cut off from his traditional culture, he asserts himself for a moment as a solitary and challenging figure. He denies both the society from which he originated and that of North America. When he thrusts himself outward, it is not to unite with what surrounds him but rather to defy it. This is a suicidal gesture, because the pachuco does not affirm or defend anything except his ex-

asperated will-not-to-be. He is not divulging his most intimate feelings; he is revealing an ulcer, exhibiting a wound. A wound that is also a grotesque, capricious, barbaric adornment. A wound that laughs at itself and decks itself out for the hunt. The pachuco is the prey of society, but instead of hiding he adorns himself to attract the hunter's attention. Persecution redeems him and breaks his solitude: his salvation depends on his becoming a part of the very society he appears to deny. Solitude and sin, communion and health become synonymous terms. . . .

Inequality Under Law and Other Problems of Mexican Americans in the 1940's: An Anglo's View

During recent struggles that various minorities have waged for civil rights, one complaint has been fairly common—inequality under the law. Many private organizations and governmental agencies have collected reports to document claims that members of minorities have made against the law enforcement officers for illegal arrests, brutality, harassment, or failure to protect them.

Few single events could more dramatically illustrate a common complaint of many members of minorities against public servants paid to protect them than the account of the riots in Los Angeles in 1943. The selection, which is from *North from Mexico* by Carey McWilliams, is preceded by another reading from Mr. McWilliams—testimony he gave before the Los Angeles Grand Jury less than a year before the riots about other injustices which Mexican Americans suffer. At the time he testified, Mr. McWilliams was Chief of California's Division of Immigration and Housing.

Testimony of Carey McWilliams Before the Los Angeles County Grand Jury

Speaking at a meeting in Los Angeles on September 16, 1942, Vice-President Henry Wallace declared that nowhere is Mexican-American friendship more strikingly demonstrated than in California. "The present offers a unique case here in California," he said, "of what might have been a sore spot, but which actually has become instead a fusion ground of two cultures."

No one entertains a greater admiration for Vice-President Wallace than I do, but, in this case, it seems to me that the wish was father to the thought. While California, for historical and geographical reasons, should be a place where the two major cultures of the Western Hemisphere have fused, such, most emphatically, is not the case. I mention this at the outset because it seems to me that the problem of Mexican youth in Los Angeles County is, in the widest sense of the term, a problem of cultural conflict.

California not only might have been, as Mr. Wallace notes, a "sore spot" but, in point of fact, it actually presents just such a situation. The reason that I stress "cultural conflict" as being at the root of our local problem is, that I know of no scientific warrant for the doctrine that there is any biological predisposition on the part of any race toward certain types of behavior.

Dr. Ruth Benedict, one of our leading anthropologists, has said that: "Man is not committed in detail by his biological constitution to any particular variety of behavior." "Culture," as she notes, "is not a biologically transmitted complex."

Even the very term "race" has generally come to be regarded as being almost meaningless. Tendencies toward certain types of behavior are to be found, not in the bloodstream of a people, but in their cultural heritage. Cultural conflicts produce certain patterns of behavior, not only in individuals but in groups, and these patterns of behavior have been carefully studied of recent years. There are, in fact, recognized techniques for dealing with the varied problems which result from such conflicts. Only the most unfortunate consequences, therefore, are likely to flow from any misguided attempt to stress allegedly "biological factors" in such a problem.

Our local problem, in truth, is merely one aspect of a much larger national problem. This becomes immediately apparent when the question is asked: Just how large is the Mexican population in the United States? Due to incomplete methods used by census enumerators, it is impossible to give exact totals, but certain figures can be cited. In 1940, according to the census, there were 1,861,400 white persons in the United States who listed Spanish as their mother tongue, mother tongue being defined as the principal foreign language, if any, spoken in the home of the person in his earliest childhood. Even this enumeration, in my judgment, falls far short of the total number of persons who might be called Mexican, at least in the sociological sense.

For example, the National Resources Planning Board has placed the total as high as 3,500,000. In any case, the total constitutes a sizable part of our population; a proportion that is likely to increase in relation to the general population in the future; and a proportion, by reason of its concentration, which is quite high in certain states.

Generally speaking, there are two major divisions or categories into which resident Spanish-speaking groups fall: First, the long-resident Spanish-speaking or so-called Spanish-Colonial population; and, second, the immigrant group, or those who have entered this country, say, since 1900.

The Spanish-Colonial group is largely located in New Mexico and the San Luis Valley of Colorado. Over 51 percent of the population of New Mexico is of Spanish or Mexican descent; both Spanish and English are official languages in New Mexico. Many of these New Mexicans are the direct descendants of the original Spanish colonists and, as such, they represent families who have lived in New Mexico for upwards of three hundred years. Yet so deeply rooted is Spanish culture in the area that, to this day, most of these people still speak Spanish and know very little English.

The immigrant group however is numerically much more important. For example, it is generally estimated that between 1900 and 1930, about one million immigrants from Mexico entered this country. Some 300,000 are supposed to have returned during the depression, which would leave the present total of the immigrant group at around 700,000. Many of these original immigrants have, however, lived in this country for long periods of time; ten, fifteen, twenty, and thirty years. And a great many of them, of course, have American-born children.

Getting back to the census figures for 1940: These figures show 416,140 Spanish-speaking people in California. Of this total, 136,700 were listed as foreign-born; 215,740 were listed as native-white, foreign, or mixed parentage; and 63,700 were listed as native-white, native-parentage.

The figures for the City of Los Angeles were as follows: 107,680—of whom 38,040 were foreign-born, 51,280 were of native-white, foreign, or mixed parentage, and 18,360 were listed as native-white, native-parentage.

These figures for California, as well as similar figures for Texas, indicate that both states have a heavy percentage of the immigrant Spanish-speaking group. The percentage of Mexican immigrants in both states is much higher, for example, than in New Mexico, where nearly 90 percent of the Spanish-speaking people fall within the native-white, native-parentage category.

In 1933 President Hoover's Research Committee on Social Trends in the United States (Vol. 1, p. 562), had this comment to make of the Mexican immigrant group: "Since the Mexicans are the newest of the large immigrant groups, there has not been sufficient time to rear a large second generation born of parents of this nationality."

This comment, you will note, was made as recently as 1933. In other words, we are just beginning now, in 1942, to feel the impact of this second-generation problem in the Mexican group. It is for this reason that most of the rather elaborate studies of the Mexican problem made between 1920 and 1930 fail to deal with the second-generation problem, for during these years it had not yet assumed major proportions.

The general pattern of the second-generation problem among immigrant groups has long been recognized. The root of the problem is not traceable to the mere fact that a child happens to have parents who were born outside this country. The problem is created, as Dr. Florence Cassidy has said, "by social conditions and attitudes which make the child constantly aware of a sense of difference. It is intensified when children grow up in families having standards quite at variance with the standards which the children see in the world outside their homes; when they are subjected to and at the same time rebel against a kind of home discipline that tends to become more and more authoritative as the parents feel their own position socially and economically less and less secure. As a result the children often copy the things that are least lovely in American life and discard the things that are best in their own nationality community, on the theory that by so doing they will gain status in the American community. The problem grows in acuteness according to whether the child belongs to a nationality group or to a family which seems conspicuously different from the general pattern of American life about him. Conversely, the problem is least acute in nationalities whose manners and customs are most like our own." (When Peoples Meet, 1940).

Applying what Dr. Cassidy says to the situation in Los Angeles County, it is immediately apparent that certain factors exist which naturally make for an acute second-generation Mexican problem. There is, in the first place, the matter of color differentiation. Mexicans are listed in the census as "white persons" and, ethnically, there is no doubt but that the classification is correct. Nevertheless, it must be recognized that many Mexicans have what might be called a degree of color visibility.

And as Dr. Robert E. Park of the University of Chicago has said: "The races of high visibility are the natural and inevitable objects of race prejudice." Not only are Mexican youngsters victimized by this degree of visibility, or physical difference, but, in point of time, their parents were recent immigrants to this country. The parents come from a cultural background which is to be sharply distinguished from that in this country. Inherent in this situation, therefore, are possibilities for conflict. These possibilities are much more pronounced among Mexicans as a group than they would be, say, among a group of English immigrants.

You will note also that Dr. Cassidy stressed that it was social conditions and attitudes which, to a large extent, created the second-generation problem. Generally speaking the social conditions that prevail in typical Mexican settlements in California are most deplorable.

I want to read you a brief report which I received from one of our inspectors in the Division of Immigration and Housing. It is dated March 26, 1942, and refers to a Mexican settlement in Los Angeles County. The report reads:

"There were 156 cottages containing from 3 to 7 rooms. The population of the camp approximated 150 men, 140 women, and 536 children. All were Mexicans, either born in Mexico or in this country. The original portion of the cottages are still in fair structural condition; however the tenants have added to these with shack construction. It was found that the roofs leaked in rainy weather in approximately 50 percent of the homes; that doors, windows, and screens were in need of repair.

"The flimsy foundation of the tile flues tacked up on the side of the buildings were noted in many cases to constitute a fire hazard and they should be repaired. Very few of these cottages had kitchen sinks, generally the slops were thrown out the door in the backyard to the chickens or used for irrigation around the shrubbery, and those few who did have sinks had open drains for this disposal. Many of the houses had concrete hoppers near the back door, connected to open drains. Only four cottages out of a total of 156 cottages had modern plumbing and flush toilets. The rest were using the outside privy. All of these were in poor structural and bad sanitary condition and infested with flies. No disinfectant was noticed as being used and fly-breeding was evident in nearly all the pits. Many families had cluttered up their backyards with poultry, rabbits, and animal pens. The pens were usually arranged one on top of the other. Several had cows and horses and one had hogs. All these pens were filthy and dirty. Much garbage and refuse was in evidence all through the camp. There was also evidence of rats in the camp. Although the exterior appearance of the camp was bad, invariably the interiors were kept clean and neatly painted and papered, and many of them were fairly well furnished—a few of the five-room houses contained as many as 8 to 12 occupants, indicating evidence of serious overcrowding."

I could match this report with literally dozens of similar reports referring to conditions throughout Southern California: in Carpinteria, Santa Paula, Oxnard, Pomona, Colton, Riverside, Azusa, and San Bernardino.

As to living conditions generally among Mexicans in California, may I refer you to: "How Mexicans Earn and Live," a study by Dr. Constantine Panunzio of the University of California at Los Angeles, published by the University of California Press in 1933; and to "Mexicans in California," an exhaustive report prepared by Governor C. C. Young's special Mexican Fact-Finding Committee in 1930.

These reports will substantiate my statement that living conditions among the Mexican population of California are extremely bad. Many of our Mexican shack-towns or Jim-towns, as they are called, came into existence during the First World War, with the great influx of Mexican immigrants which then took place.

Most of these settlements are as bad today as they were in 1918; little if any improvement can be noted. Mexican settlements in California generally represent an unofficial type of segregation. Mexicans are segregated, not by statute or ordinance, but simply because they originally clustered in these settlements upon their arrival here, largely because rentals were cheap, and here they have remained.

Intentionally or otherwise, however, segregation,

as such, exists. Segregation narrows the range of employment opportunities; reduces the opportunities for cultural adjustment, both for groups and for individuals, and also makes for discrimination. It would be folly indeed to deny that Mexicans are victimized by race prejudice in Los Angeles County, and, for that matter, in many other areas.

The "Zoot Suit" Riot of 1943

One of the severest outbreaks against Mexican Americans occurred during the Second World War at a time when Mexico was our ally. It was the first of a series of riots that summer which in part reflected the tension of a country at war.

The anti-Mexican riots in Los Angeles raged from June 3, 1943, until June 9. This was wartime; a nearby naval base made Los Angeles the mecca for sailors' leaves. The riots were touched off on June 3 by two incidents. Some servicemen walking through a deteriorated street in a Mexican section of the city were beaten up by a gang of Mexican boys. In a nearby precinct on the same evening some Mexican boys returning from a "club" conference at the police station on how to avoid gang strife were beaten up by a gang of non-Mexican boys. It does not seem as if the two incidents were connected. The police took no immediate action, but then after their regular duty was over, a so-called "vengeance squad" set out to clean up the gang that had attacked the sailors. They found no one to arrest, but great newspaper publicity was given to the incidents and to the policemen who had made the fruitless raid.

The following night about 200 sailors hired a fleet of 20 taxicabs and cruised the Mexican quarter. The Mexican adolescent boys had a fad of wearing long, draped jackets (zoot suits). Four times the taxicab brigade stopped when it sighted a Mexican boy in a zoot suit and beat up the boys, leaving them lying on the pavement. There was no mobilization of police. One police car did intercept the caravan and nine sailors were taken into custody, but no charges were preferred against them. In the morning papers the war news was pushed off the front page with stories of the night before on a triumphal note of the sailors' move to clean up "zoot-suited roughnecks." The third night, June 5, scores of sailors, soldiers, and marines marched through the Mexican quarter, four abreast, stopping and threatening anyone wearing zoot suits. No sailors were arrested, either by the police, the shore patrol, or the Military Police, although twenty-seven Mexican boys were arrested. In various bars Mexicans were beaten up or their jackets torn off and ripped up. The police announced that any Mexicans involved in rioting would be arrested.

On the night of June 6, six carloads of sailors cruised through the area, beating up teen-age Mexicans and wrecking establishments. The police came after them in mopping-up operations and arrested the boys who had been beaten up. In the morning forty-four severely beaten Mexican boys were under arrest.

Whipped up by the press, which warned that the Mexicans were about to riot with broken bottles as weapons and would beat sailors' brains out with hammers, the excitement erupted and two days of really serious rioting occurred, involving soldiers, sailors, and civilians, who invaded motion picture houses, stopped trolley cars, and beat up the Mexicans they found, as well as a few Filipinos and Negroes. At midnight on June 7, the military authorities declared Los Angeles out of bounds for military personnel. The order immediately slowed down the riot. On June 8, the mayor stated that "sooner or later it will blow over," and the chief of police announced the situation "cleared up." However, rioting went on for two more days. Editorials and statements to the press lamented the fact that the servicemen were called off before they were able to complete the job. The district attorney of an outlying county stated that "zoot suits are an open indication of subversive character." And the Los Angeles City Council adopted a resolution making the wearing of zoot suits a "misdemeanor."

The Meaning of Chicano

The two selections that follow focus attention on differing points of view regarding words used to describe Mexican Americans.

While most younger Mexican Americans appear to prefer the term *Chicano*, there are many who reject the word. Such a point of view is that of the Reverend Thomas Sepulveda, an Army Chaplain, who expressed his views in a letter to the *Los Angeles Times* on January 5, 1970. Since the newspaper had been using the term to identify Mexican Americans, one of the editors explains his point of view in a note that follows the letter.

The second article was written for the *Los Angeles Times* by Ruben Salazar, one of its staff reporters. Mr. Salazar was formerly head of the newspaper's Mexico City bureau.

The Use of Chicano

The constant barbaric use by Mexican Americans and the general public of the word chicano instead of Mexicano urged me to break my long silence against the wrong use of the word.

According to Vastus's "Diccionario Enciclopedico de la Lengua Castellana" the word chicano or chicana signified *mentiroso*—liar or embustero—tricky.

The meaning of this word chicano is even worse if one interprets it etymologically. So, I hope this statement will help the general public and the people who have pride in calling themselves chicanos, when they really mean to call themselves Mexicanos.

I feel real proud to be a Mexicano and I forbid people to call me and my people chicano or chicanos because when they do they are calling us all mentirosos—liars—*embusteros*—tricky—and something worse.

REV. THOMAS SEPULVEDA
Chaplain, General Hospital
Denver, Colo.

The fact that the Mexican-American Law Students Assn. from UCLA, Loyola, and USC has changed its name to the Chicano Law Students Assn. indicated the popularity of the term with young activists. Chicano may be best understood by comparing it to black. Negroes at one time may have felt that to be called black was an insult. Now many insist on it. The same with Mexican Americans who at one time didn't want to be called chicanos. Now they insist on it. Chicano and black are political, cultural, and social terms and have nothing to do with erudite dictionaries.

Who Is a Chicano? And What Is It the Chicanos Want?

A Chicano is a Mexican-American with a non-Anglo image of himself.

He resents being told Columbus "discovered" America when the Chicano's ancestors, the Mayans and the Aztecs, founded highly sophisticated civilizations centuries before Spain financed the Italian explorer's trip to the "New World."

Chicanos resent also Anglo pronouncements that Chicanos are "culturally deprived" or that the fact that they speak Spanish is a "problem."

Chicanos will tell you that their culture predates that of the Pilgrims and that Spanish was spoken in America before English and so the "problem" is not theirs but the Anglos' who don't speak Spanish.

Having told you that, the Chicano will then contend that Anglos are Spanish-oriented at the expense of Mexicans.

They will complain that when the governor dresses up as a Spanish nobleman for the Santa Barbara Fiesta he's insulting Mexicans because the Spanish conquered and exploited the Mexicans.

It's as if the governor dressed like an English Redcoat for a Fourth of July parade, Chicanos say.

When you think you know what Chicanos are getting at, a Mexican American will tell you that Chicano is an insulting term and may even quote the Spanish Academy to prove that Chicano derives from chicanery.

A Chicano will scoff at this and say that such

Mexican Americans have been brainwashed by Anglos and that they're Tio Tacos (Uncle Toms). This type of Mexican Americans, Chicanos will argue, don't like the word Chicano because it's abrasive to their Anglo-oriented minds.

These poor people are brown Anglos, Chicanos will smirk.

What, then, is a Chicano? Chicanos say that if you have to ask you'll never understand, much less become a Chicano.

Actually, the word Chicano is as difficult to define as "soul."

For those who like simplistic answers, Chicano can be defined as short for Mexicano. For those who prefer complicated answers, it has been suggested that Chicano may have come from the word Chihuahua—the name of a Mexican state bordering on the United States. Getting trickier, this version then contends that Mexicans who migrated to Texas call themselves Chicanos because having crossed into the United States from Chihuahua they adopted the first three letters of that state, Chi, and then added cano, for the latter part of Texano.

Such explanations, however, tend to miss the whole point as to why Mexican-American activists call themselves Chicanos.

Mexican Americans, the second largest minority in the country and the largest in the Southwestern states (California, Texas, Arizona, New Mexico, and Colorado) have always had difficulty making up their minds what to call themselves.

In New Mexico they call themselves Spanish-Americans. In other parts of the Southwest they call themselves Americans of Mexican descent, people with Spanish surnames or Hispanos.

Why, ask some Mexican Americans, can't we just call ourselves Americans?

Chicanos are trying to explain why not. Mexican Americans, though indigenous to the Southwest, are on the lowest rung scholastically, economically, socially, and politically. Chicanos feel cheated. They want to effect change now.

Mexican Americans average eight years of schooling compared to the Negroes' ten years. Farm work-

ers, most of whom are Mexican American in the Southwest, are excluded from the National Labor Relations Act unlike other workers. Also, Mexican Americans often have to compete for low-paying jobs with their Mexican brothers from across the border who are willing to work for even less. Mexican is the synonym for inferior in many parts of the Southwest.

That is why Mexican-American activists flaunt the barrio word Chicano—as an act of defiance and a badge of honor. Mexican Americans, though large in numbers, are so politically impotent that in Los Angeles, where the country's largest single concentration of Spanish-speaking live, they have no one of their own on the City Council. This, in a city politically sophisticated enough to have three Negro councilmen.

Chicanos, then, are merely fighting to become "Americans." Yes, but with a Chicano outlook.

Among the Valiant

Mexican Americans have always been loyal and served their country well in war as well as in peace. During the Second World War, they mixed with Anglos in military units and each group learned much about the other. Mexican Americans set a brilliant record for valor during World War II.

They have earned more high military decorations, including the Congressional Medal of Honor, than any other group. Their high casualty rate stems from the very high percentage who served in the front lines.

At the beginning of World War II, the Mexican-American population in the United States was approaching two million, and Mexican-American youths were quick to volunteer for service. The many military honors and decorations they won attest to their loyalty and courage. Similarly, a very high percentage of eligible Mexican Americans served with honor and courage both in the Korean War and in Vietnam.

In recent years, as opposition to American involvement in Vietnam has become widespread among the nation's young, some Mexican-American youths have begun to reexamine their attitudes toward military service. Like other young Americans everywhere, some have refused to go into service because of their opposition to the war. Others have refused because they believe the draft system discriminates against minorities, taking the sons of the poor in place of those whose parents have influence with draft boards or whose economic means enable them to get college deferments.

Obviously, the resistance of young Mexican Americans does not mean that they are any less patriotic; it simply means that they are redefining their patriotism, like other young Americans.

The two readings that follow discuss the valor and casualty rates of Mexican Americans in military service. The first, "GI's Ultimate Act of Bravery Saves Buddies," originally appeared in the *Los Angeles Times* on February 21, 1966. And "Mexican-American Casualties in Vietnam" is from a progress report of a Mexican-American Study Project in 1967.

GI's Ultimate Act of Bravery Saves Buddies

Cu Chi, South Vietnam—"When he spotted the grenade, he lunged on top of it without hesitation. He hollered, 'Move out, you people' and then it went off."

Spec. 4 James McKeown of Willingboro, N.J. was talking about Spec. 4 Daniel Fernandez of Sunray, Texas, whose ultimate act of bravery saved the lives of four of his buddies. But the blast ended the life of Dan Fernandez, 21.

Last Friday, Fernandaz was in a reinforced squad lying in ambush outside the 25th Division's 2nd Brigade perimeter, 25 miles west of Saigon. The Americans were hit by a much larger Viet Cong force using a 50-caliber machine gun, a light machine gun, automatic weapons, and plenty of grenades.

"The grenade hit Dan on the foot as he was crawling," McKeown said Sunday. "When it went off, it tore into his groin, abdomen and right leg."

Pvt. David R. Masingale of Fresno, Calif., a medic, told Fernandez while they were waiting for a medical evacuation helicopter, "Hang on, buddy."

Fernandez replied, "I'm going to hang on." But he added: "I never believed it would hurt so much."

Platoon buddies of Fernandez said he was a friend to everyone, generous with his money when others had run out, a likable guy.

Fernandez, whose father, Jose, lives at Los Lunas, N.M., already had served one stint in Vietnam, a 90-day volunteer tour as a door gunner on armed helicopters. He earned the Air Medal and a Purple Heart during that tour.

He returned to Vietnam last month with the 1st Platoon C Company of the 5th Mechanized Infantry's 1st Battalion.

He was still volunteering.

"He was in the same spot the night before and volunteered to go out on patrol again even though he hadn't had any sleep for 48 hours," 2nd Lt. Joseph D'Orso of Norwalk, Conn., said. "He was always volunteering."

Masingale, one of those saved by Fernandez's lunge stop of the grenade, said his friend "had a girl back home he planned to marry when he got back. He also wanted to get a new truck for his father's ranch."

One member of the platoon said: "After it happened, I asked somebody, 'Who was his closest friend?'"

Supplying his own answer, the soldier added, "Everyone was."

Members of the platoon chipped in $40 for a wreath for Fernandez's funeral.

"He was one of the best men in the platoon," D'Orso said. "He was ready to do anything. And he was always cheerful."

Fernandez was hit by a rifle bullet after the grenade exploded. He lived to get back to the brigade hospital. Doctors fought for two hours to save him, but the internal bleeding was heavy.

The Viet Cong paid a price, too. Seventeen of them were killed and five others were believed killed and carried away by comrades.

Fernandez's officers are recommending him for the Congressional Medal of Honor.

Mexican-American Casualties in Vietnam

American servicemen of Mexican descent have a higher death rate in Vietnam than other GI's. Analysis of all combat and non-combat deaths between January 1, 1961 and February 28, 1967 indicates that a large number of young people from this minority group reach the Southeast Asia theater of war and that a considerable number of them are involved in hazardous duty.

Servicemen from the five southwest states of Texas, New Mexico, Arizona, Colorado and California suffered 1,631 deaths in the aforementioned six-year period. Of these, 19.4 percent had Spanish surnames. This figure appears high when compared with the share of Spanish-surname population in the total for the region (11.8 percent in 1960). It is still high when the comparison is based on males of military age, i.e., individuals between age 17 and 36 years in 1967 (esimated at 13.8 percent).

While these figures are estimates, they are sufficient to indicate orders of magnitude. If one were to project birthdate, immigration and other factors, the statistical relationship would not be substantially different. Spanish-surname individuals would probably be slightly more numerous.

War deaths by branch of service suggest that relatively large numbers of Mexican Americans are involved in high-risk duty. For example, Spanish-surname individuals represented 23.3 percent of all Southwest Marine Corps deaths, 19.4 percent of the Army, 9.1 percent of the Air Force and 7.3 percent of the Navy. Marine Corps deaths, which are high in all the five southwestern states, include a substantial number of casualties of presumed Mexican background. In New Mexico, for example, 13 of the state's 25 Marine Corps casualties had Spanish surnames. In Colorado 37 Marines died for both combat and non-combat causes. Nine of these had Spanish last names.

The Department of Defense classifies casualties as combat and non-combat. (Only deaths are included in our analysis.) There were 1,335 combat deaths of Southwest servicemen in Vietnam in the period under discussion, and 296 non-combat. Over 20 percent of all servicemen dying in combat and 14 percent of the non-combat casualties had Spanish surnames. Combat deaths result from military action against the enemy. Non-combat deaths may result from illness, accidents (as in the case of the U.S.S. *Forrestal*), and similar causes.

Since Mexican Americans are a highly urbanized population, the majority of their war casualties came from the cities of the Southwest. However, statistics show, Mexican-American servicemen have about the same high casualty rate whether they come from the urban or rural sectors (19.5 percent of the urban total and 18.1 percent of the rural total).

An adequate interpretation of the data is impossible without further information. Spanish-surname servicemen may be overrepresented in the Vietnam casualties because they are overrepresented in the armed services generally or in the units assigned to Vietnam. Since relatively few young ethnics go on to college, they have less of a chance to be deferred by local draft boards (which usually include few representatives of minority groups). Poverty and a yearning for the greater social acceptance in the armed services than in civilian life may cause more Mexican Americans to seek service and obtain the extra pay associated with high-risk duty. For some of them, the armed forces offer the first opportunity to escape from the barrios. In any event, the casualty figures seem to confirm the experience of World War II and Korea that is so vividly described by Raul Morin in *Among the Valiant.*

MEXICAN-AMERICAN LITERATURE

Most Mexican-American literature has been lost through neglect or indifference of both Mexican Americans themselves and the Anglo majority. While there has been an intellectual elite among Mexican Americans, the majority has had neither the time, money, nor educational background for such intellectual and cultural luxuries as literature.

In recent years, however, as more and more Mexican Americans seek higher education, they find that Mexican-American literature is far more prevalent than they thought. As they search deeper and deeper into their cultural backgrounds, they find more and more literature from the pens of Mexican Americans.

Journals, such as *Aztlan, El Grito, La Raza, Regeneracion,* and the *Journal of Mexican-American Studies* are bringing to light again almost forgotten chapters of Mexican-American literature. And such journals are offering young Mexican-American writers a chance to find their place in letters.

I Am Joaquin: An Angry Mexican American Issues a Cultural Declaration of Independence

"I Am Joaquin" is one of the most interesting pieces of Mexican-American literature, and it is, at the same time, an extraordinarily powerful political and sociological document.

No one was listening to Mexican-American poets before, not even their own people. Many Mexican Americans were mostly indifferent to the struggle for justice and equality or were too busy trying to be Anglos to gain acceptance.

Most activists in the struggle took various courses. Cesar Chavez proved that the dollar could be used as a weapon during the grape strike. Other leaders used different means, but few picked up the pen to use as a weapon during the struggle. One who did is Rodolfo Gonzales, the author of "I Am Joaquin," and he proved that the pen can be a powerful weapon.

Mr. Gonzales lives in Denver where he works in the area of education and community organization. He advocates the concept of Aztlan, a socially and economically separate society of Mexican Americans within the United States.

I Am Joaquin

By Rodolfo Gonzales

I am Joaquin,
Lost in a world of confusion,
Caught up in a whirl of an
*   Anglo society,*
Confused by the rules,
Scorned by attitudes,
Suppressed by manipulations,
And destroyed by modern society.
My fathers
*   have lost the economic battle*
and won
*   the struggle of cultural survival.*
And now!
*   I must choose*
*   Between*
*   the paradox of*
Victory of the spirit,
despite physical hunger
*   Or*
*   to exist in the grasp*
of American social neurosis,
sterilization of the soul

Yes,
I have come a long way to nowhere,
Unwillingly dragged by that
   monstrous, technical,
   industrial giant called
     Progress
and Anglo success . . .
   I look at myself.
    I watch my brothers.
     I shed tears of sorrow.
      I sow seeds of hate.
   I withdraw to the safety within the
Circle of life . . .
      MY OWN PEOPLE

Now
   I bleed in some smelly cell
  from club.
  or tyranny.
I bleed as the vicious gloves of
   hunger cut my face and eyes,
as I fight my way from stinking
   Barrios to the glamour of the Ring
    and lights of fame
     or mutilated sorrow.
My blood runs pure on the ice caked
hills of the Alaskan Isles,
on the corpse strewn beach of
  Normandy,
the foreign land of Korea
        and now
        Viet Nam.

Here I stand
   before the Court of Justice
        Guilty
for all the glory of my Raza
    to be sentenced to despair.
Here I stand
   Poor in money
    Arrogant in pride
     Bold with Machismo
      Rich in courage
        and
     Wealthy in spirit and faith.
My knees are caked with mud.
My hands calloused from the hoe.

I have made the Anglo rich
        yet
   Equality is but a word,
    the Treaty of Hidalgo has been
    broken
   and is but another treacherous
   promise
My land is lost
   and stolen,
My culture has been raped,
   I lengthen
    the line at the welfare door
and fill the Jails with crime
    These then
are the rewards
      this society has
For sons of Chiefs
    and Kings
     and bloody Revolutionists.
I shed tears of anguish
as I see my children disappear
behind the shroud of mediocrity
never to look back to remember me.
I have endured in the rugged
   mountains of our country
I have survived the toils and slavery
   of the fields.
      I have existed
in the barrios of the city,
in the suburbs of bigotry,
in the mines of social snobbery,
in the prisons of dejection
in the muck of exploitation
and
in the fierce heat of racial hatred.

And now the trumpet sounds,
The music of the people stirs the
      Revolution,
Like a sleeping giant it slowly
rears its head
to the sound of
      Tramping feet
     Clamoring voices
    Mariachi strains
    The smell of chile verde and

Soft brown eyes of expectation for a
                              better life.
And in all the fertile farm lands,
            the barren plains,
The mountain villages,
smoke smeared cities
            We start to MOVE.
Mejicano!
   Espanol!
     Latino!
          Hispano!
          Chicano!
or whatever I call myself,
       I look the same

I feel the same
I cry
    and
Sing the same

   I am Joaquin
The odds are great
but my spirit is strong
          My faith unbreakable
          My blood is pure
I am Aztec Prince and Christian
   Christ
       I SHALL ENDURE!
       I WILL ENDURE!

INDEX